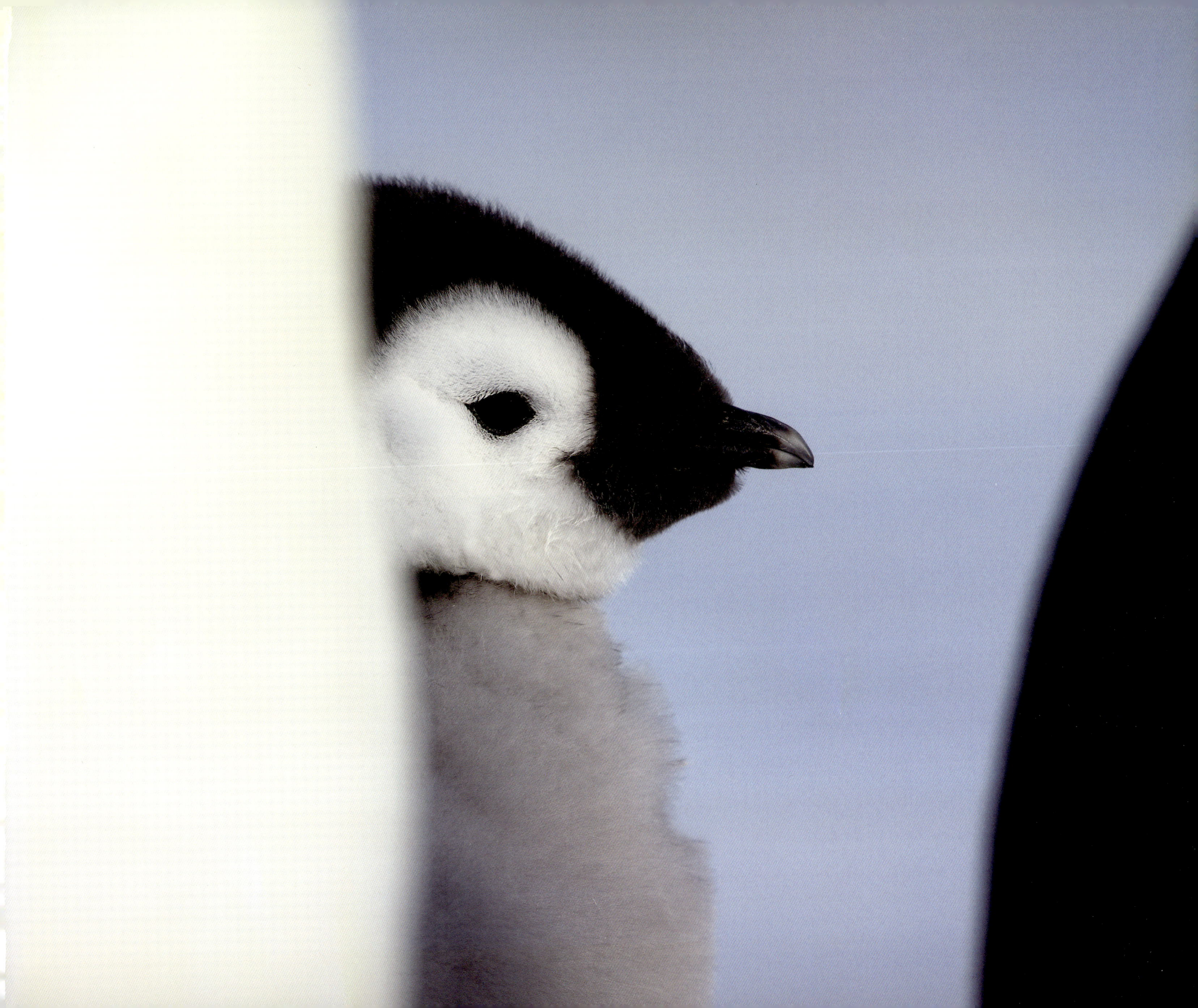

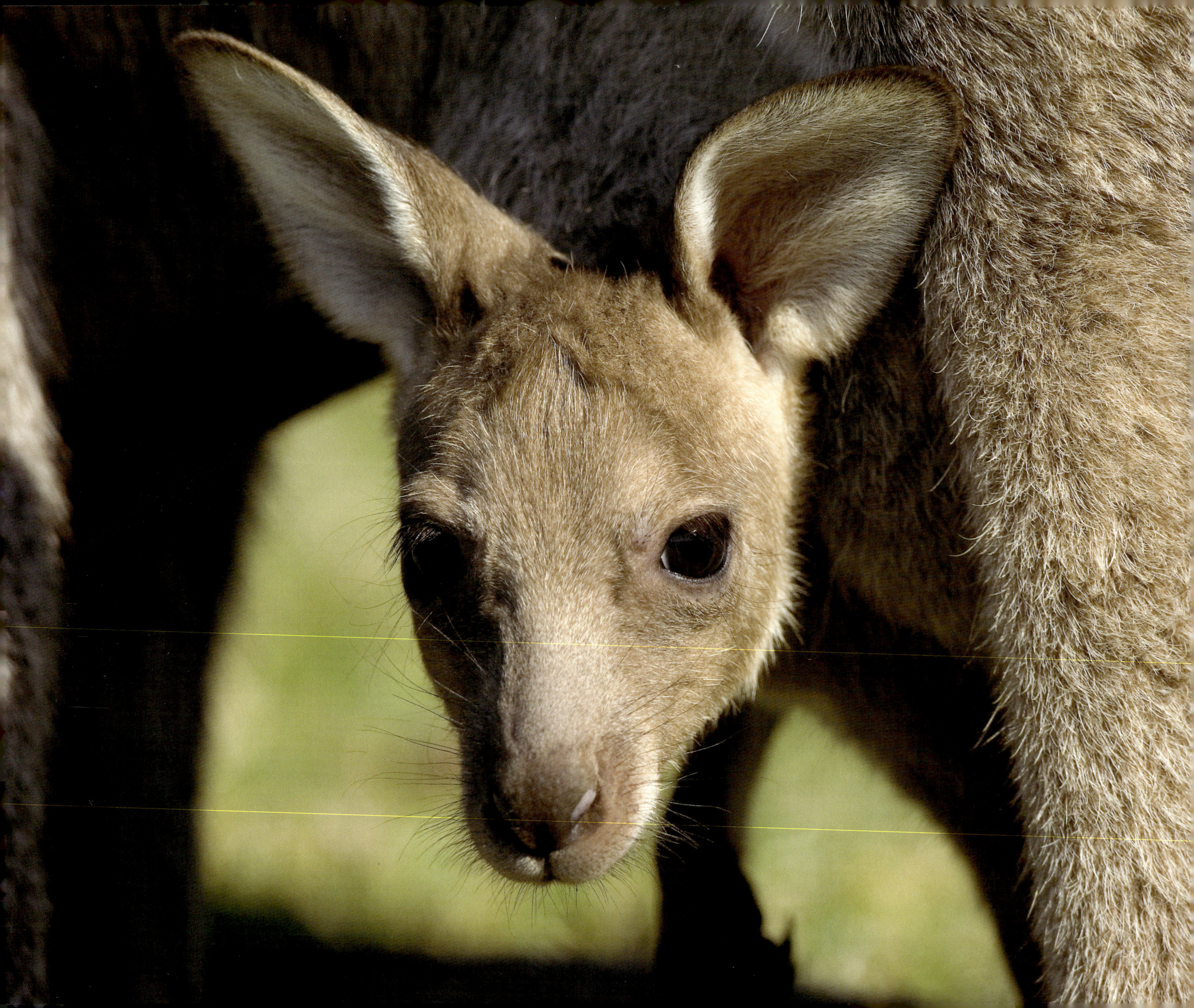

Growing up Wild

Concept and photographs by Thorsten Milse
Text by Uta Henschel

BUCHER

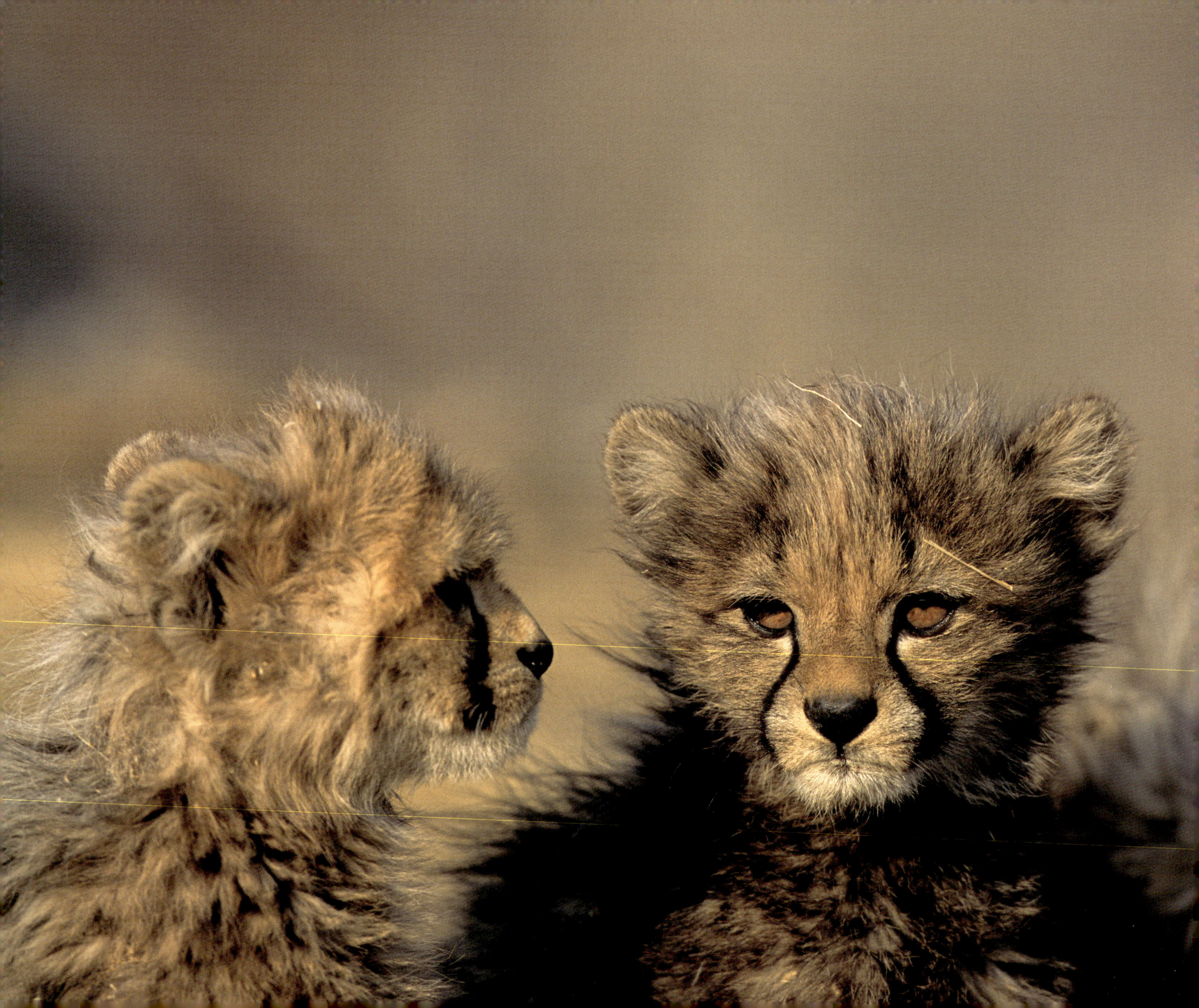

Contents

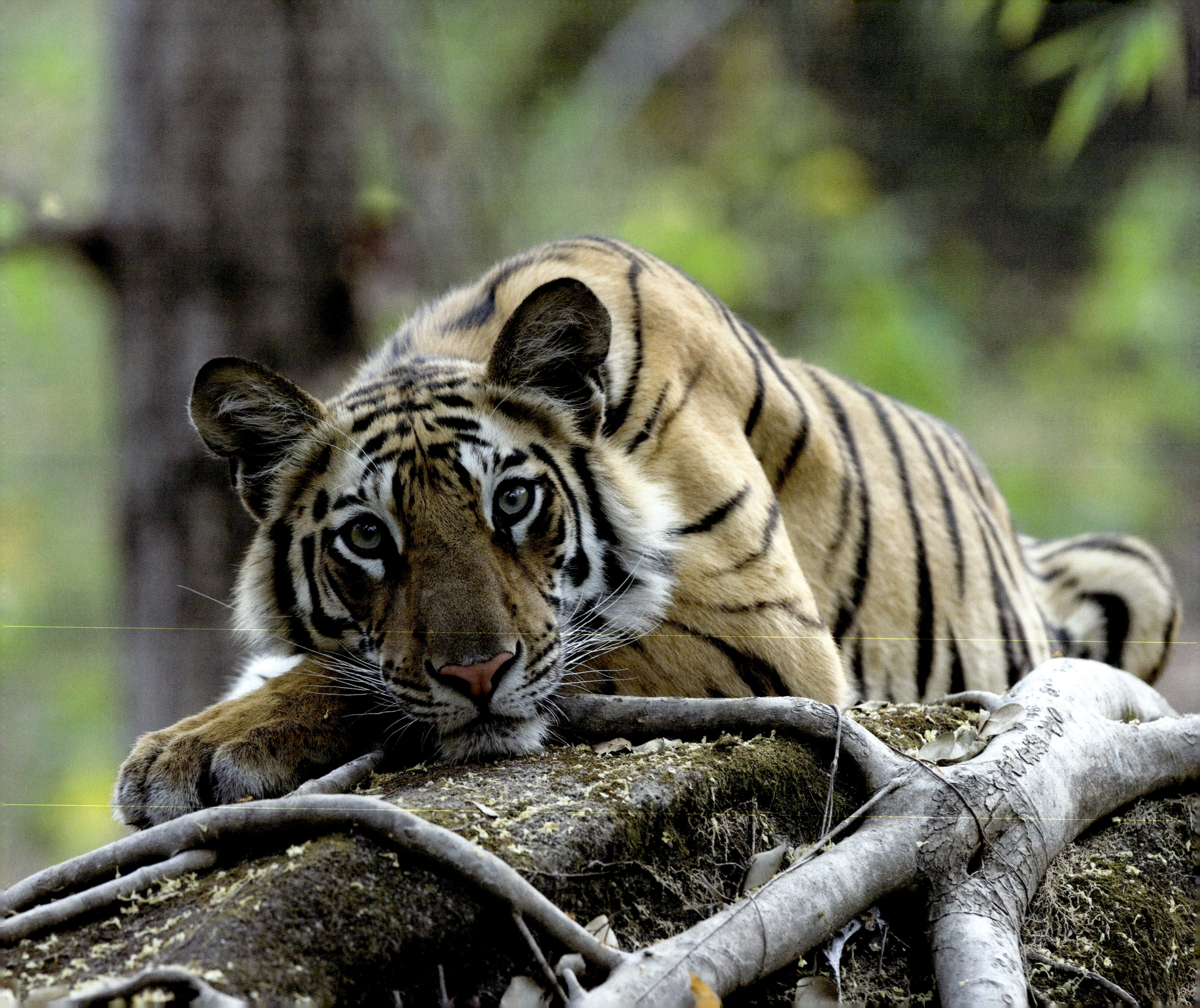

Preface

As editor of *BBC Wildlife* Magazine, I have seen thousands of images of wildlife, and even those that are technically excellent and attractively composed rarely stop me in my tracks. But one photographer's work never fails to catch my eye.

Thorsten Milse's images are always fresh and exciting, intimate and evocative, beautifully framed and perfectly executed.

It's easy to take the natural beauty of wildlife for granted and assume that with a mere press of a button, a photographer can capture that beauty. But as anyone who has attempted to photograph a wild animal knows, it's much harder than it looks. It takes exceptional vision, talent and patience to take the perfect shot.

Not only must you have a creative eye and passion for your subject, you must also be prepared to suffer for your art. Like many wildlife photographers, Thorsten has had to endure uncomfortable conditions to realise his vision. When he returned from Canada's Wapusk National Park, he told me that the cold wind constantly stung his face like a thousand tiny needles, but the second he saw a polar bear's black nose poking out of a hole in the ice he forgot the pain – "such magical moments are the most exciting and beautiful of my life."

Thorsten seems to relish the challenge of photographing familiar species – tigers, polar bears and emperor penguins – and revealing new facets of their behaviour.

When he embarked on his quest to photograph polar bears three years ago, there seemed to be no aspect of these charismatic bears' lives that had not already been documented by countless other professional photographers. Yet Thorsten discovered a new side of these top predators – the tenderness of a mother bear with her playful cubs.

For those of us who will never see such things for ourselves, Thorsten paints a picture so vivid you feel as if you are crouching beside him, witnessing these intimate moments through his camera lens.

The rich colours, low perspectives and wide angles that characterize Thorsten's wildlife portraits not only transport the viewer to these far-flung places, you can actually feel the heat of the African sun beating down on a young cheetah's woolly back and the bite of the frigid Antarctic wind sweeping over the huddled emperor penguin colony.

Many of the species featured in this book are perilously endangered. As the polar bear's ice world melts, the tiger is poached to extinction and the gorilla's forest home is felled, Thorsten's photographs not only showcase the beauty and majesty of these creatures, they remind us that these animals are special – and that they need our help.

Sophie Stafford
Editor-in-Chief of *BBC WILDLIFE* magazine

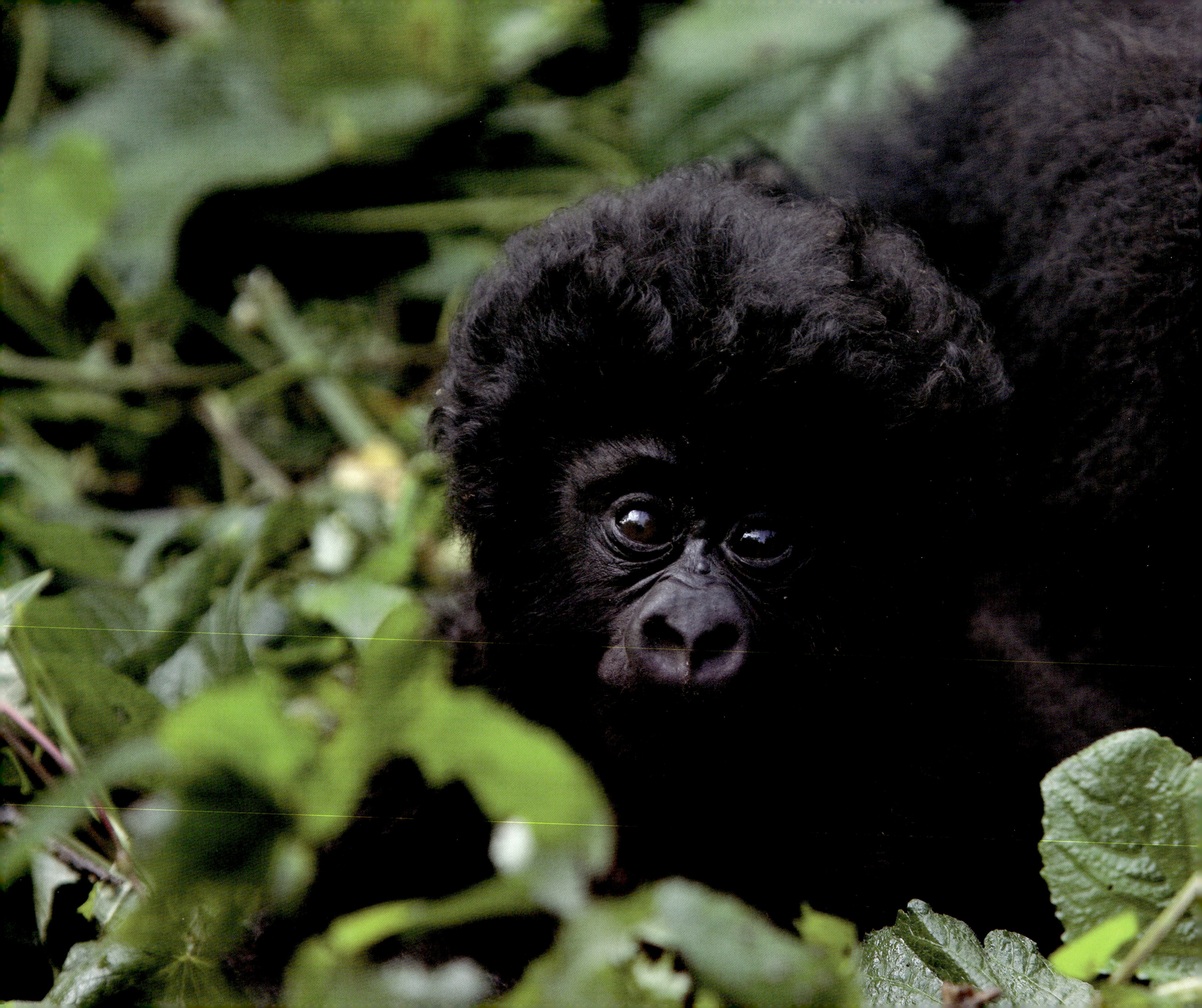

Introduction

Having children is among the most natural occurrences in the world and evolution's ultimate purpose. But rearing the little ones is another matter entirely. Amazing as it may seem, there is no patent recipe for the challenge of bringing them up – neither for human beings, nor for the 30 million or so animal species on earth. It's hardly surprising, then, that the majority of animal parents invest little in the way of care for their children. What they lack in devotion, they make up for in the numbers of offspring they produce. And they might easily justify this apparent negligence by arguing that a few of the little ones are bound to make it anyway. This is actually true. Judging by statistics alone, there can be few objections to this careless method of reproduction.

And yet evolution has continued to grapple with the theme of child-rearing, and after several hundreds of millions of years has finally produced some species that invest far more in their young than mere eggs and sperm.

Many species of bird and mammal take infinite pains with their young, building nests, excavating caves, traveling halfway around the world to offer their little ones the best breeding ground. They feed, protect, warm and clean their young, cuddling them tenderly and fighting their battles – and often enough providing a first-class education in the process.

Some animals spend weeks caring for their young; others sacrifice months and years of their lives. A close bond grows between these parents and their offspring. Amid the wilderness, with all its dangers, a social niche is created, an enclave of shelter and security in which the protected children thrive and grow strong and are finally able to deal with the hazards of their environment on their own.

The challenge of rearing young has thus been countered by the emergence of a host of biological options for getting parenting right. This book examines the "nurseries" of six species of animal and describes the burdens that animal mothers face – occasionally with the assistance of the fathers and family clans – to ensure that their offspring grow up safely. The pictures and texts published here are choice examples taken from a fount of incredible diversity. They introduce readers to wonderful beginnings of fascinating life stories, the outcome of which remains unknown.

Every animal childhood is different. Each follows its own storyline and responds to specific needs. Each is a model of success, having completed a test phase measured in geological eras. Again and again nature has rejected aspects of development that failed to work, shaking new tricks and variations from her sleeve until, finally, she accomplished what is on show today: the most advanced, reliable, empathic form of child-rearing ever in the entire history of life on earth. Reason for a standing ovation if ever there was one.

On the following pages, readers can watch helpless baby animals grow into competent adults. How parents not only hand down their DNA and their instincts, but also their personal experience, their hunting methods, their preference for specific sources of food, their alertness, and their reliability within their community.

Readers are eye-witnesses to the irresistible adorability with which evolution has armed young animals in the present era; they experience the effects of bright, front-facing eyes, round heads, short ears and muzzles, soft limbs and clumsy movements, and they feel touched by emotions generated by the sheer vulnerability of animal babies. Their need for protection appeals to our mothering instincts.

And why not?

We are, after all, the most recent species in an ancient evolutionary line that is focused on affectionate devotion, tenderness and compassion. As human co-mammals, members of the same biological class, we respond to similar visual signals as mother animals do when they succumb to the charm of juvenile cuteness, unable to do otherwise than give their all for the well-being of their young.

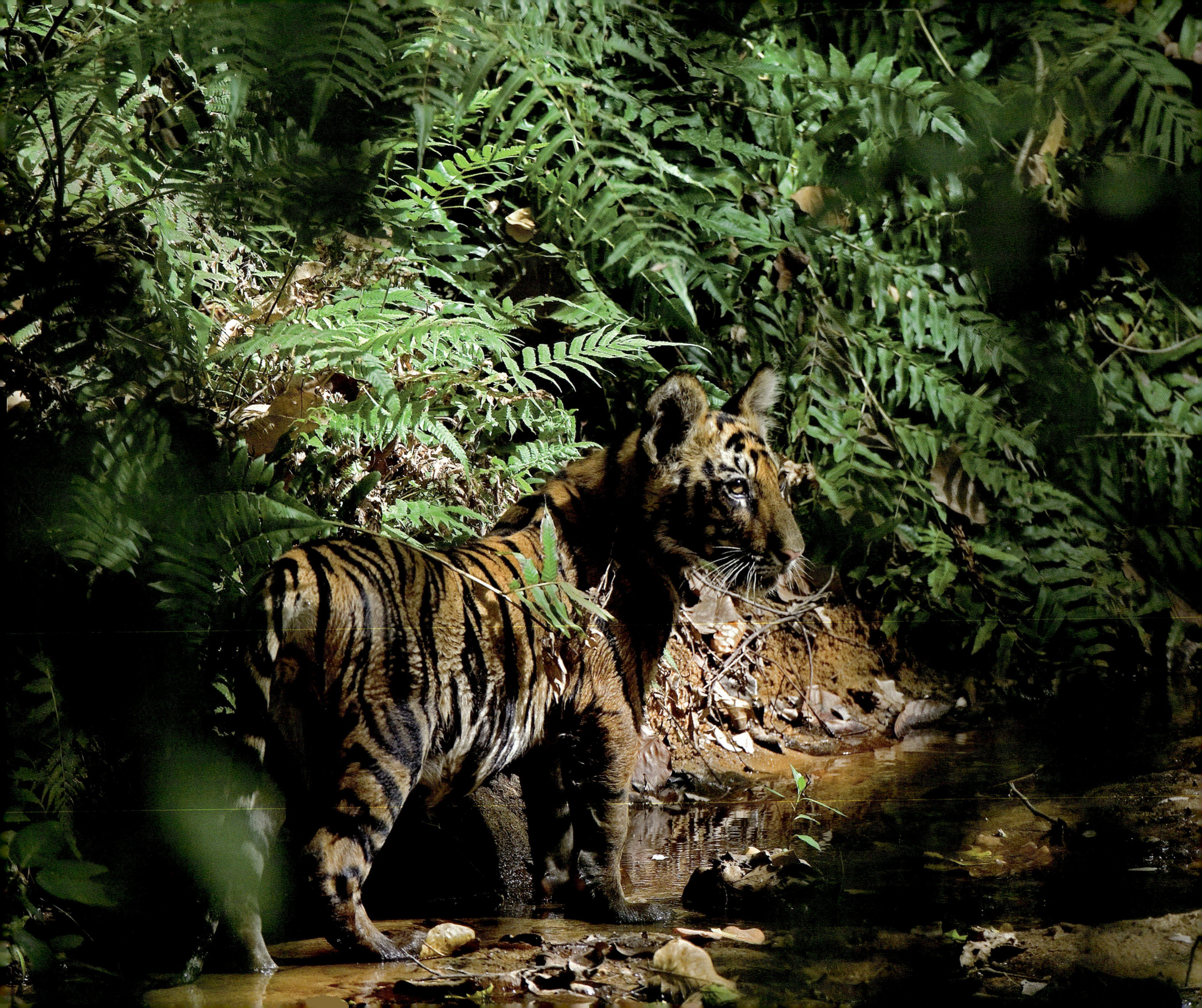

Indian Tigers

Softly Softly

There it is again – that sound that recently made such an impression on her. The memory sears through her body like a jolt of electricity. Her muscles tensed, she rears her head, pricks up her ears and briefly concentrates her gaze on the large clearing.

Only an hour before, the young tigress had left the forest of Bandhavgarh, the moon sailing over its spreading tree crowns and dappling the ground with silver brightness. The great cat crept from shadow to shadow until she reached the bamboo thicket on the edge of the great grassy plain. There she sank down, blending into the deep darkness at the foot of the stems. And then she waited. Patient and immobile, as her mother had taught her during the last year. A long training course.

How difficult it had often been to do what was expected of her. Particularly when, aged scarcely twelve months, she was allowed to accompany her mother hunting. At first she did not understand why she was not allowed to play with her two brothers while stalking the prey. Attacking their throats, ambushing them from behind, lifting a threatening paw – all this was watched by her mother with such affection in those relaxed hours under the resin-scented shorea trees, and she occasionally even participated, but none of this seemed to meet with approval when hunting lessons began. The young tigress made herself equally unpopular when she tried to capture the tip of her mother's tail bobbing so enticingly in front of her nose, or took a swipe at a butterfly. Even when she was dreadfully bored and just itching to move she had to remain still and lie in wait, imitating her teacher. And after a while, when nothing at all had happened, the three apprentices' heads grew heavy and sank down onto their front paws. Their eyes closed, and they fell asleep.

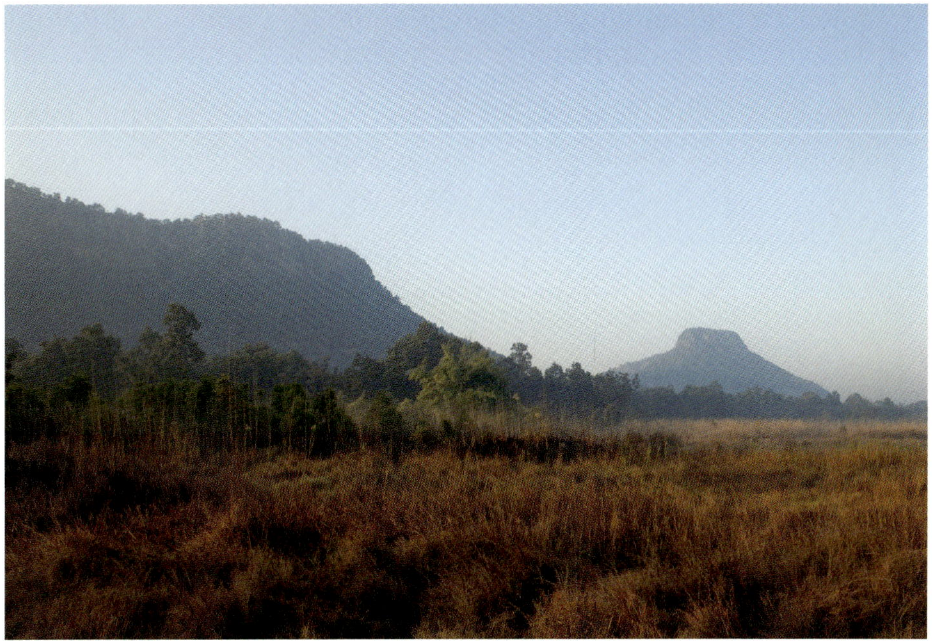

But being too eager also proved to be a stumbling block for the three young hunters. Again and again, a clumsy step would make leaves rustle under the weight of a paw, or a bush would quiver suspiciously, breaking their camouflage, because the young tigers had underestimated the dimensions of their bodies. On such occasions they earned a stern glare from their mother. But worse still was the sound of their prospective dinner making a swift escape.

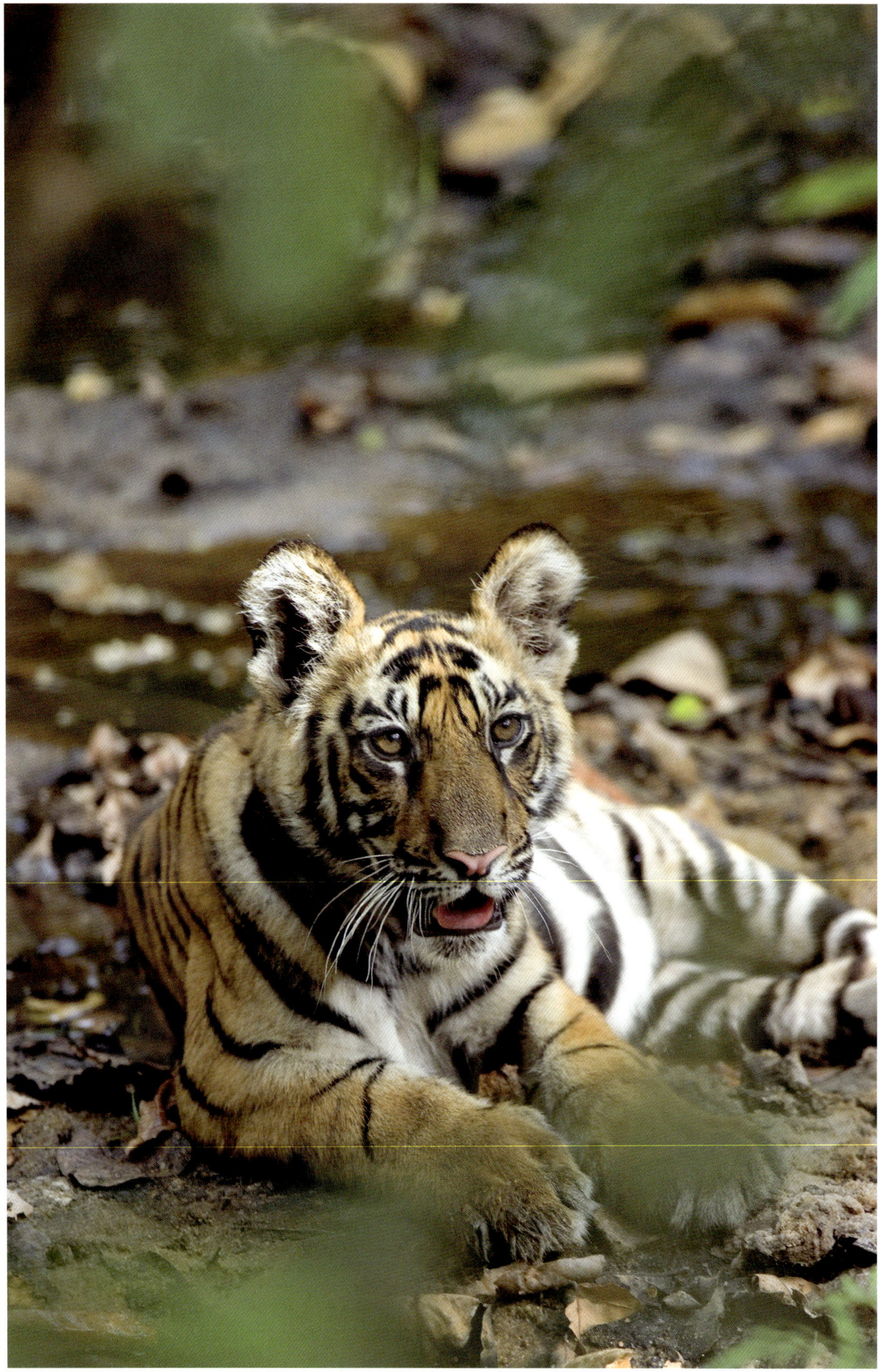

After these mishaps, they had no choice but to roam for many kilometers in their search of prey and to hope for another chance, their stomachs growling. These lessons were not quickly forgotten. With each new expedition the young tigress grasped more clearly that hunting is not a pastime, but a crucial activity. To avoid starvation, she had to learn how to be an efficient predator.

From that time on she pulled herself together, checking her childish high spirits, and followed her mother like a shadow. And yet even that experienced teacher succeeded only one time in eight – she, too, experienced mishaps. For example, when a mistrustful sambar deer spotted the concealed tiger family. Although the deer was not even earmarked as prey, its echoing DONK! DONK! call informed the whole jungle that danger was in the offing, and every living creature in the jungle suddenly held its breath.

As much as the young tigress endeavored to do everything right, she learnt the most from her mistakes. Twenty, even 30 times her prey escaped at the last moment before the big cat finally managed to capture something – a duck or rabbit, a careless chipmunk or a monkey.

But she gradually succeeded in coordinating her movements, in stalking noiselessly and restraining her hunting urge until she had crept up to within a single bound of her prey. In the very final moment, the key was to gauge the distance precisely by sight. To do this she carefully stretched out her neck and drew it back towards her body to improve her focus. Only when she had gathered her entire strength and rehearsed every possibility did she launch herself from the ground with her hind paws, stretching out her legs, throwing herself forward in a single eight-meter (26 feet) bound and burying her claws in the prey's soft hide.

Occasionally, she tried to catch up with a fleeing ungulate, but after a mere 500 meters (1,600 feet) she threw herself down into the grass and panted for air. Now she understood why her mother gave up immediately instead of accompanying her in her pursuit: gazelles and deer are far fleeter than big, heavy cats, and have far more stamina. At the age of almost two, this member of the *Panthera tigris* species finally understood the tigers' recipe for success for millions of years – stalk, leap, bite – and began to follow it.

Until that night a few weeks ago, when her mother suddenly demonstrated an astonishingly different strategy. Her actions had been triggered by that sound, the strange clicking that was audible above the hubbub of animal voices in the nocturnal jungle. It was the first time she had noticed it. And while she was still pricking up her ears, she remarked in surprise the effect the sound had on her mother. Abandoning her stalking, the huntress threw camouflage to the winds and crashed through the vegetation with the force of a winter monsoon.

Just as her daughter does now. The bamboo canes part swiftly before her, twigs whip her ears, thorns rake her coat, but she hardly notices. Now she has to reach the spot like lightning in order to surprise two axis deer locking antlers in the glade. In the ferocity of their rivalry, they are oblivious to everything around them. They ignore the flight of their herds. They do not hear the warning calls of a group of their fellow creatures on the edge of the forest. They do not notice what is approaching in the dappled moonlight. A second too late, the rivals attempt to separate. But their antlers are firmly entangled.

The tigress leaps at both deer in full flight and hurls them to the ground. Clumps of grass are flung through the air, fountains of dust rise. One deer leaps to his feet and flees, hooves beating a tattoo of fear in the dry grass. The other lies buried under 150 kilos of muscle. His legs attempt to take flight, but manage no more than a feeble quiver. The tigress has turned the deer's head back towards her with both paws, and her yawning jaws encircle the exposed throat and clamp shut.

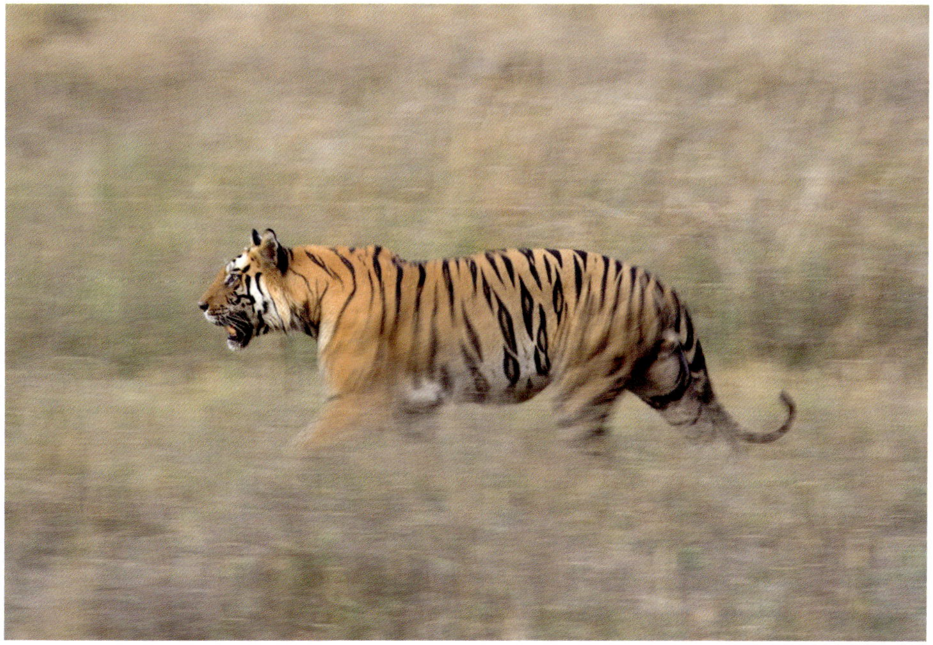

Soon the last spark of resistance is extinguished, the last breath expired. The huntress carefully releases her bite and lifts her head, her lips dripping with blood. Panting with exertion, her tongue lolling, she rests for a while.

When she has recovered, she grasps the dead deer by a back leg and drags the 80-kilo carcass, walking backwards to her spot near the bamboos, around 200 meters (650 feet) away. Although she is starving, she will not be able to devour much more than 15 kilos at a single sitting; however, the remains are now well hidden.

In the darkness she rubs her whiskers down the lie of the fur to locate the rump, the meatiest part of her prey. Then she begins to eat. She can take her time, because now she need share her meal with nobody. The prey she has caught is hers and hers alone.

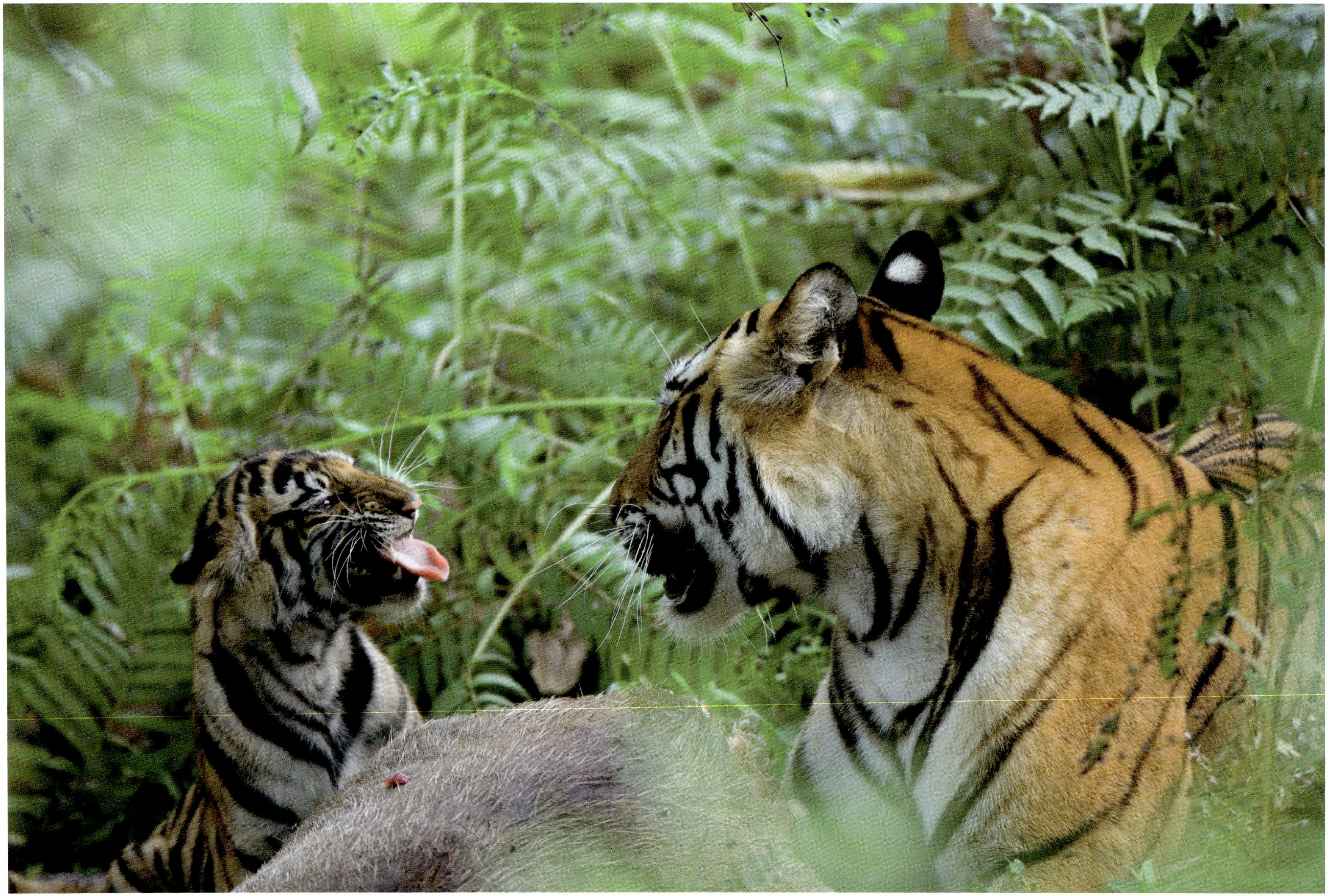

Female tigers allow their young to get away with almost anything.
The headstrong cubs are even permitted to spit at their mother when squabbling over the best place at the carcass she has killed. She merely growls briefly in reply and withdraws until the cubs have eaten their fill.

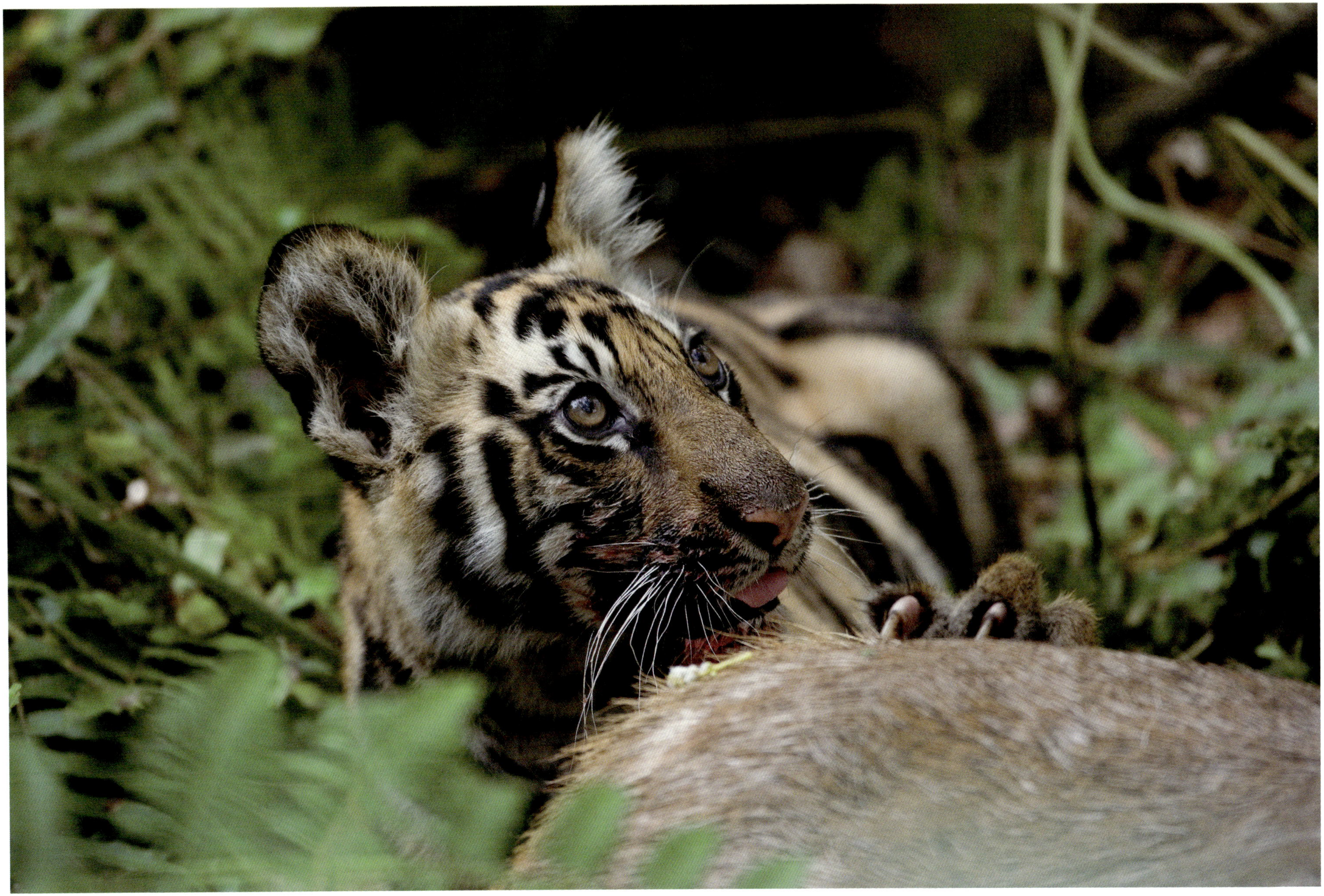

When eating, young tigers possessively lay a paw on the carcass killed by their mother.
At four months, a cub is still far too small to hunt for itself. Without the groundwork by its mother, who tears open the sambar deer's hide with her powerful predator's teeth, her cub would not even be able to get to the meat.

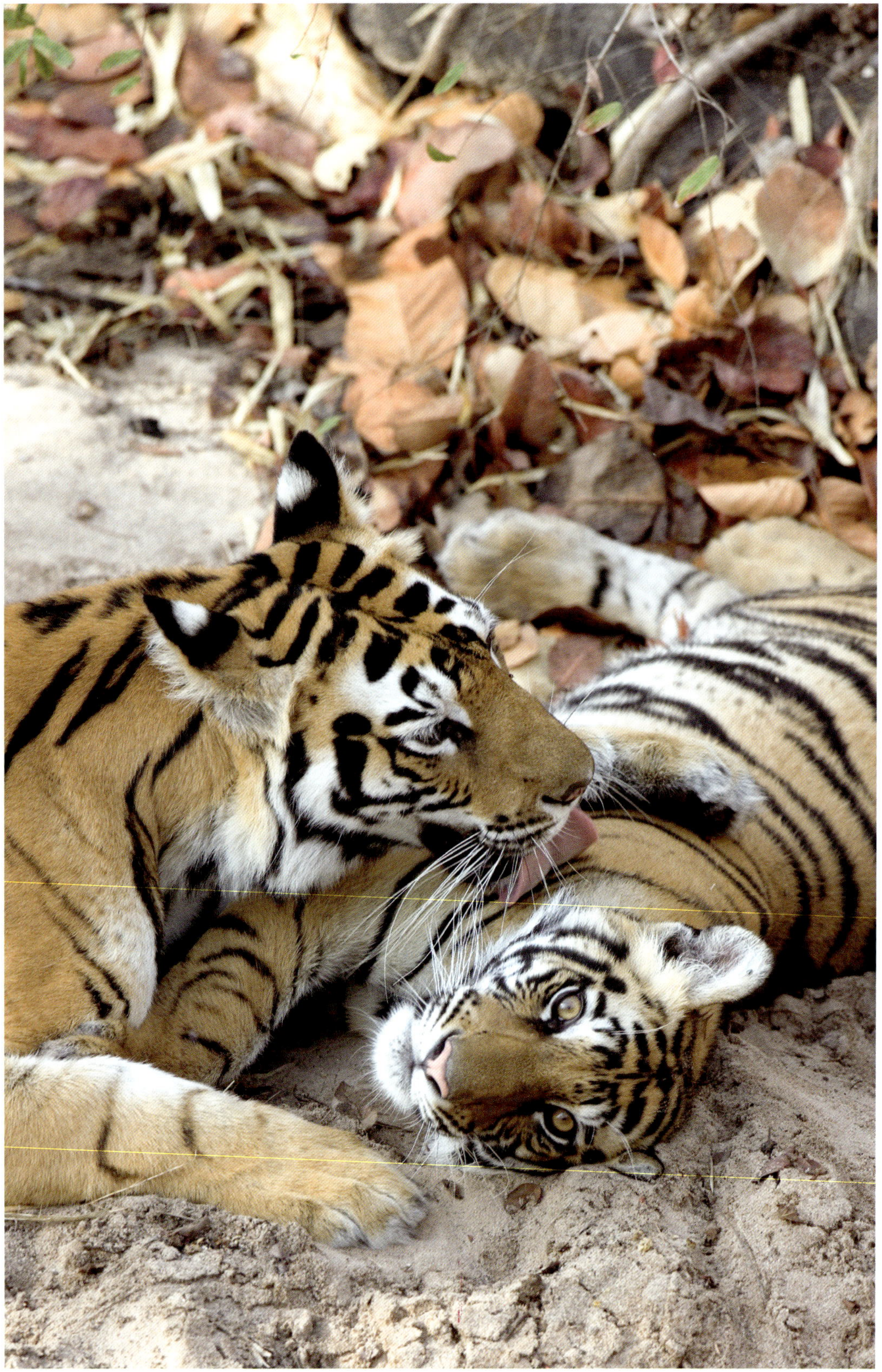

When her mother was still hunting to feed the family, her two brothers were always the first to fall on the kill. They grew faster and were more powerful than their sister, attempting to drive away their rival by growling and spitting, each trying to appropriate the bounty for himself. But the adolescent tigress did not move an inch, and bared her fangs threateningly. She knew it was all show. However greedily the three tigers tore at the prey, their one-year-old jaws were still too undeveloped to do more than scratch the surface of the kill. If their mother had not skinned a portion for them, they would have starved to death next to the fresh carcass.

Only now, at the age of 18 months, are the tigress' teeth complete, an arsenal of deadly weapons. The most impressive are the slightly curved canines, seven centimeters (2.75 inches) long, and the characteristic feature of all big cats. Only a few moments ago, these dagger-sharp tools had slit open the trachea and a jugular vein of the Axis deer, which bled to death while it was being choked.

When combined with the tonnes of pressure exerted by the tigress' jaws, these four conical projections can prize apart the neck vertebrae of a small gazelle and break its neck with a single bite in an attack from above – though this is not her preferred method. Her design is that the prey falls to the ground, losing balance, the slim legs fluttering helplessly in the air.

When eating, the young tigress primarily uses her eight fangs, four on each side: two upper and two lower. They are shaped like mighty scraping-knives and can hack off portions of meat like twin guillotines. The tigress tilts her head to one side to bite off chunk after chunk and devour them whole. She usually does not bother to chew. As a finale, she licks the remnants of meat from the bones using her tongue, which has a surface as rough as a file.

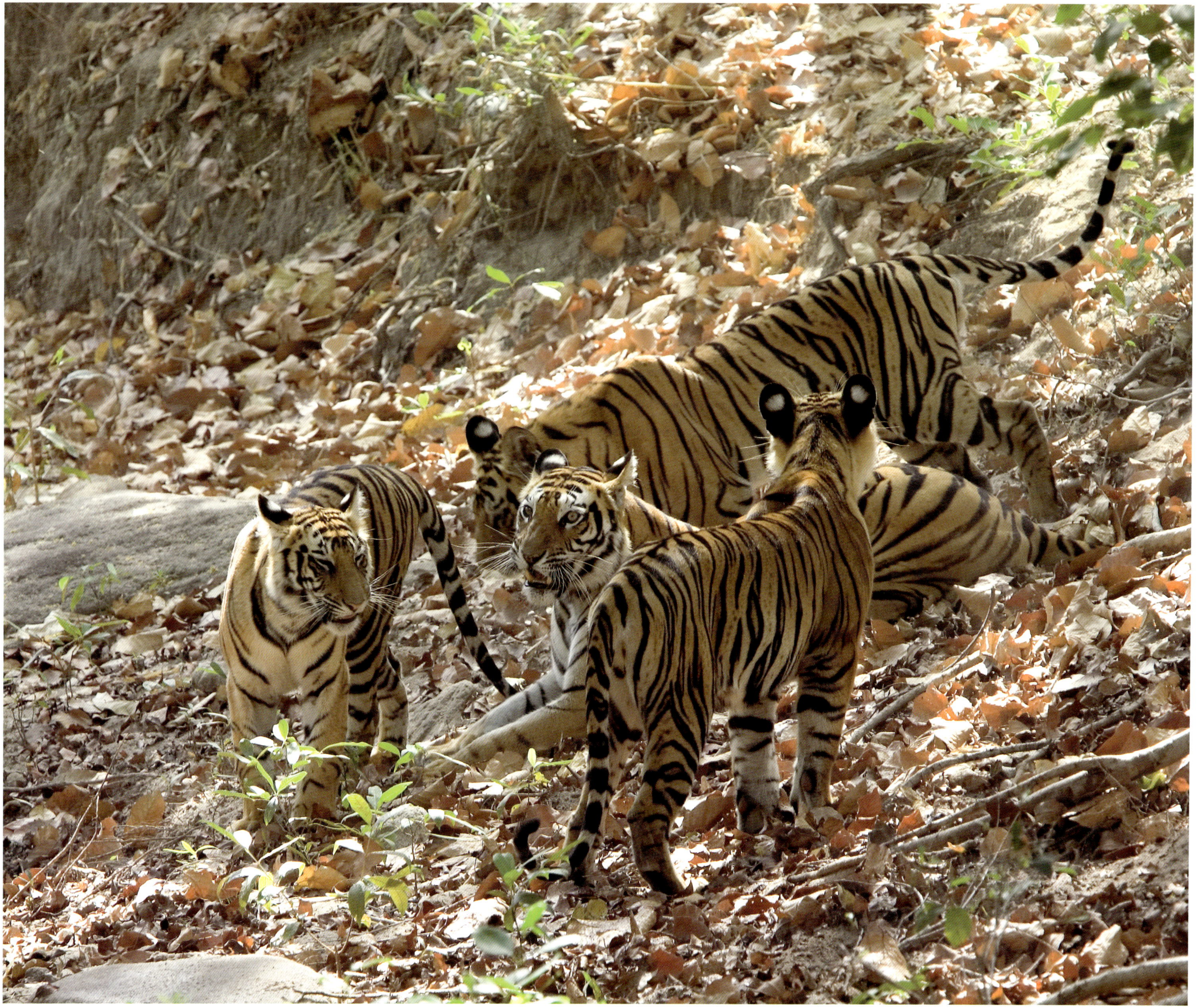

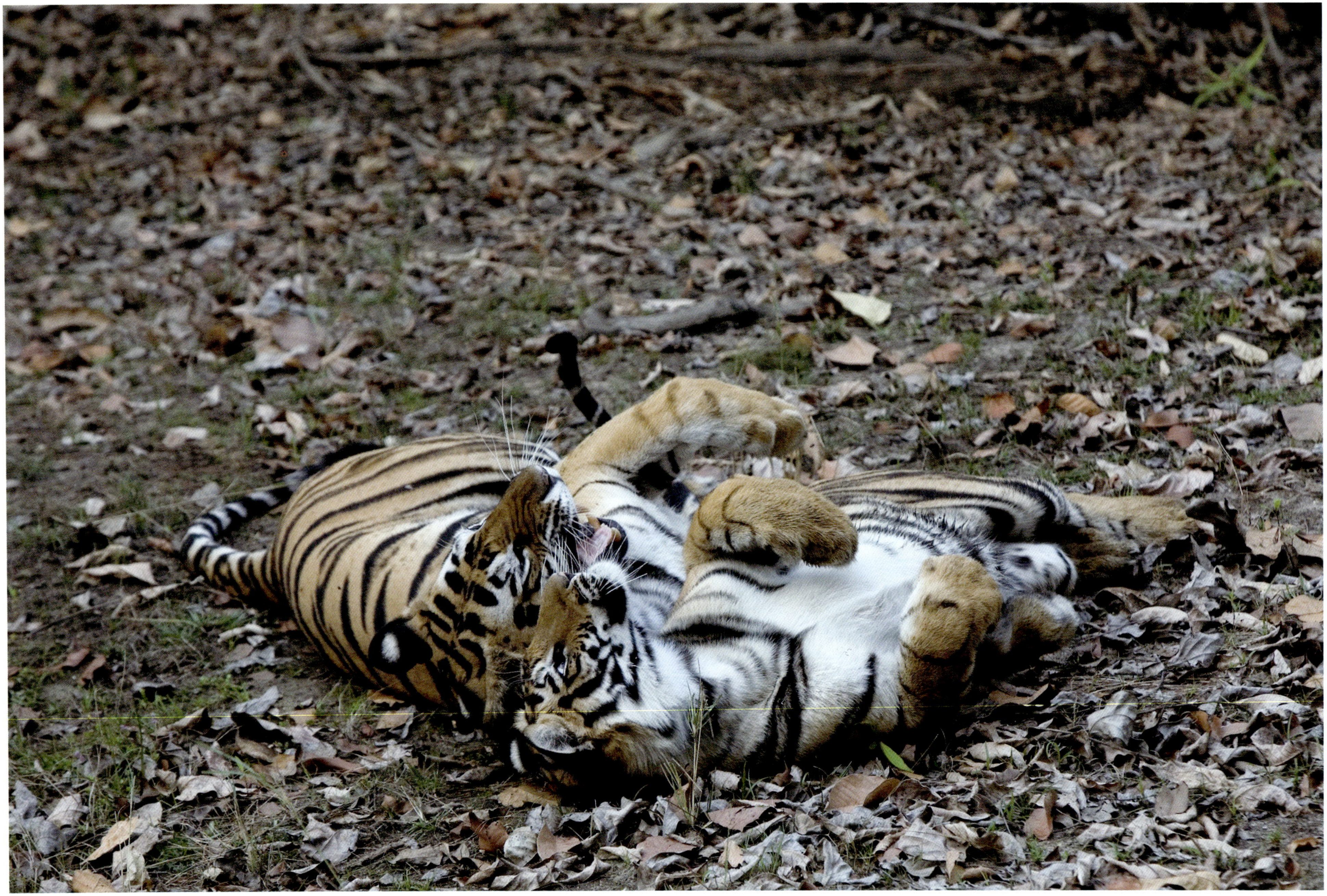

No other animal can afford to spend the day in such a relaxed pose, its vulnerable belly exposed.
A mother tiger and her 15-month-old cub raptly cuddle.
Only Bandhavgarh's tigers, the kings of the reserve, know a life free from fear.

She is finally satisfied – and thirsty. With the confident swagger of the huntress, she strolls over to the water hole. The axis deer on watch over the herd sends up a warning, and the startled group on the edge of the forest immediately moves close together to form an indistinguishable mass, even the kids now invisible in the press of bodies. Attempting to hunt them now would be futile. The tigress knows this from experience. She will not try to hunt again today.

Having, by now, acquired a vast store of experience concerning the other animals in the jungle, their routines, habits, hiding places and pathways, the young predator spares herself unnecessary effort. She sets off on a hunting expedition almost as if it were a predetermined appointment. As important as physical strength may be in the final phase, success comes only when everything has been minutely calculated, every eventuality carefully mapped out in the mind. This is because the species the tiger has singled out as prey are constantly watchful, aware of the tiniest change in their environment. They generally move in herds, with many eyes and ears, many noses and a sensitive intuition of danger. Their suspicion is their key to survival. The huntress, however, is alone, pitting her cunning against that of many. Her strategy always takes into account her victims' potential escape routes.

There is no such thing as luck in hunting. Or almost no such thing. The first male sambar deer, a sturdy animal of 300 kilos which the tigress brought down a few days before, practically ran into her open jaws. First trumpeting his usual DONK! DONK! warning to announce her hiding place, he then raised his ruff of fur, threw up his short tail, trampled his hooves and marched stiff-legged towards the bushes in which the big cat was crouched waiting to pounce. It is a strange characteristic of male sambar deer that they like to check whether their suspicions are well founded – whether an enemy actually is hiding in the spot they believe. And just a moment before this deer died, his suspicions were confirmed.

As the young tigress wades into the water and drinks deeply, the axis deer are still standing stiffly, necks extended. However, they gradually realize that this time there is no danger. The tension gradually leaves their bodies. Some lower their heads and begin to graze. Others trot nervously on the spot for a while.

The young tigress sees her mother less and less frequently; recently, encounters have taken place only once a week. At these times the big cats stage an emotional reunion, licking each other, rubbing their heads and bodies against each other. Later, the two spend a few hours together on the rocks, snuggled closely together and dozing away the hottest hours of the day. But the harmony will soon be over when the next litter of small siblings comes along. The two cats already spend much of their time avoiding each other.

The two brothers, boisterous daredevils as befits male tigers, did not survive their youth. One fell onto the rocks while pouncing on a langur monkey, and sprained his hip. Unable to accompany the family on hunting trips, he grew thin and weak and was finally eaten by a python. While attacking a Sambar deer, the other received a battery of kicks which shattered his jaw – an injury from which he later died.

The young tigress is now approaching the end of her sheltered childhood, her training for life as a predator. She is almost fully grown. In general, young tigers must leave their home, with all its familiarity – the forest, the bamboo groves, the water holes, the river, the clearing and its passing herds of antelopes, the hiding places. The advent of independence means she must seek her own living and hunting grounds – or perhaps conquer those of a rival by waging battle.

But it seems as if the young tigress will be allowed to stay. As if she will inherit a share of her mother's 20-square-kilometer (7.8-square-mile) territory. And the neighbor on the other side of the border has long since ceased staking her claims by leaving scratches and scent marks of urine. If things stay this way, the young predator will have acquired a prime jungle site, including a route to the water hole and the terrain on both sides of it. A predator that has learnt to wait patiently and crouches concealed in the hollows will never go hungry in game-rich Bandhavgarh. ■

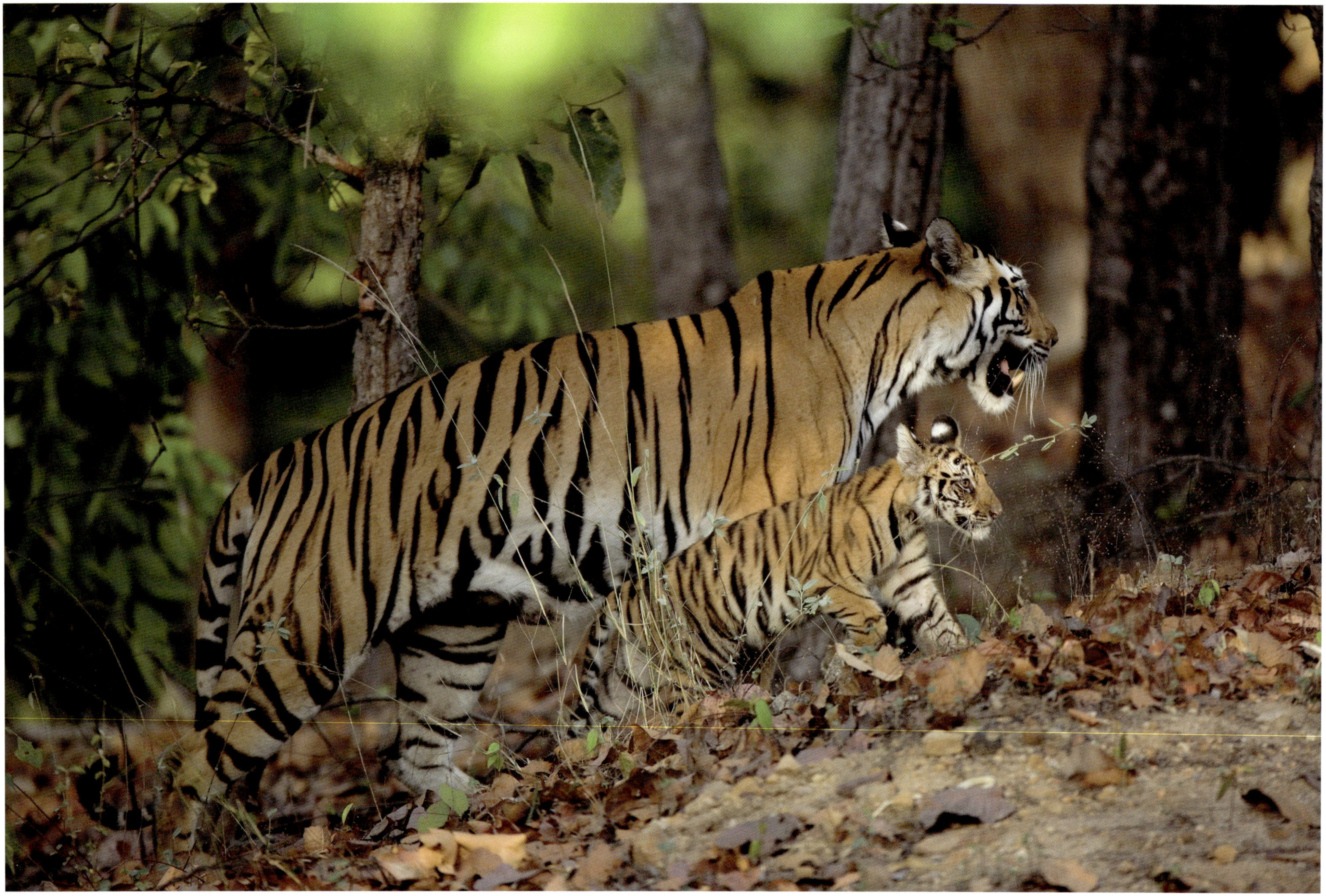

Every tiger has unique markings. The majority have broad dark stripes and stripes that merge at the tips. The flamed pattern probably developed from original rosette-shaped markings, which extended further and further during the course of evolution; this would explain the "gap" at the center of many stripes.

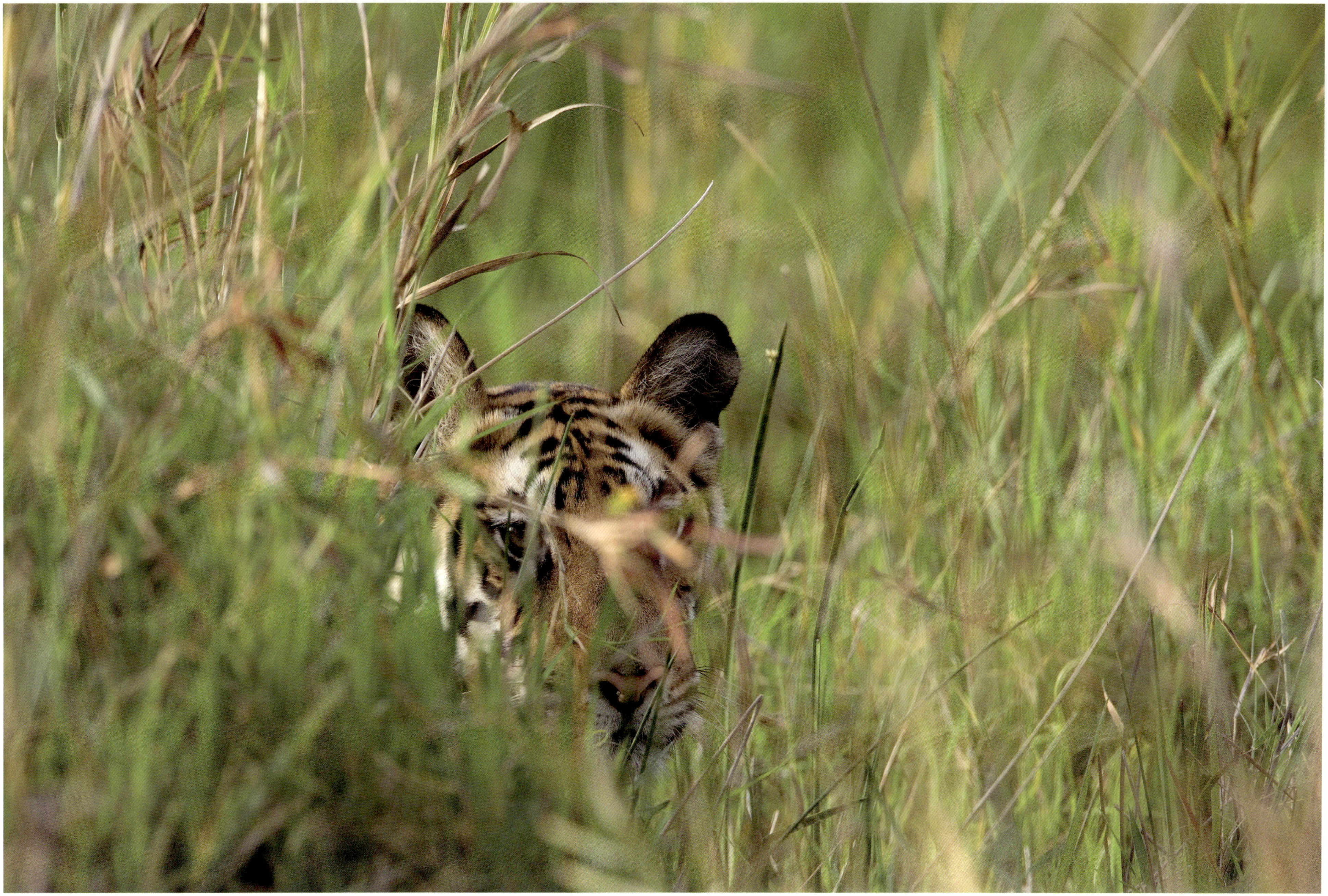

A young tigress relies on her coat for camouflage in the high grass. At the age of 20 months this big young female already hunts by herself. She lies down near the water hole in the late afternoon and waits patiently. As soon as twilight falls countless thirsty antelopes will have to pass her hiding place to reach the water.

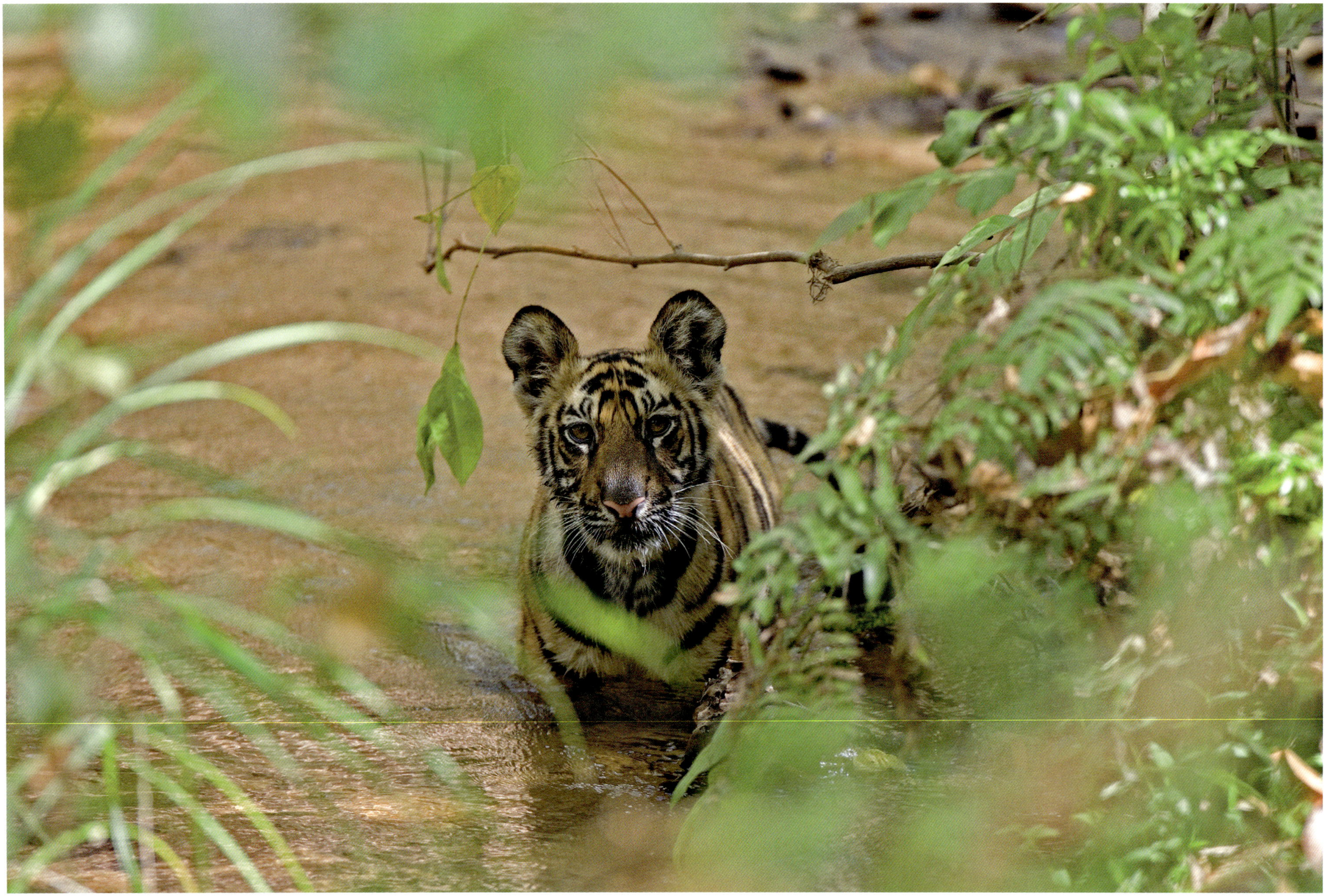

The tigers of Bandhavgarh prefer to spend the hottest hours of the day in pools and ponds.
Unlike most other big cats, tigers have no fear of water.
The four-month-old cub has just eaten and is now taking a cleansing bath.

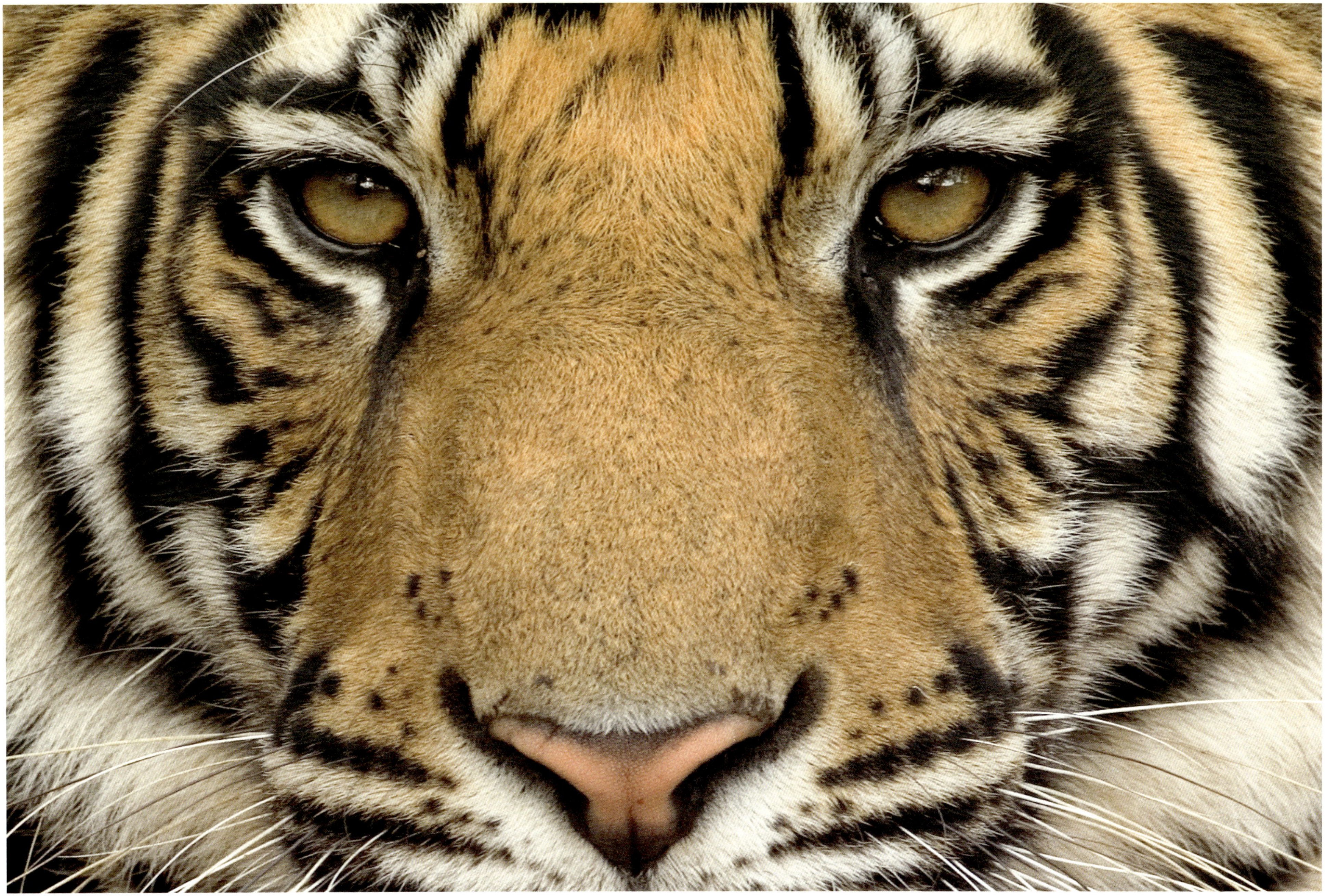

The eyes of this confident young tiger shimmer like amber. The nocturnal hunters have excellent eyesight even in the deepest twilight, thanks to a reflective layer at the back of their eyes, which redirects light back to the retina and stimulates it with new optical information. Even in darkness, the sensitive eyes of big cats miss little.

Indian Tigers – at a glance

Their place in the animal kingdom

- They belong to the phylum of vertebrates
- to the class of mammals
- to the order of predators
- to the cat family

Their scientific name

Panthera tigris tigris

Their closest relatives

Four to six million years ago, prehistoric cats began to evolve into the panther family. The clouded leopard was the first new species to develop, followed by the snow leopard and, around two million years ago, the other big cats – including tigers.

Where tigers live (population numbers)

Today there are five subspecies of tiger living in a wide variety of habitats. Tigers need territories with ample game stocks and with a supply of water. Around 5,000 animals live in the furthest eastern reaches of Russia and in North Korea, China, Sumatra, Thailand, Malaysia, Laos, Cambodia and Vietnam. One subspecies, the Indian tiger (pop. 3,000–4,000), can be found in India, Bangladesh, Nepal, Bhutan and Myanmar.

Tigers in figures

- Tigers are the **biggest living cats** in the world.
- Indian tigers are the **second largest** subspecies after the Siberian tiger;.
- Females grow to a **length** of 270 centimeters (around 9.0 feet), while male tigers can be up to 320 centimeters (10.5 feet) long.
- The **weight** of a male tiger is around 280 kilos, while females weigh approximately 180 kilos.
- Tigers can devour up to 30 kilos of meat at a **single meal**.
- Tigers can reach **speeds** of 60 kilometers (37 miles) per hour over short distances.
- They are powerful **jumpers**, clearing heights of 5 meters (16.5 feet) and lengths of 10 meters (33 feet).
- Female tigers reach **sexual maturity** at the age of three, males not until the age of four.
- Tigers require **territories** of up to 100 square kilometers (39 square miles), encompassing several territories of females of around 20 square kilometers (around 7.7 square miles) each.
- Their average **gestation period** is 103 days.
- Tigers have a **life expectancy** of approximately 20 years.

Indian tigers' characteristic features

A tiger's most striking feature is precisely what makes it so inconspicuous in the jungle: its markings. Indian tigers have particularly bold markings, with thick dark stripes against an orange background and sharply edged areas of white. Tigers are particularly effectively camouflaged in grass, where their black stripes imitate the shadows of the stalks. Their whiskers, or vibrissae, are highly sensitive, enabling the tiger to find its way through the thick jungle foliage at night.

What tigers eat

Although tigers are skilful hunters, they bring down prey only around one time out of ten. They eat anything they can catch – antelopes, elephant calves, water birds – and may also kill animals larger and heavier than themselves by the sheer force of their attack, and by the stealth with which they surprise their unsuspecting prey. They kill by giving a powerful bite to the neck or throat.

Indian tigers' lifestyle

Tigers spend up to twenty hours a day in an inactive state, resting in the shade or cooling themselves by bathing in shallow pools. Adult tigers are solitary, and do not tolerate other tigers in their territories. Females generally live with their cubs. Territorial battles among tigers are frequent and violent. Tigers regularly patrol their territory to establish whether the tigresses in their smaller sub-territories are in heat. When a male finds a receptive female, he mates repeatedly with her for several days; ovulation is induced by the frequency of copulation. After around 103 days, the female gives birth to two to four cubs in a hidden place or cave.

How tigers raise their young

Male tigers protect the territory in which their young grow up, repelling intruding males that may harm their cubs. While they occasionally visit their family, the females alone are responsible for the care and training of the cubs. Although cubs may nurse for up to six months, they begin to eat meat at eight weeks of age. Young tigers pick up hunting skills by playing and by watching their mother – a training period of almost two years, after which it is time for them to hunt their own prey and seek their own territory.

Dangers to tigers

Only 25 per cent of all tiger cubs survive their first year; the rest are killed by other tigers or fall prey to jackals, wild dogs or pythons. Tigers are endangered by illegal trade.

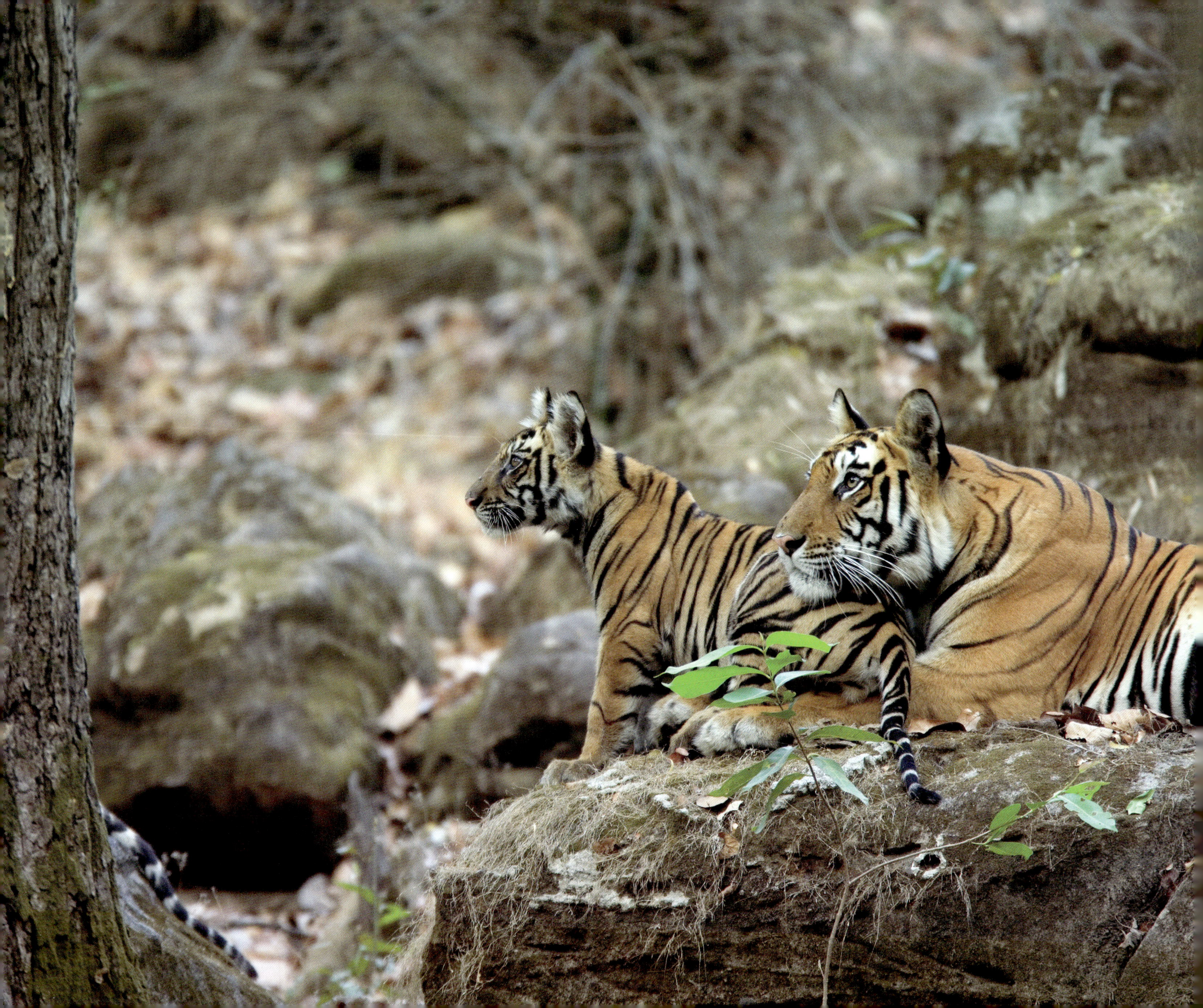

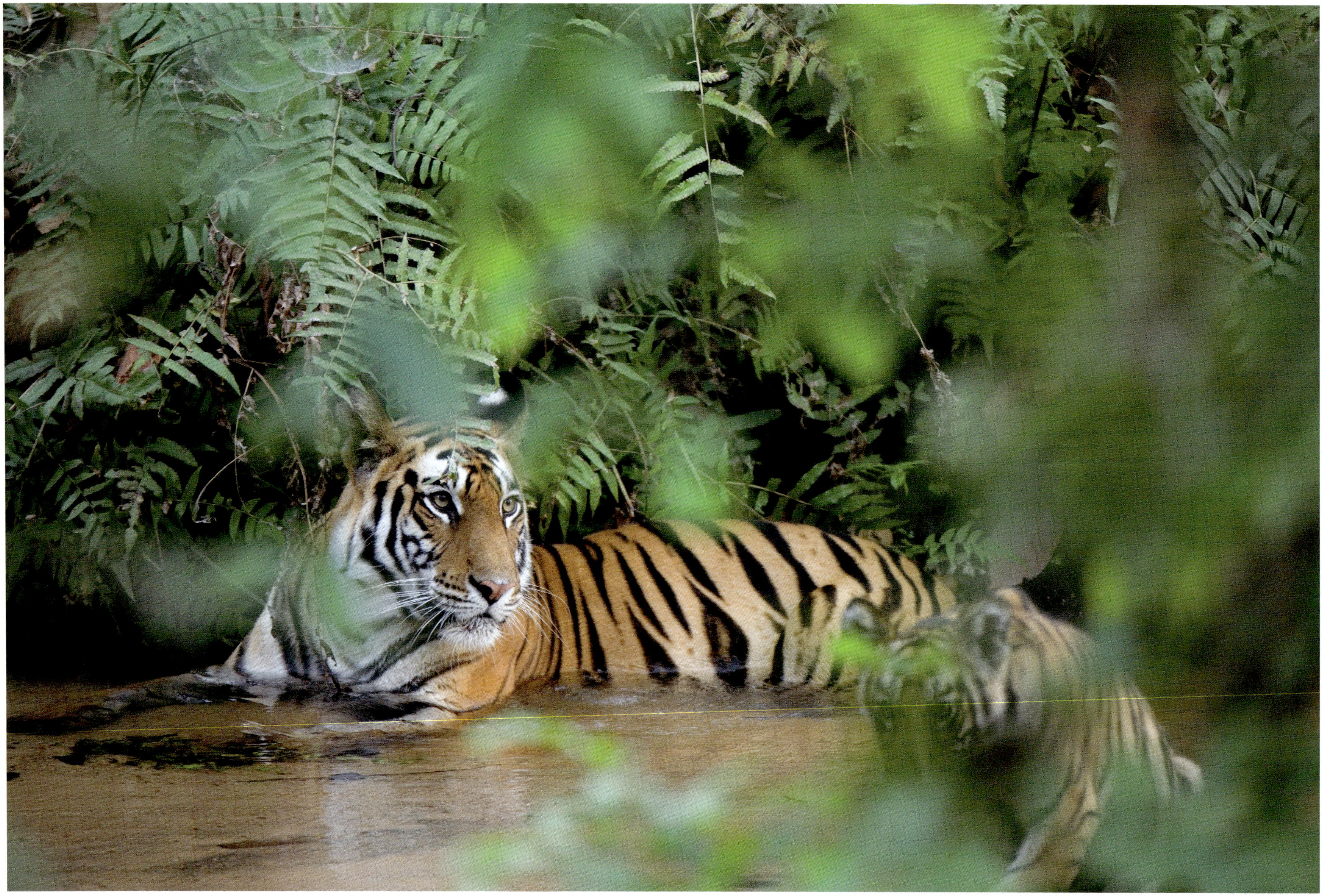

Bandhavgarh Tiger Reserve is full of water holes, ponds, pools and streams – an attractive location for tigers. During the summer months the big cats need a cooling oasis. The geographical location of these refreshing spots is one of the elementary lessons taught to the cubs by their mothers.

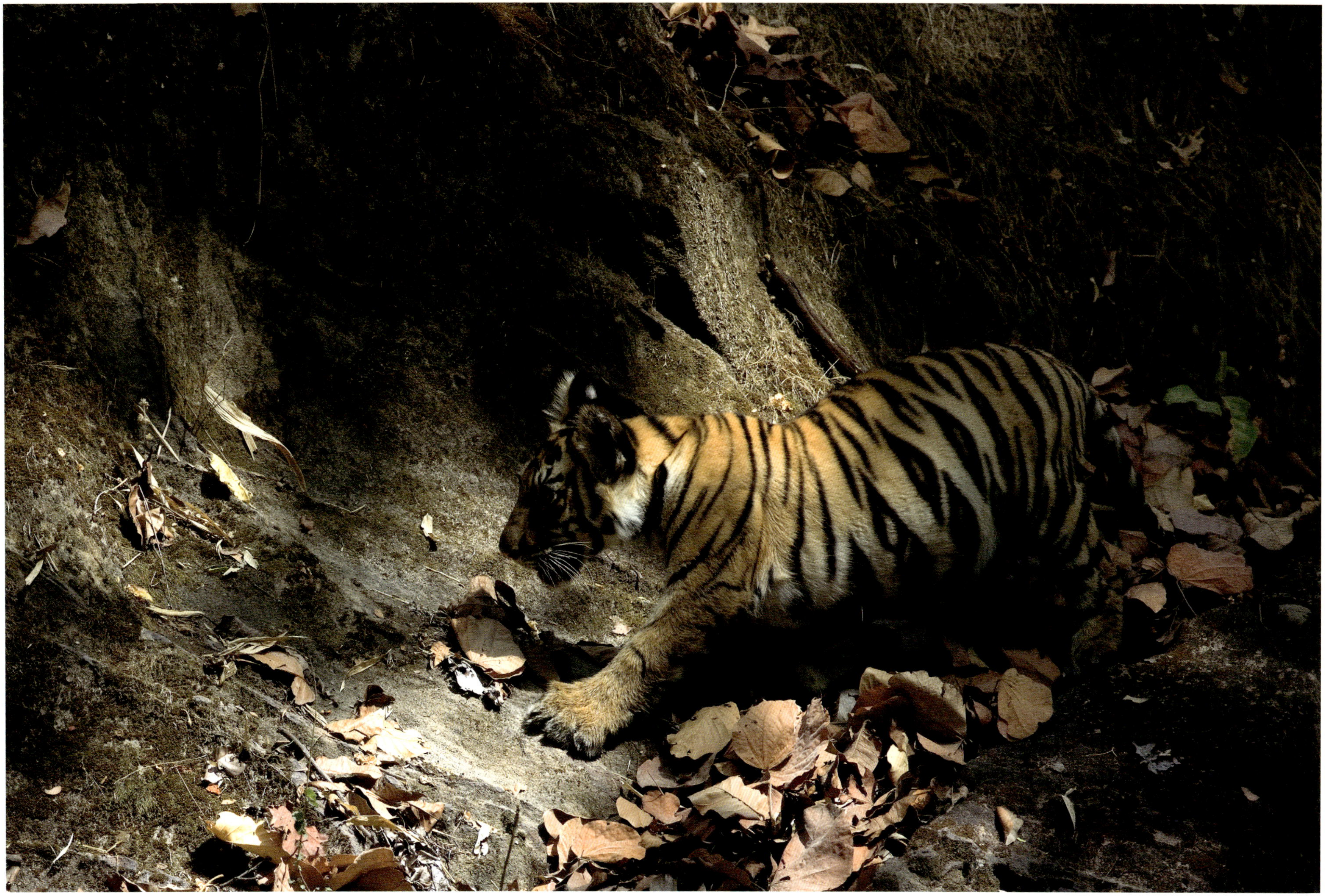

The four-month-old cub has eaten well and now hauls his distended stomach into the shade.
Tigers spend a good 20 hours a day doing nothing.
They prefer to lie in a slightly elevated place, perhaps a rocky outcrop, with an occasional breeze.

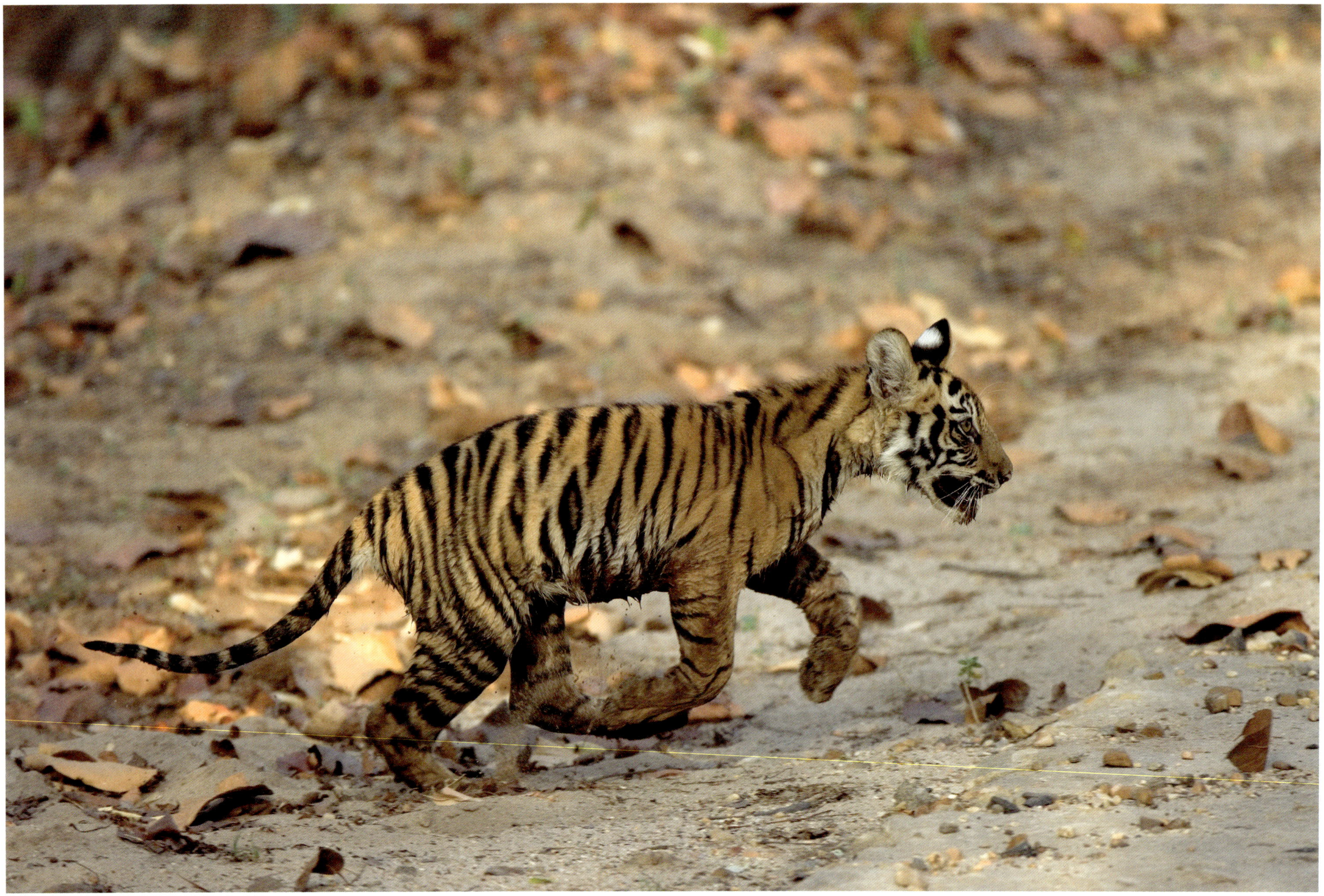

The three-month-old cub, coat dripping, crosses a sandy track in Bandhavgarh Tiger Reserve. Supervised by his mother, he has been bathing and now follows her back to one of the higher-set caves in the park which are part of every tiger's territory. Here, mothers hide their cubs before they go hunting.

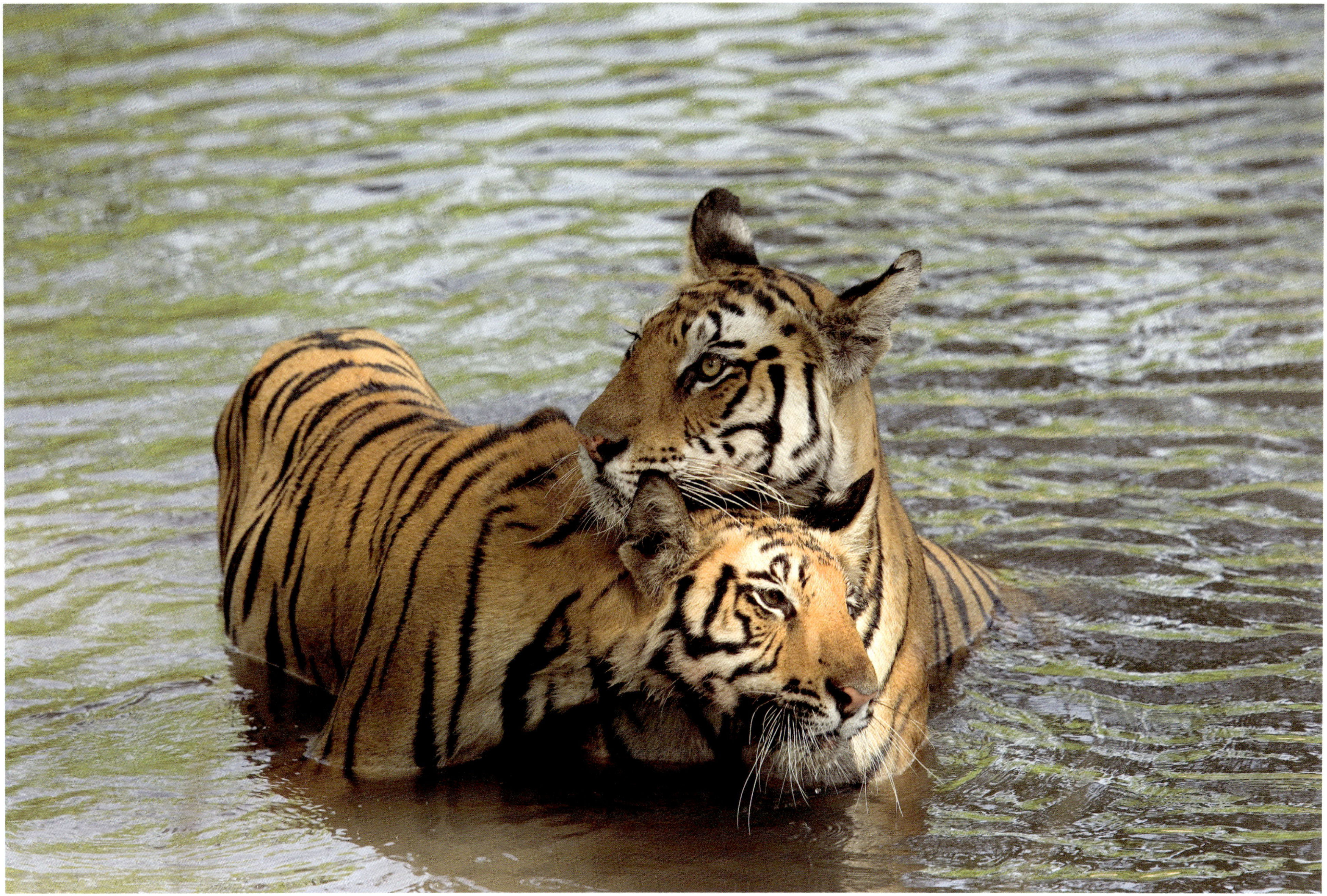

A mother tiger and her 17-month-old cub have just been romping in the water. Now they rub each other's whiskers and snuggle up to each other tenderly. Tiger cubs spend a long time with their mothers, learning the art of the predator before they are able to look after themselves.

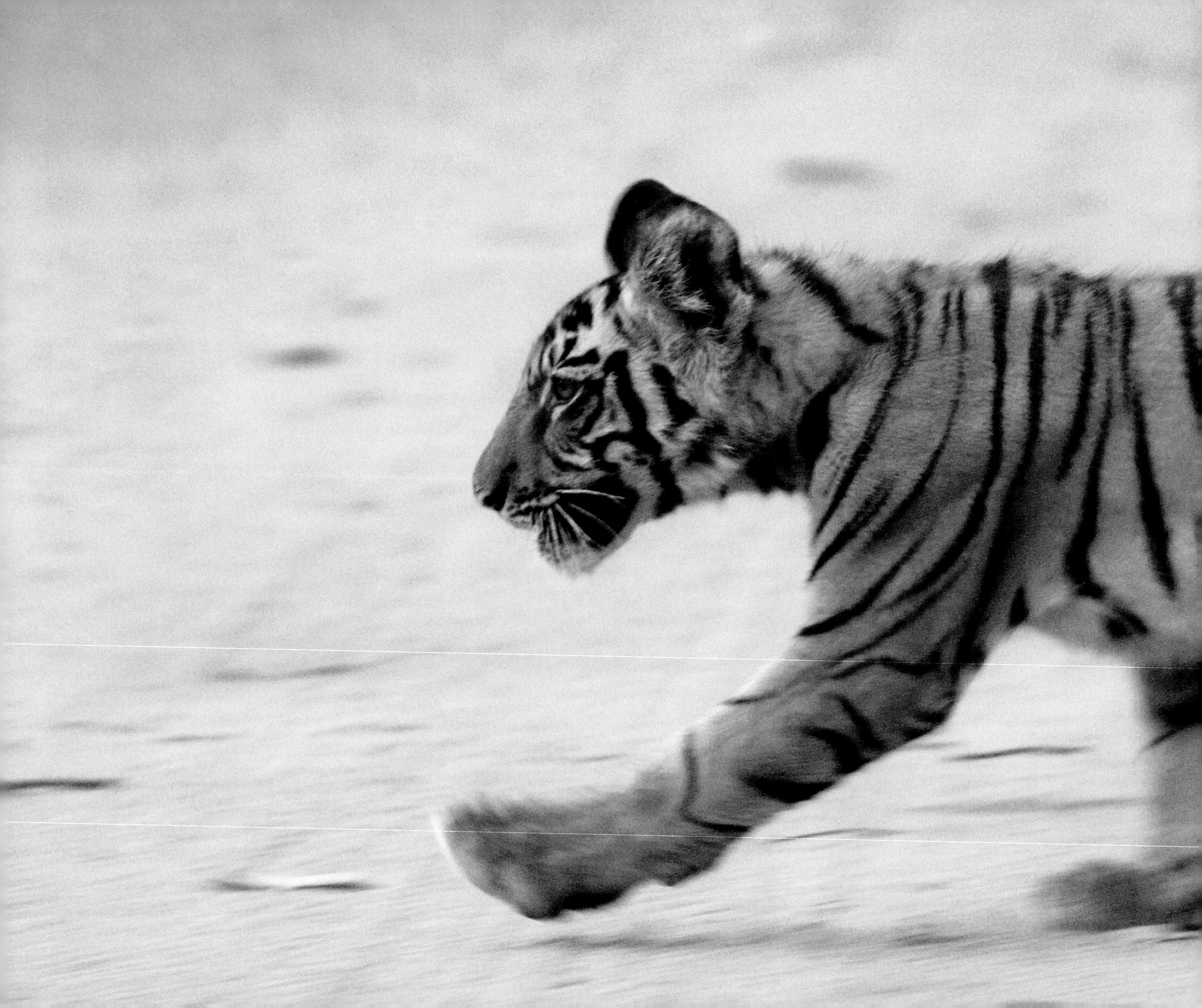

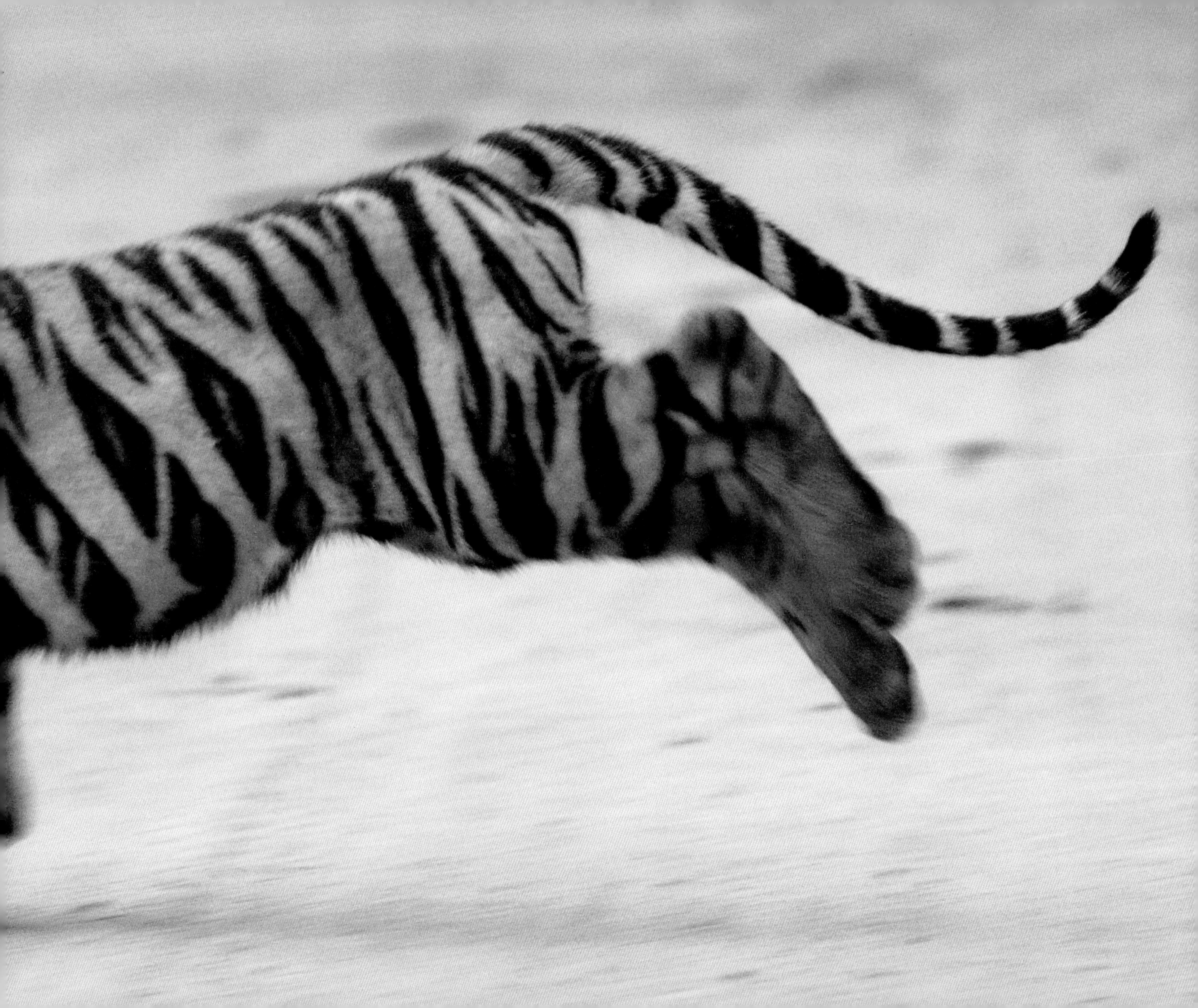

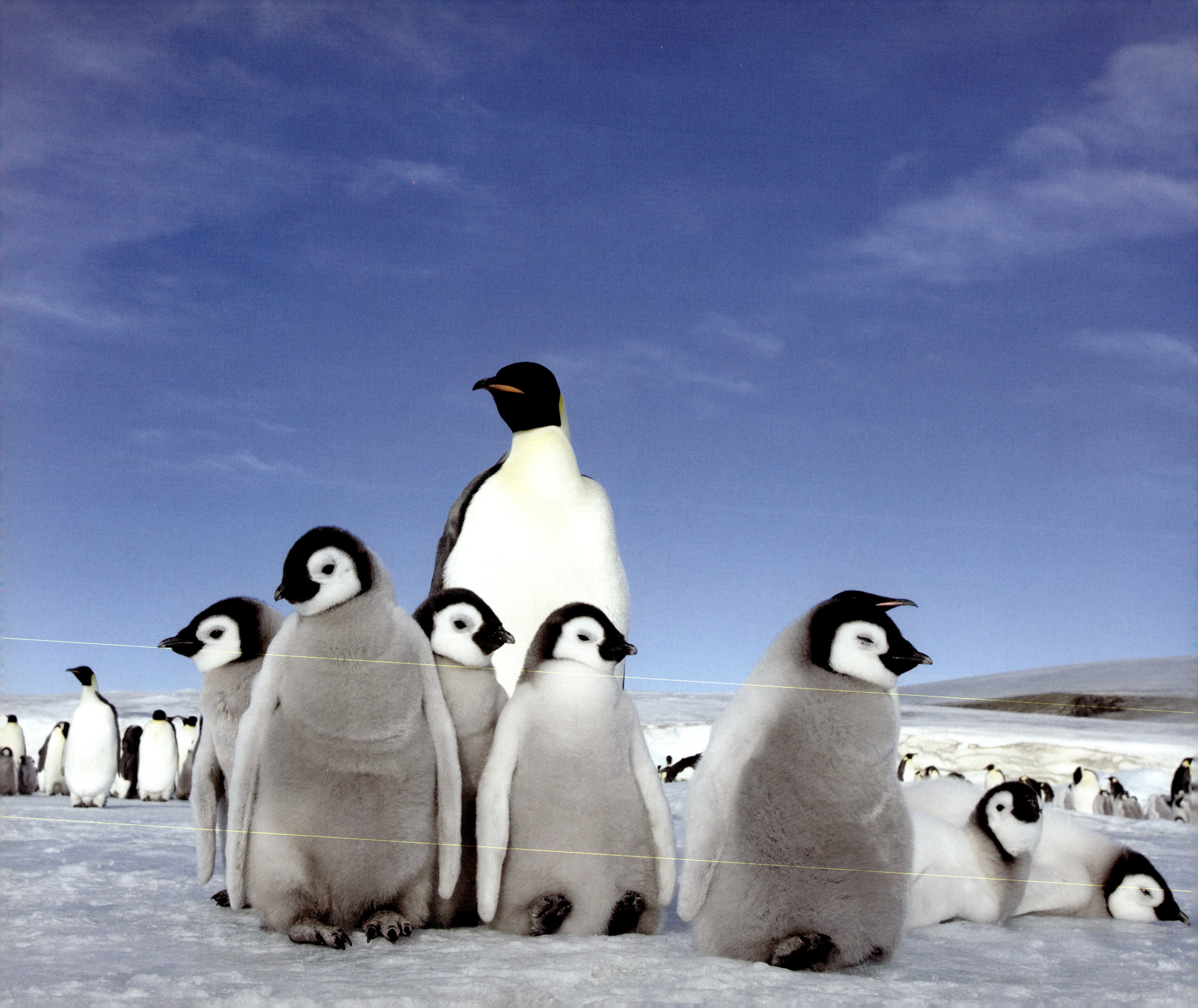

Emperor Penguins

A Colony of Huddlers

As if shot from an underwater launching pad, several dozen emperor penguins break the turbulent surface of the ocean, describing a low parabola before landing on the ice with both feet. An acrobatic tour de force at the end of the world. The birds take only a moment to regain their balance and rearrange their ruffled feathers before marching onward.

Over a meter (3.28 feet) tall, the figures make an endearingly clumsy impression as they waddle along. As if at any moment they could tumble over in a thoroughly un-imperial fashion. In fact, emperor penguins use twice as much energy when walking as any other animal of the same size, because of their short legs. Their muscles have to work overtime, delivering the impetus to move a considerable weight of 30 to 40 kilos. However, the clownish swaying recoups 80 percent of the energy loss by generating forward momentum. The birds cover heroic distances with their waddling gait – up to 200 kilometers (124 miles) if necessary.

And for the female emperor penguins that have just emerged from the icy Weddell Sea off Snow Hill Island, the outermost tip of the Antarctic peninsula, walking is imperative. They choose the worst time to do it – the first half of July, the Antarctic winter, with temperatures of minus 40 degrees Celsius and winds of up to 200 kilometers (124 miles) per hour. The birds must travel a good 50 kilometers (31 miles) before they reach the traditional breeding grounds of their population. And they hurry as if they are already rather late for an appointment. Their fat feet and downward pointing toes drum incessantly onto the ice.

Exactly how they find their destination in the trackless white of the pack ice and snowdrifts, exactly how their sense of orientation functions, is unknown. Since the female penguins left the breeding ground many weeks ago and marched to the ocean, the border of frozen salt water surrounding Snow Hill Island has roughly doubled in size, so that the return journey is twice as long and the terrain largely unfamiliar.

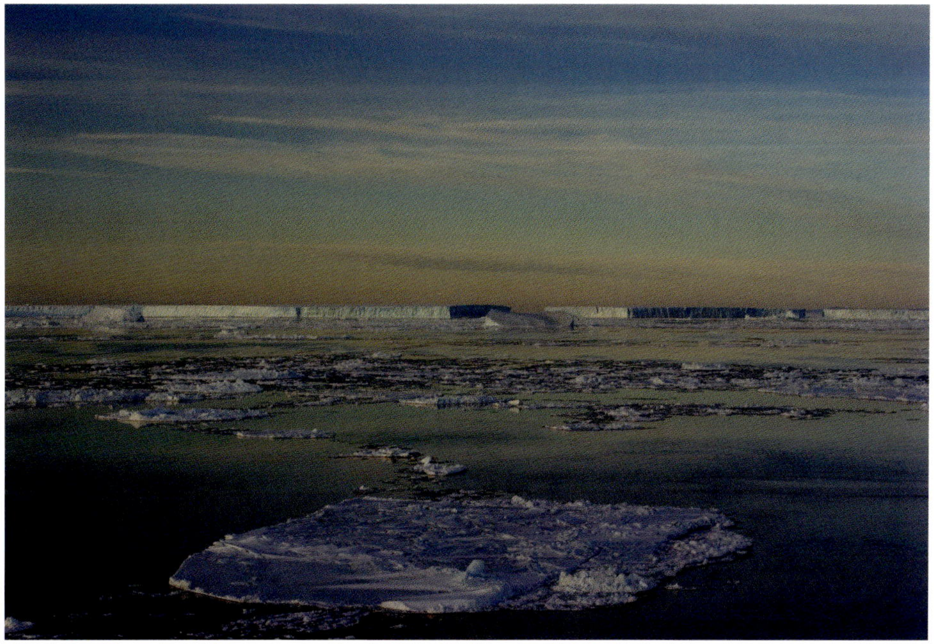

They cross ice plates, surmount hillocks and blocks, skirt the steep cliffs of icebergs frozen fast in the sea. They traverse a desert of crystals that they have never seen before. And yet all the females determinedly head in the same direction, one after the other, a ribbon of waddling black-and-white figures. All driven by the same longing.

Even more astonishing than the female penguins' sense of direction is their punctuality. How do they know that the time has come to keep an appointment they made with their partner two months ago? Everything depends on the convoy of females reaching the breeding grounds

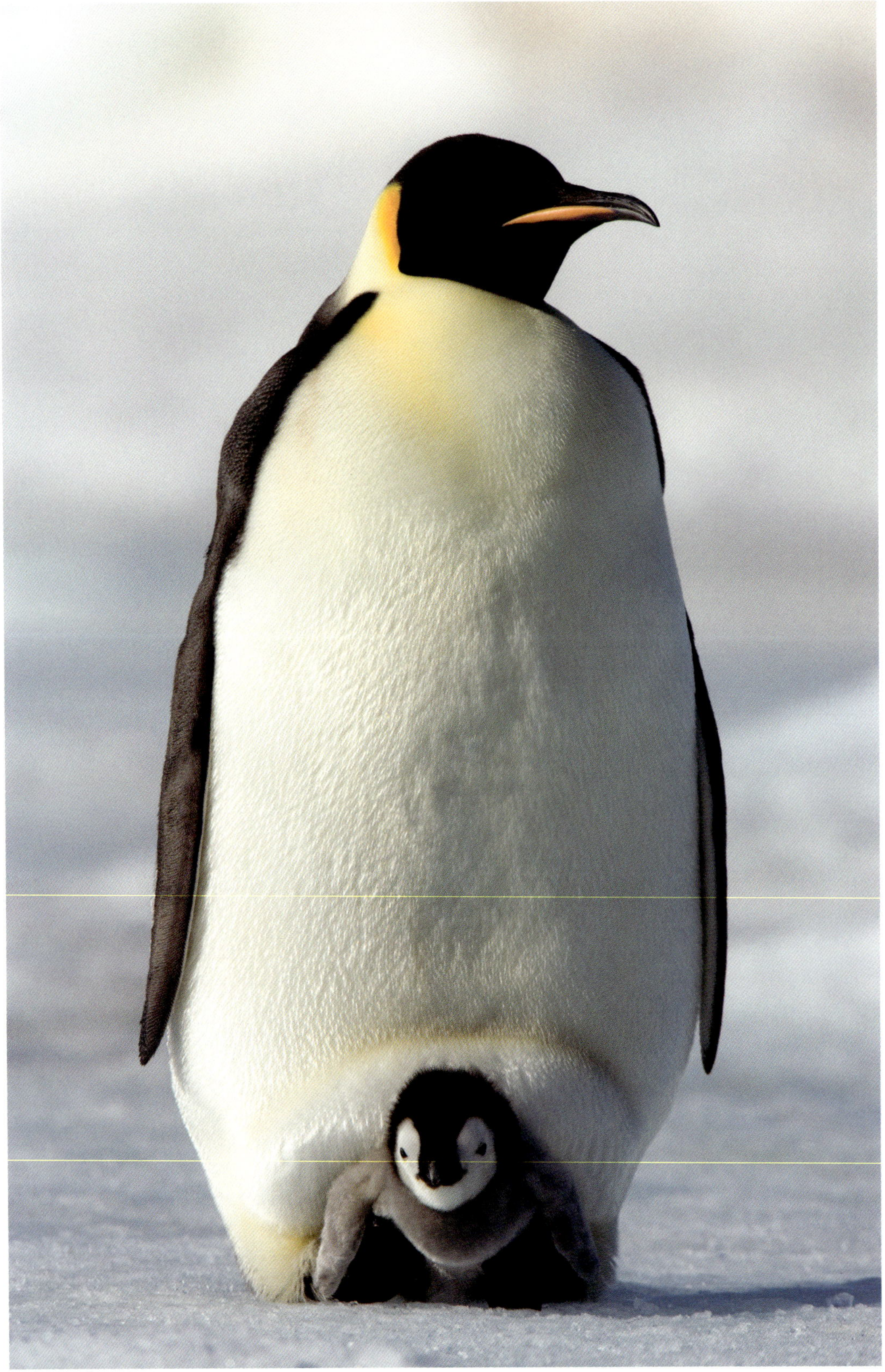

in time: the success of the whole year's breeding activities, the survival of their only chick, the genetic future of the couple. Perhaps some of the females are already mothers at this very moment as they slide down a sloping ice field on their fronts. Perhaps, far away, their chick has just hatched and is cheeping for food.

Even though they do not hatch their eggs themselves, mother emperor penguins evidently sense how their chicks are faring. All the females in the Snow Hill colony that had found a male and mated in March, laid their 500-gram egg in May, left it to the care of their partner and disappeared for an extended orgy of gluttony in the ocean. There, surrounded by an excess of food, the overwhelming feeling must have assailed them: my chick is about to hatch.

An emperor penguin embryo develops in around 65 days. It is unlikely that the female penguins consciously count the days. How would they measure time passing? Particularly since in the Antarctic winter darkness reigns for 20 hours a day, except for the polar lights flickering across the sky. But somewhere deep inside the bird's organism, a still-undiscovered biological clock starts ticking when the female lays her egg, and sounds the alarm when she is needed.

The call must be irresistible. For the penguins climb out of their true element, the sea, to begin the long, arduous march to their partner, their chick and the chance of assuring the survival of part of themselves, their biological identity.

As they approach, they hear the characteristic cawing from far away, hovering over the colony like a many-voiced vibrating cloud. 4,000 male emperor penguins stand on the same spot selected by uncounted generations before them to fulfill what is probably the hardest paternal role in the world: caring for their precious young.

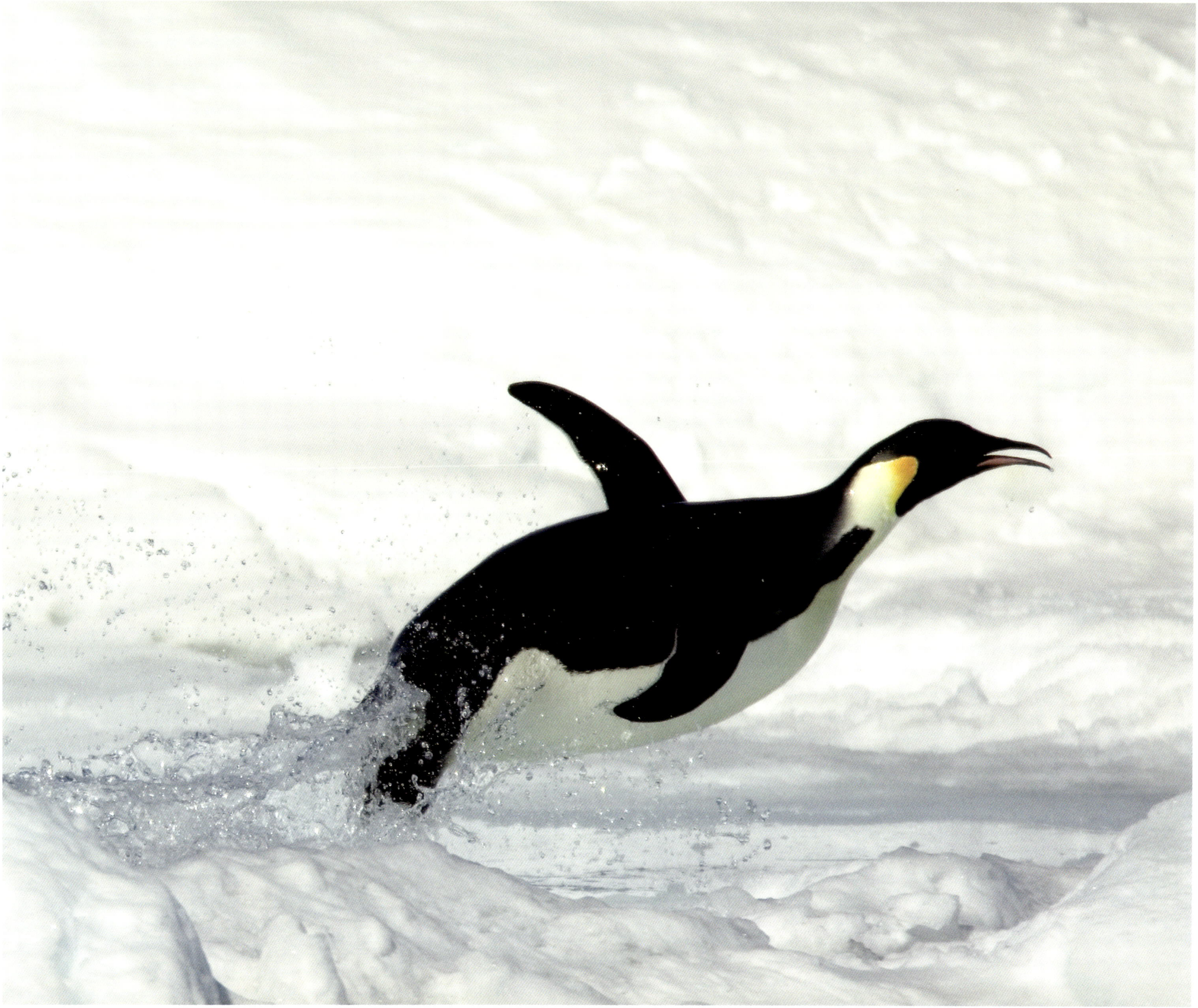

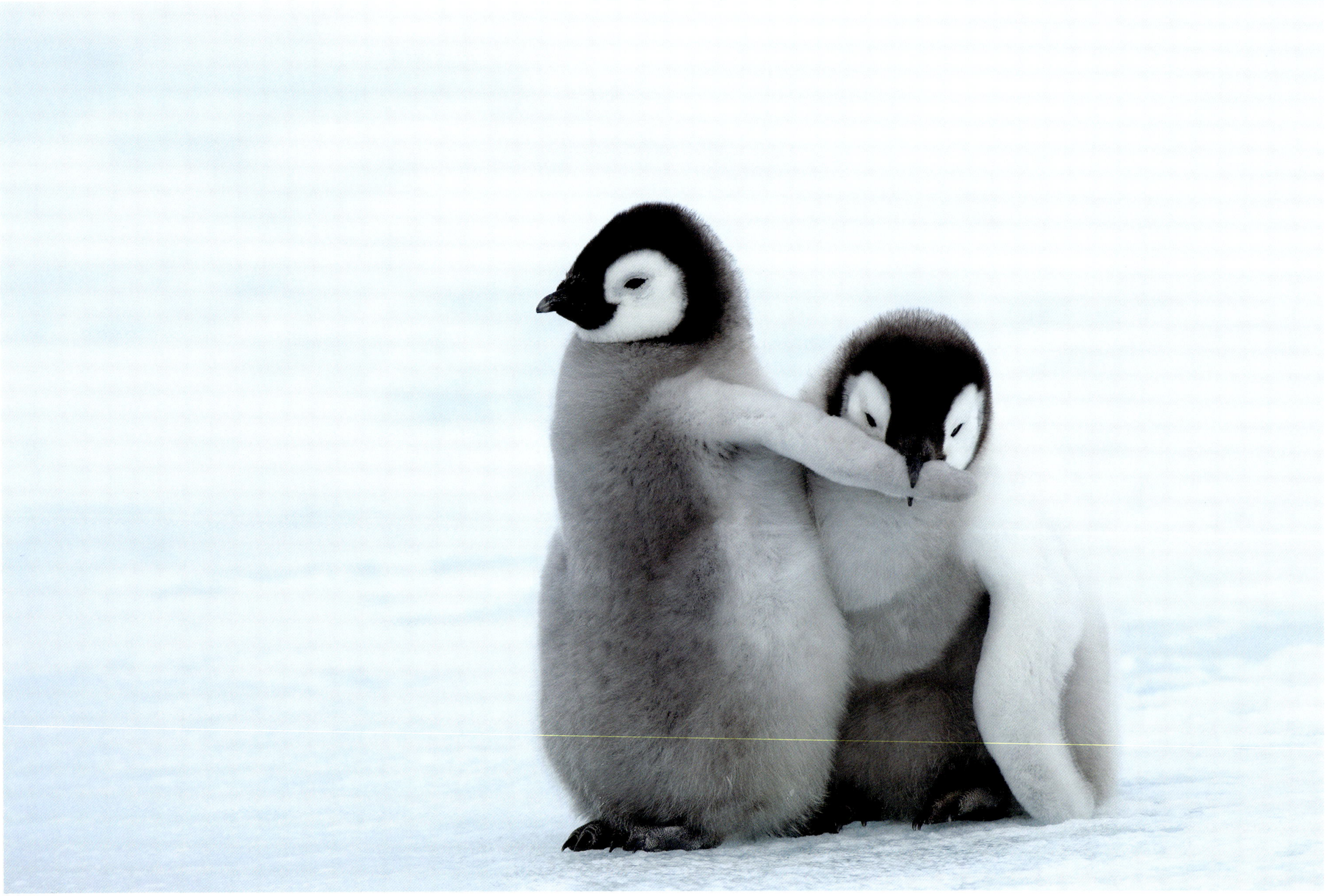

Since all emperor penguins in a breeding colony mate and lay their eggs at more or less the same time, several thousand young birds are all roughly the same age. And equally high-spirited. Wing-tweaking is one of the chicks' favourite games.

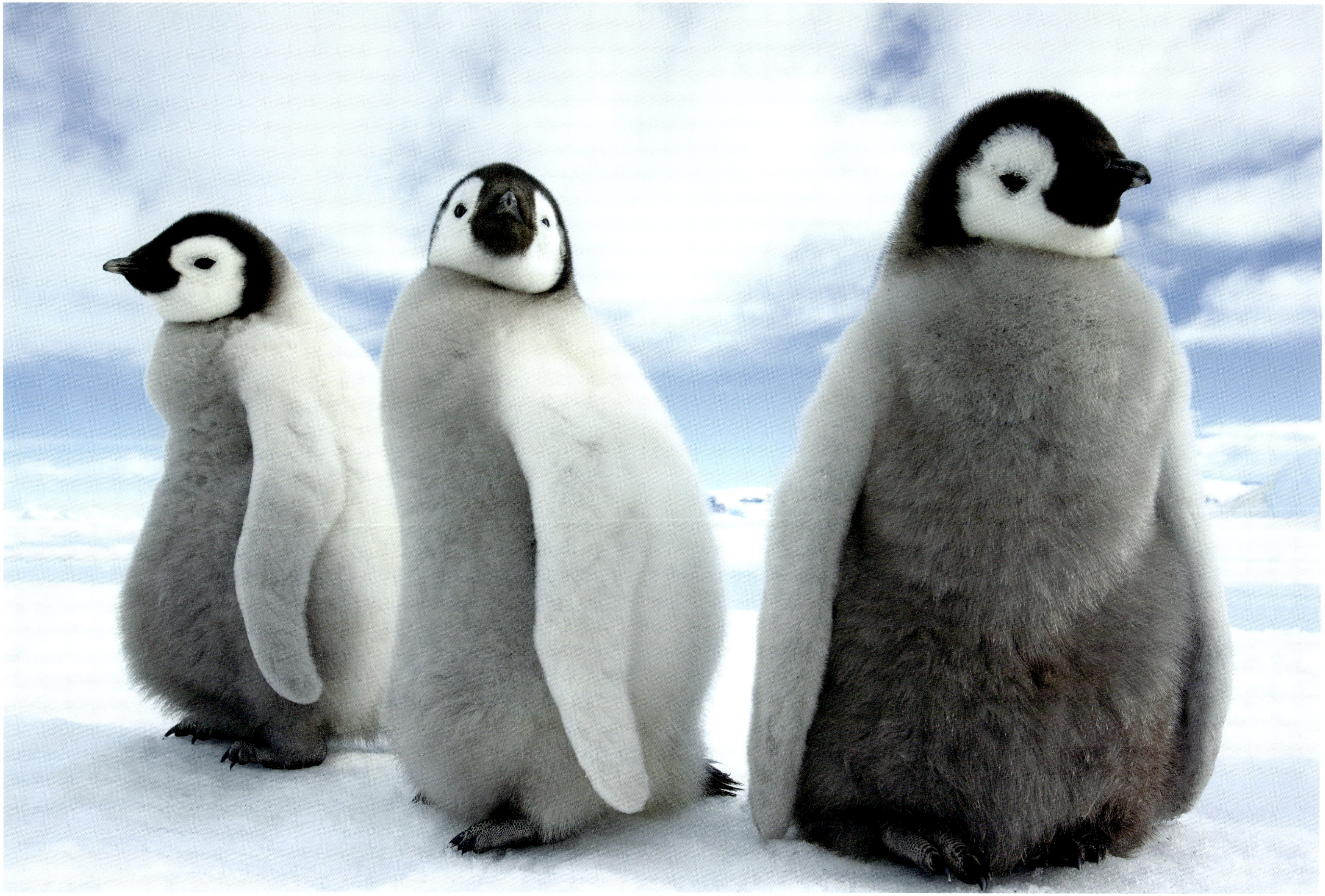

Penguin chicks are always hungry.
In good weather the down-swaddled birds stand in small groups, watching and waiting for their mother or father to return from the sea with a stomachful of fresh fish and krill.

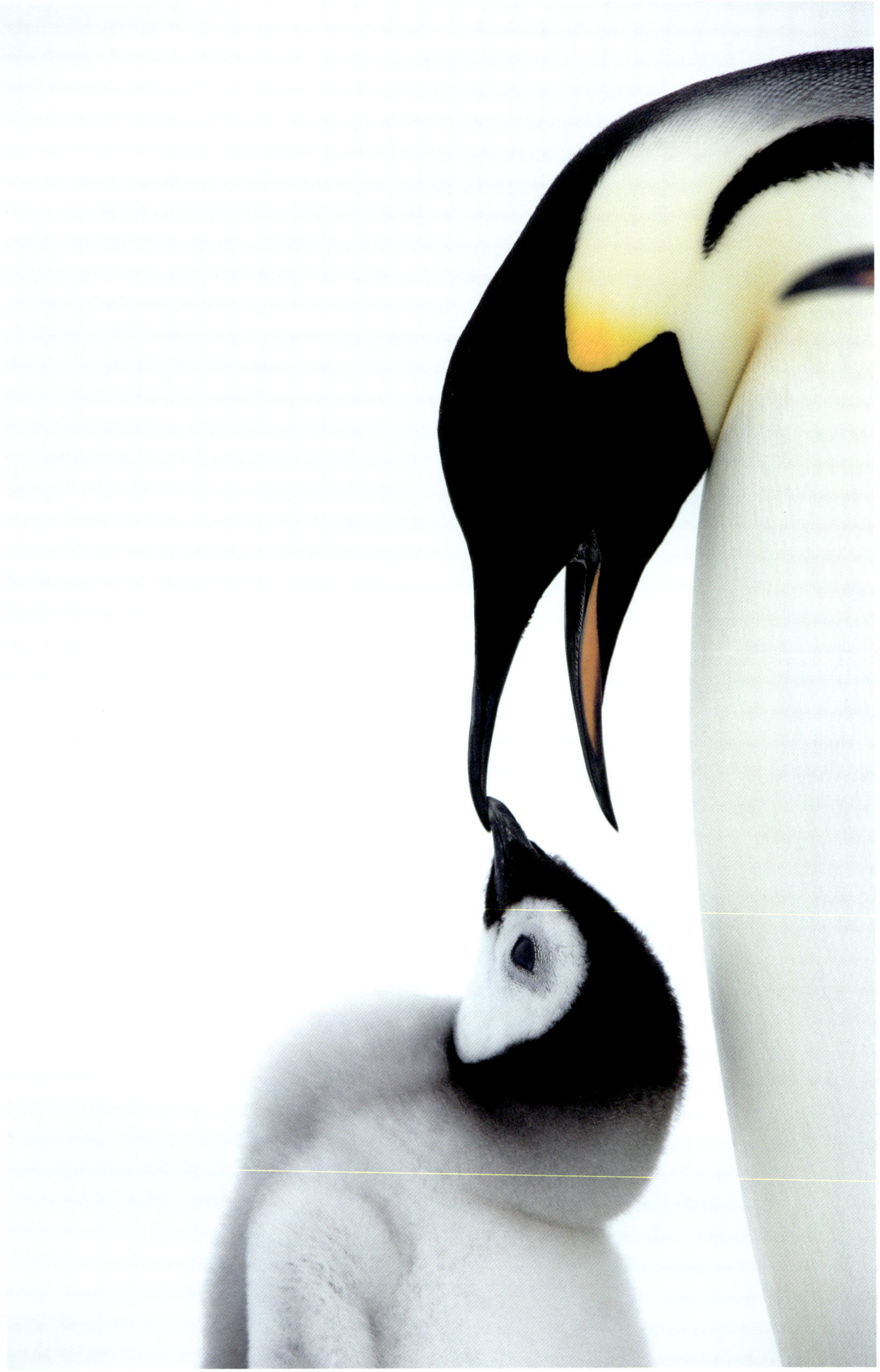

Both as egg and chick, the young penguins rest on the feet of their parents, well protected from the icy ground. In addition, the father's generous abdominal fold is spread over them like a thick tea-cozy. In this improvised brood pouch the temperature is a constant 38 degrees – ideal conditions for incubation. It remains steady when temperatures plummet to minus 57 in the icy breath of the polar cap and snowstorms howl and shriek around the colony.

Emperor penguins differ from most birds in more or less every aspect of rearing their young – beginning with the role of mother, which is initially the sole responsibility of the father. In addition, the penguins bring up their young not in spring or summer, but – of all times – in winter. They make not the slightest attempt to build a nest or even an indication of one by scraping together a little material, as other penguin species do. Their egg is mobile. It is as much a traveler as its parent, who balances it on his feet and occasionally even embarks on excursions and skating parties with his unborn offspring.

As if that were not unusual enough, penguins have also sited their reproduction in a location considered to be among the most inhospitable climates in the world. However, they are at least extremely well equipped for this extreme decision.

For one thing, they are large. Their body surface cools considerably more slowly than that of smaller animals, and their feathers are denser than those of any member of the bird family. Thirty-five feathers per square centimeter, interlinked by tiny hooks, form an elastic shield capable of deflecting even hurricanes. Under this protective coat grows a gossamer-soft layer of down in which warm air circulates. And under the skin lies what was being built up throughout the carefree summer months: a relatively thick layer of fat, providing additional insulation and accounting for roughly one third of their body weight.

The only area of naked skin which comes into contact with the ice is on the penguin's feet. To ensure that blood circulation to the feet is maintained, the birds generally stand on their heels, supporting themselves with their tail feathers to avoid falling over.

Penguins have developed an unusual strategy to protect themselves from the blizzards that often sweep over the icy ground of the earth's frost capital for weeks at a time without a break, devouring body heat and soon exhausting the energy reserves of an isolated bird. Penguins huddle. Packed together shoulder to shoulder, all the birds in the colony stand in a circle and form a living fortress defying the raging forces of nature. In this animal island of heat, up to ten penguins crowd into one square meter, each one thus saving up to 40 percent on "heating costs" and enabling it to slow down its metabolic rate and reduce consumption of its fat reserves.

The temperature is naturally highest in the center, a cozy 20 degrees. But no single member of the colony has the right to reserve the best place for itself. Penguins do not have hierarchies or individual claims to specific territory; locations are constantly reassigned. The same applies to the huddling masses. A continuous gentle shoving, shuffling and exchange of places takes place in the apparently unmoving mass of figures bent against the storm. The circle becomes a churning spiral, so that each bird in this procession takes its turn in the warm center and on the icy periphery.

It may actually be refreshing for emperor penguins to be forced to leave the crowded, bustling center of the group. Again and again, individual birds in the huddling mass stretch up their astonishingly elastic neck to exhale a cloud of steamy breath.

In the two darkest months of the Antarctic winter, father penguins incubate the egg entrusted to their care. There is no food in the icy desert. The male emperor penguins have fasted since they left the ocean in March and embarked on the pilgrimage to the colony to find a female and mate. For four whole months – a record not only for birds – the feathered heroes live from their reserves of fat and from the hope that their partner will keep her appointment, that she will return in time with a stomach full of nourishment for the baby chick.

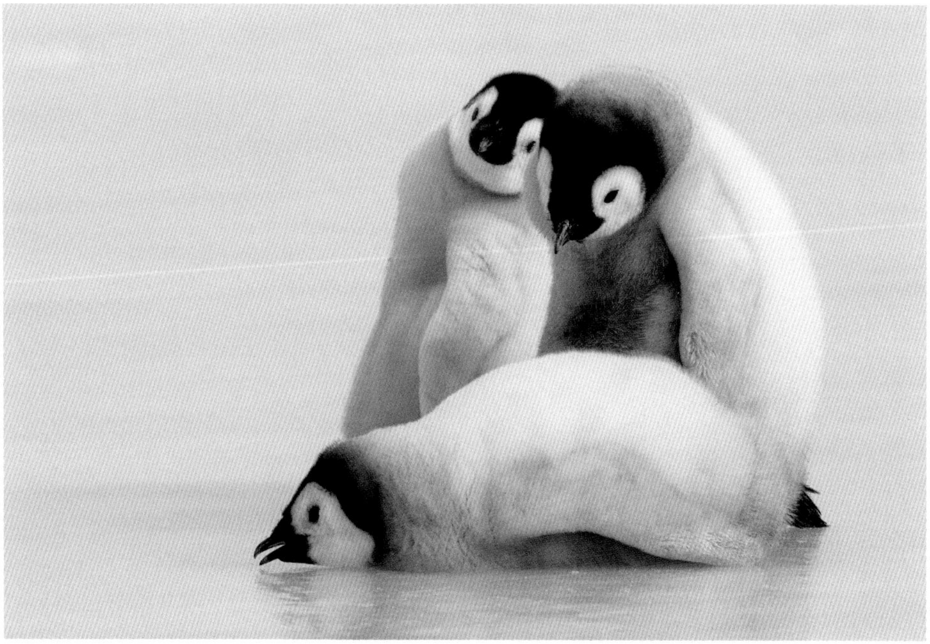

When the train of female penguins reaches the edge of the colony, they are faced with a new, seemingly insuperable challenge. How can they locate the father of their chick among the thousands of almost identical males?

There follows a "couples challenge" in which both birds must rely on their good memory. They must recall the time of courtship, mating and, above all, the sound of their partner's voice as they emitted ecstatic cries of love.

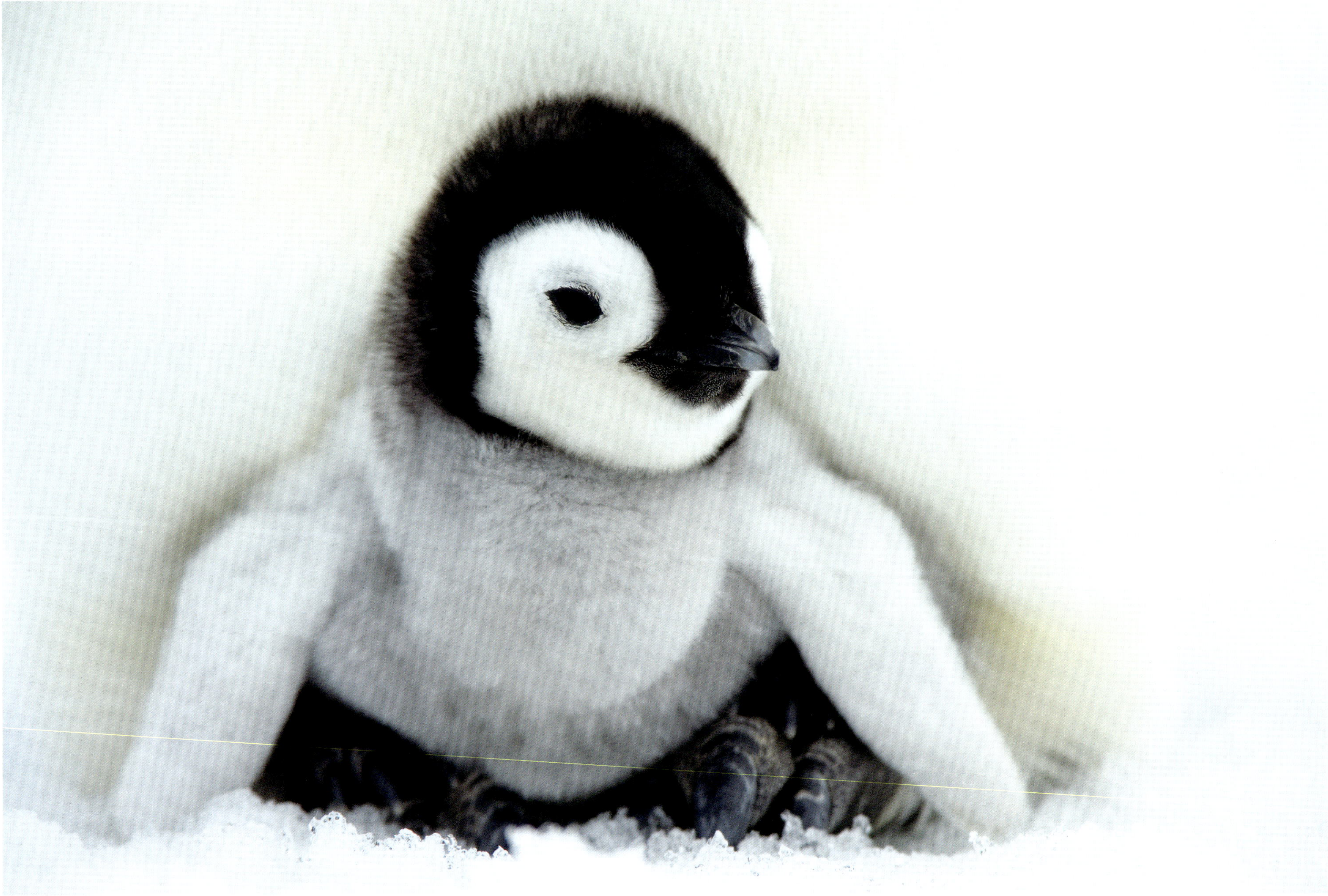

Emperor penguins initially carry their young around on their feet. These newly hatched chicks are covered in gossamer-thin down that offers no protection from the climate; however, in their parent's brood pouch they remain warm and cozy at a steady 38 degrees Celsius, even when icy winds and temperatures of up to minus 40 reign outside.

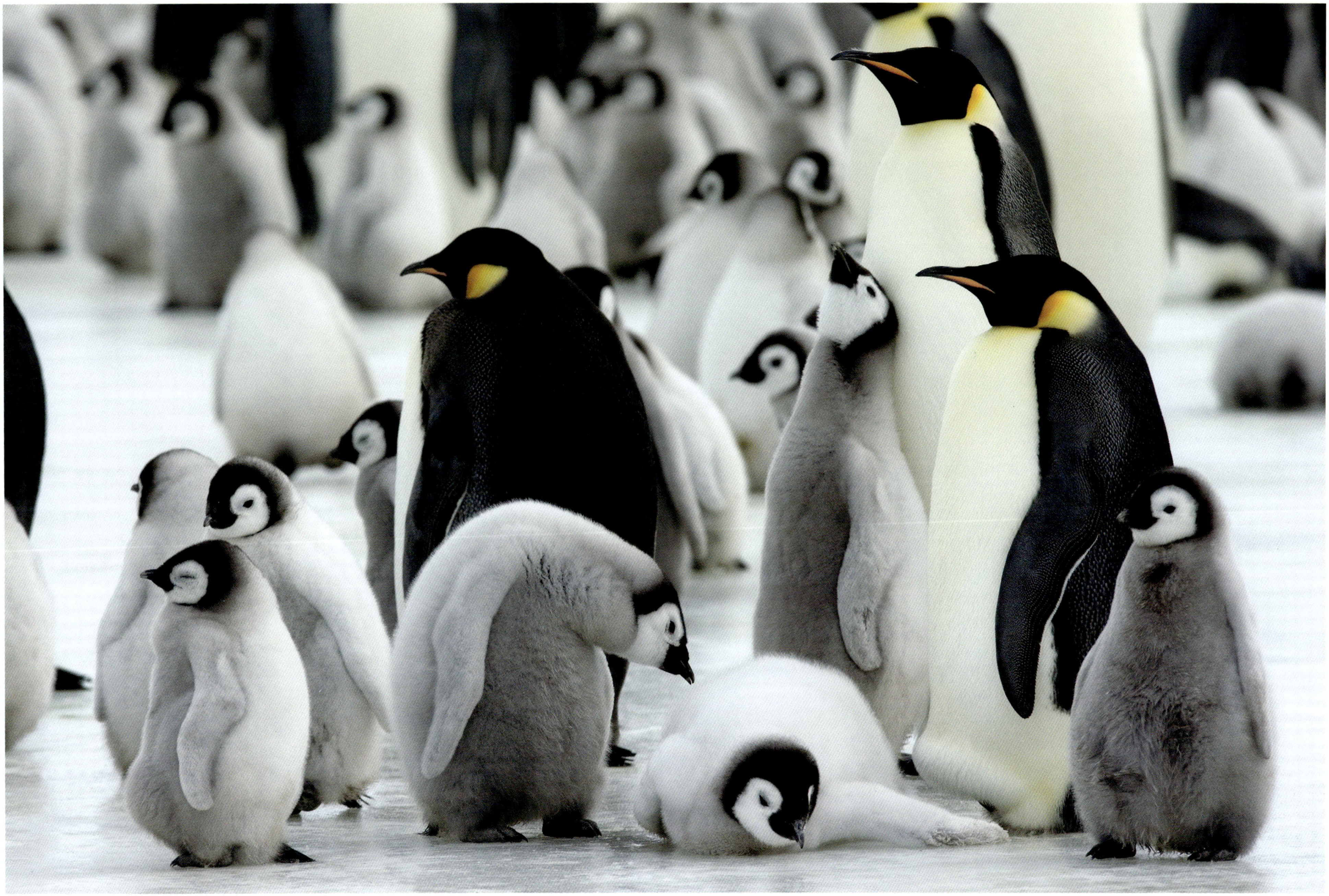

If the weather gets too warm for penguin tastes, the chicks throw themselves down on the ice and spread their paddle-like wings. The underside has no insulating layer of feathers and, when in contact with the frozen seawater, helps to cool the birds.

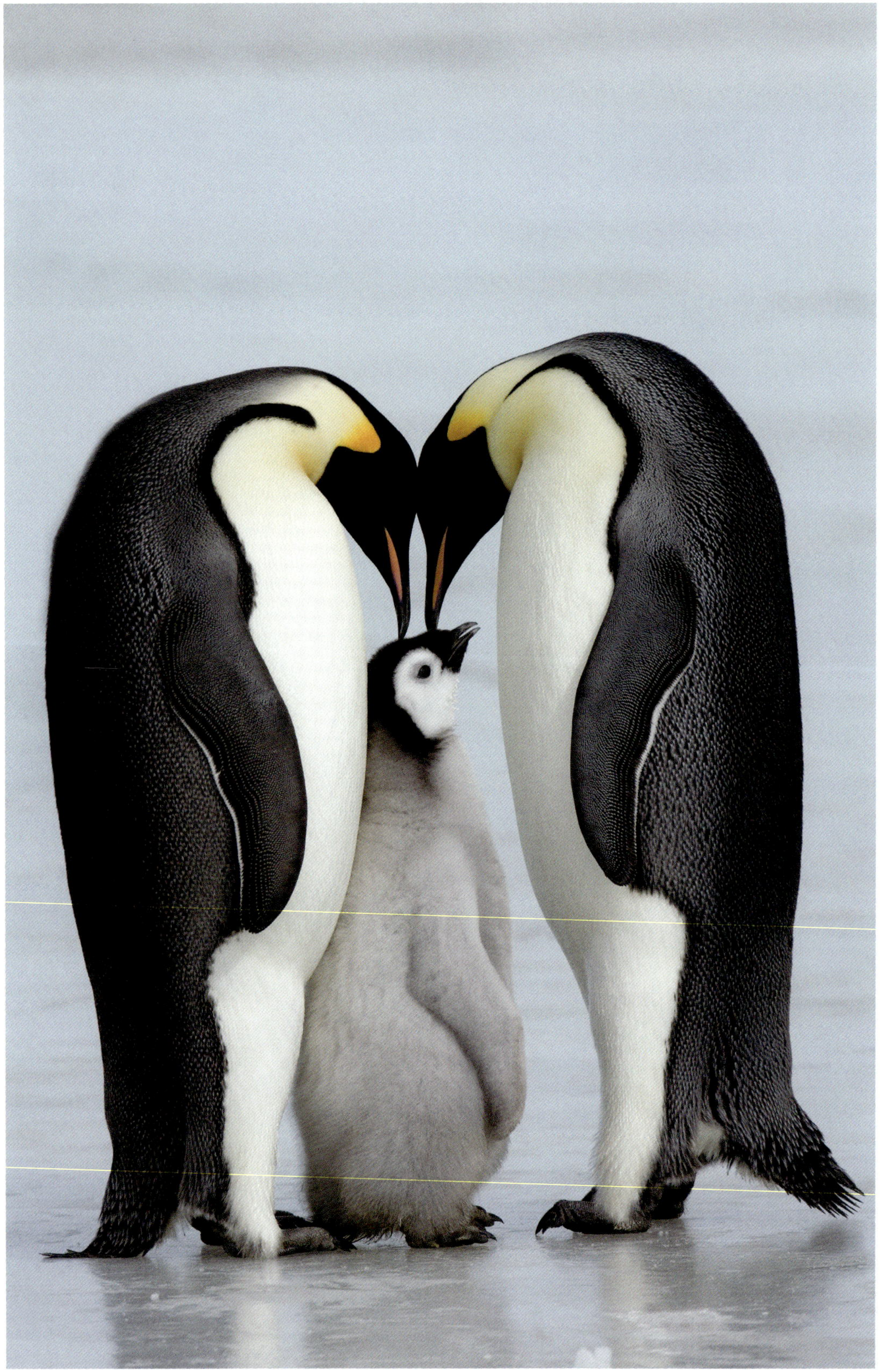

The large, well nourished females now wander through the colony of emaciated males, each one singing out and hoping that the right male will identify her voice amid the cacophonous web of sounds whirring to and fro, and recognize the familiar sound of his female.

Emperor penguins are known to possess a far more subtle ear than humans. Perhaps because they have so much more to listen to. Their call consists of not one voice, as with humans, but two voices simultaneously. If they so wished, they could sing a duet by themselves. Depending on the bird's purpose in calling, each half of its larynx produces either identical vibrations, giving a particularly rich sound, or a combination of frequencies. This double voice is a unique signature. And as the female singer repeats the syllables of her song over and over again, an acoustic signal is created that cuts through the general noise and can rapidly be filtered out by the eagerly listening partner.

When he hears her, he calls back, but does not move from the spot, waiting until the female stands before him. Again, the returned traveler sings her song, takes a couple of dancing steps, then falls still. Silently, as if rapt in thought, the two stand opposite each other for a while. Then the female examines her partner's stomach fold with growing anticipation, first with one eye, then the other. He lifts the roll of fat and releases the tiny chick, which the mother bundles into her own cozy pouch within seconds. Both penguins confirm the transfer with a final duet.

Although the fasting father should now actually be relieved, instead he appears to be disturbed and confused, repeatedly staring at his empty pouch, touching it with his beak and groaning loudly. He seems to miss what has almost been a part of his body for months on end. After more than an hour he regains his composure, and sets off on his part of the long march to the sea.

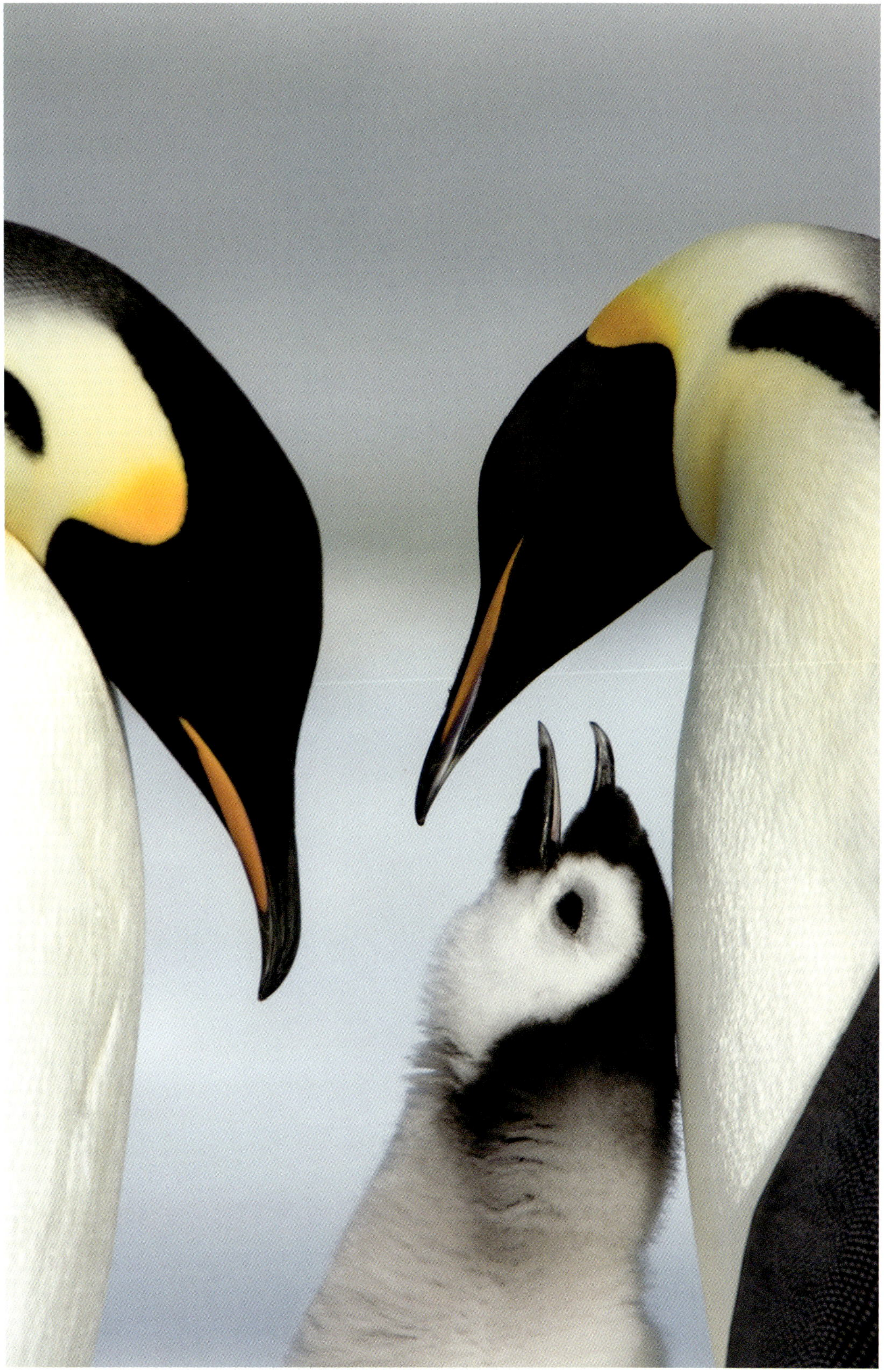

For the chick, its parents' reunion is its first singing lesson, which leaves a deep impression as it learns to distinguish their voices from all the others in the colony – a lesson that is crucial to its survival. Weighing not even 200 grams at the time of hatching and covered only in a fine coat of down, the chick is as yet unable to regulate its own body temperature. It is reliant on the body heat of its mother or father for another 50 days to avoid freezing, and must be fed for a further 150 days before it can embark on its first fishing expedition. Because the chick's survival depends on its father and mother and their care, from now on their voices mean warmth, devotion and something it now begins to demand vociferously: food.

The chick's first meal is regurgitated directly into its throat by its mother. The stores she has brought back must last until the father returns in five weeks with the next ration. While emperor penguins are feeding a chick, their digestive system is at a complete standstill; the birds are effectively fasting on a full stomach. In this phase of life, the penguin's stomach is no more than a larder.

Initially, both partners care for the chick alternately; while one is keeping it warm and taking responsibility for feeding, the other brings back food, and then they exchange roles. Every time the family is reunited, the same moving ceremony takes place: calling, seeking, recognition and jubilation.

The reunion is an occasion that emperor penguins have every reason to celebrate. Often enough a partner does not return, probably the victim of one of the orcas or leopard seals that patrol the icy coastline. This is a death sentence for the chick, too, since a single adult penguin cannot fulfill the role of both father and mother; the effort is too great. If tragedy strikes, the little one is finally abandoned.

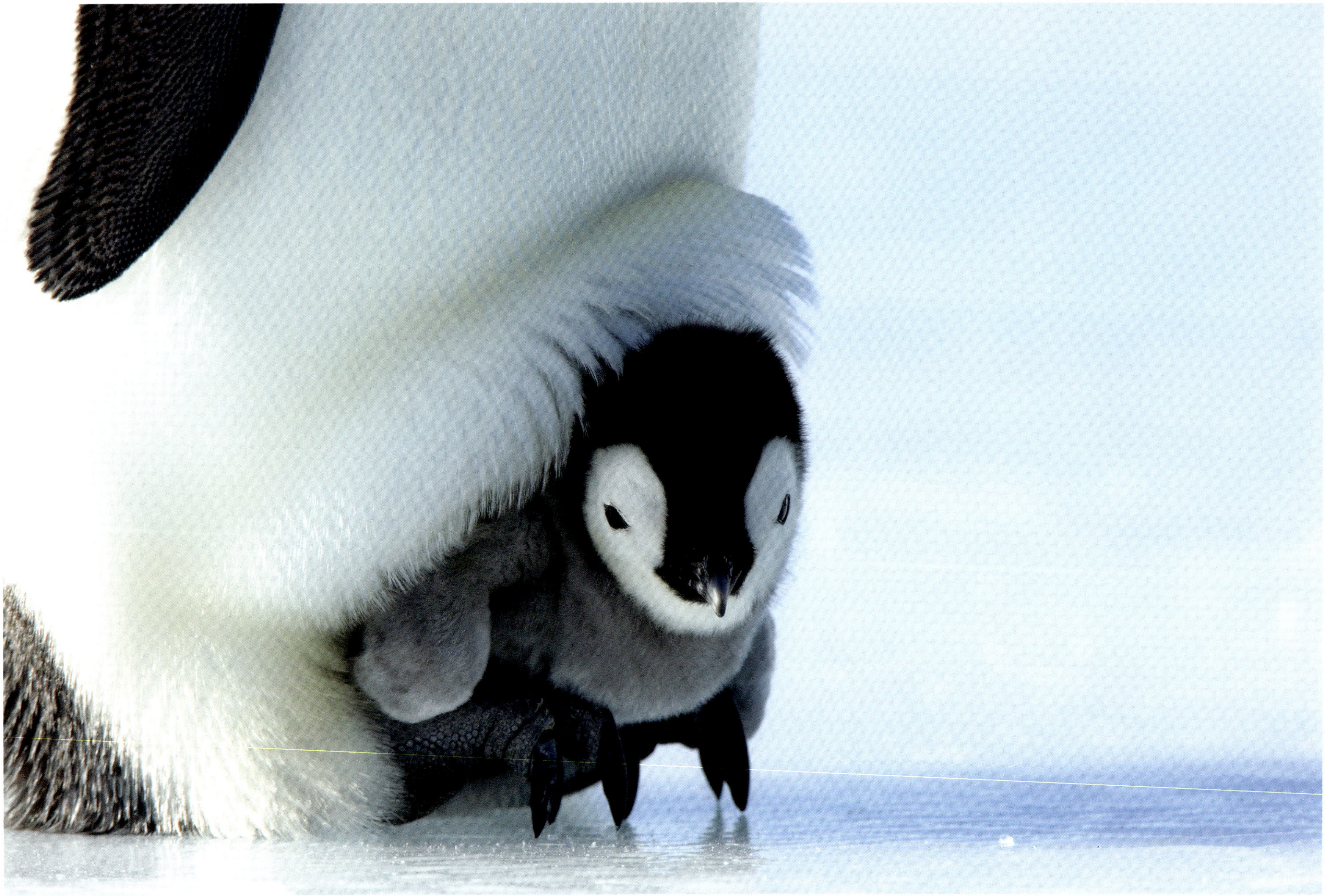

The insulating layers of feathers, down and blubber have a weak point: the penguins' bare feet. They stand on the ice for months. To prevent their extremities from freezing, the birds lean back, keeping their balance by supporting themselves on their short, powerful tail feathers. Their feet – including the chick resting on them – are thus tilted up and away from the ice, with only the claws in contact with the frozen ground.

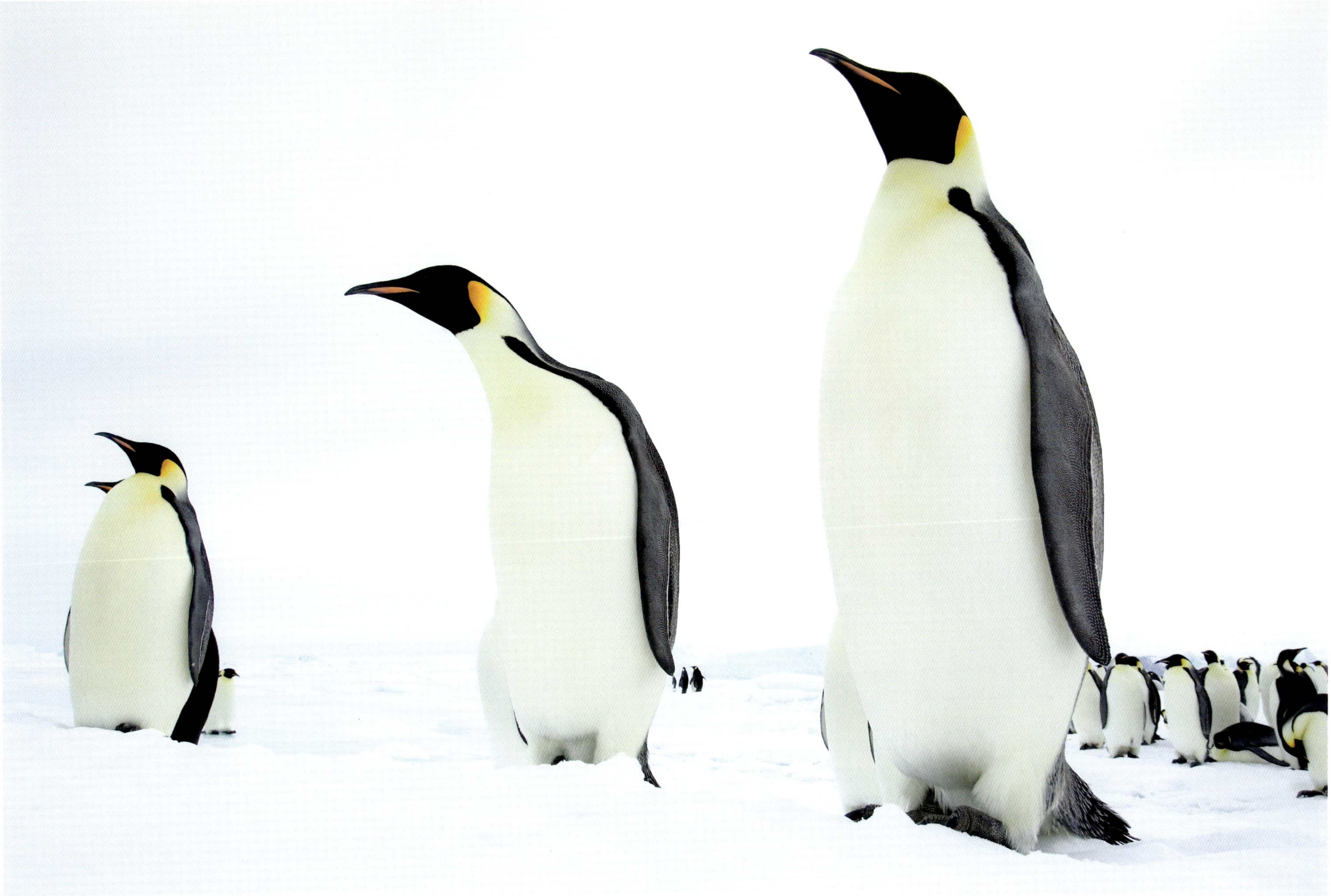

Emperor penguin colonies are not for couples only. There are some singles around, too: females unable to find a mate or birds whose chick has died. Many have an all-consuming desire to breed, "adopting" young birds whose parents have not returned from feeding in the ocean. However, no single penguin can supply enough food to rear a chick.

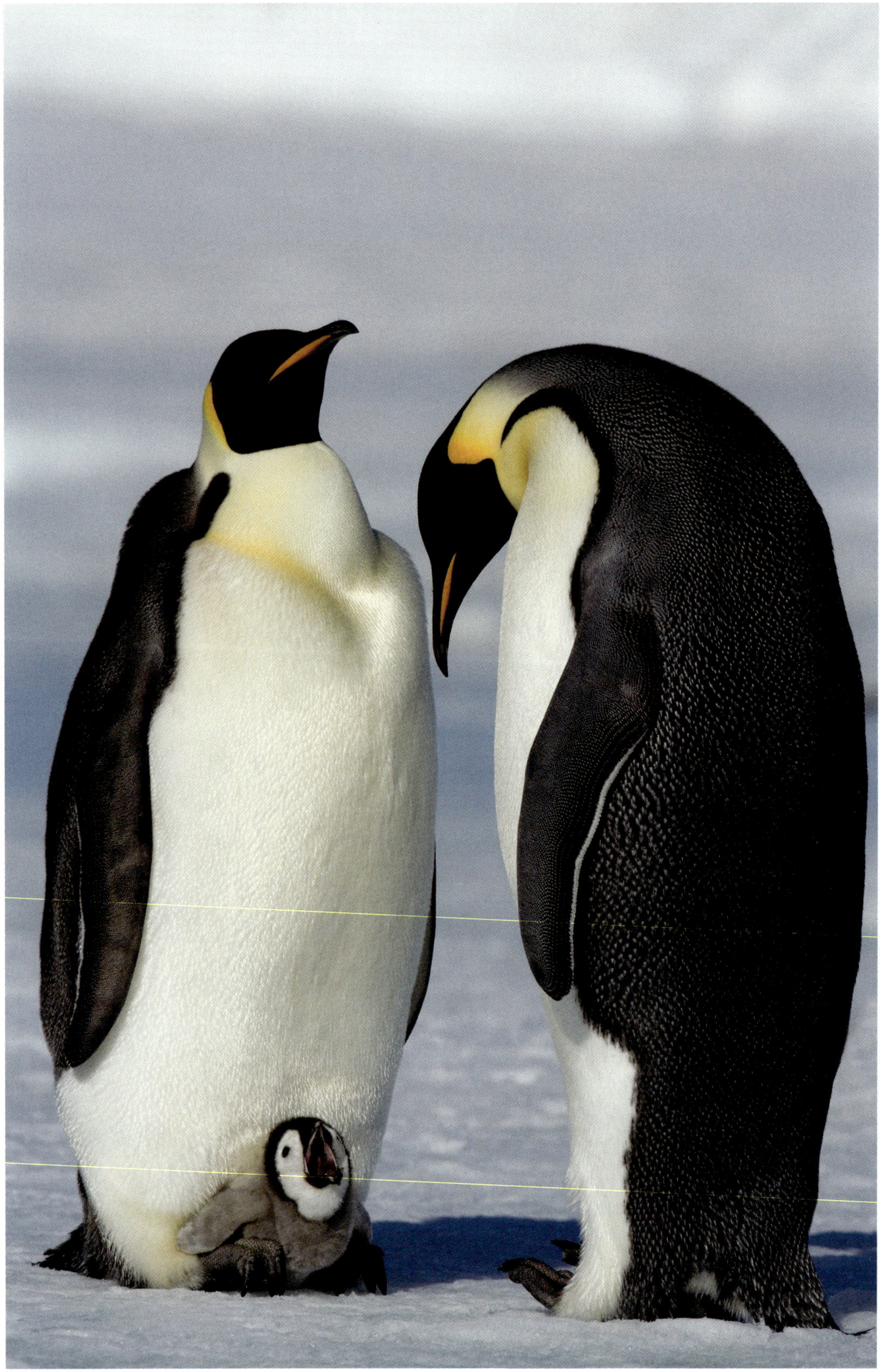

But penguins that receive care grow rapidly. After two months they have grown too big to fit under the abdominal fold and bob around full of life, kept warm by their thick gray coat of down. They join the other chicks to form a group or "crèche", while both parents go off to bring back adequate supplies of food.

After a while the route to the sea becomes a little shorter. The coldest period is now over; the days are growing longer and the sun climbs a little higher above the horizon. The pack ice creaks; gigantic floes rear groaning out of the water, crevasses yawn, and whole landscapes along the ice coast break off and float away.

Now the young penguins in their thick down comforters occasionally become too warm. When this happens they eat snow, throw themselves full-length on the ice and flap their short wings, fanning cold air over the sparsely feathered undersides. When snowstorms rise, they seek protection in their crèche, in an abbreviated version of the adult penguins' huddle – as they have learnt from an early age.

The chicks' abilities to memorize song and calls are now "tested" more and more frequently by their parents. Around once a week the adult parents appear with fresh supplies of nourishment at the periphery of the crèche in which up to 3,000 chicks sleep closely pressed together. When the parents sound their characteristic song, a tiny head immediately shoots up from the mass of bodies, a penetrating call resounds in reply, and a chick battles through the crowd of lethargic young birds to be fed. When it reaches the edge of the colony of chicks, the parents repeat their song to it – the typical ritual of return is all part of the procedure – before the fruits of their ocean-hunting expedition are produced. The growing chicks can consume up to a third of their own weight in fish at a single feed.

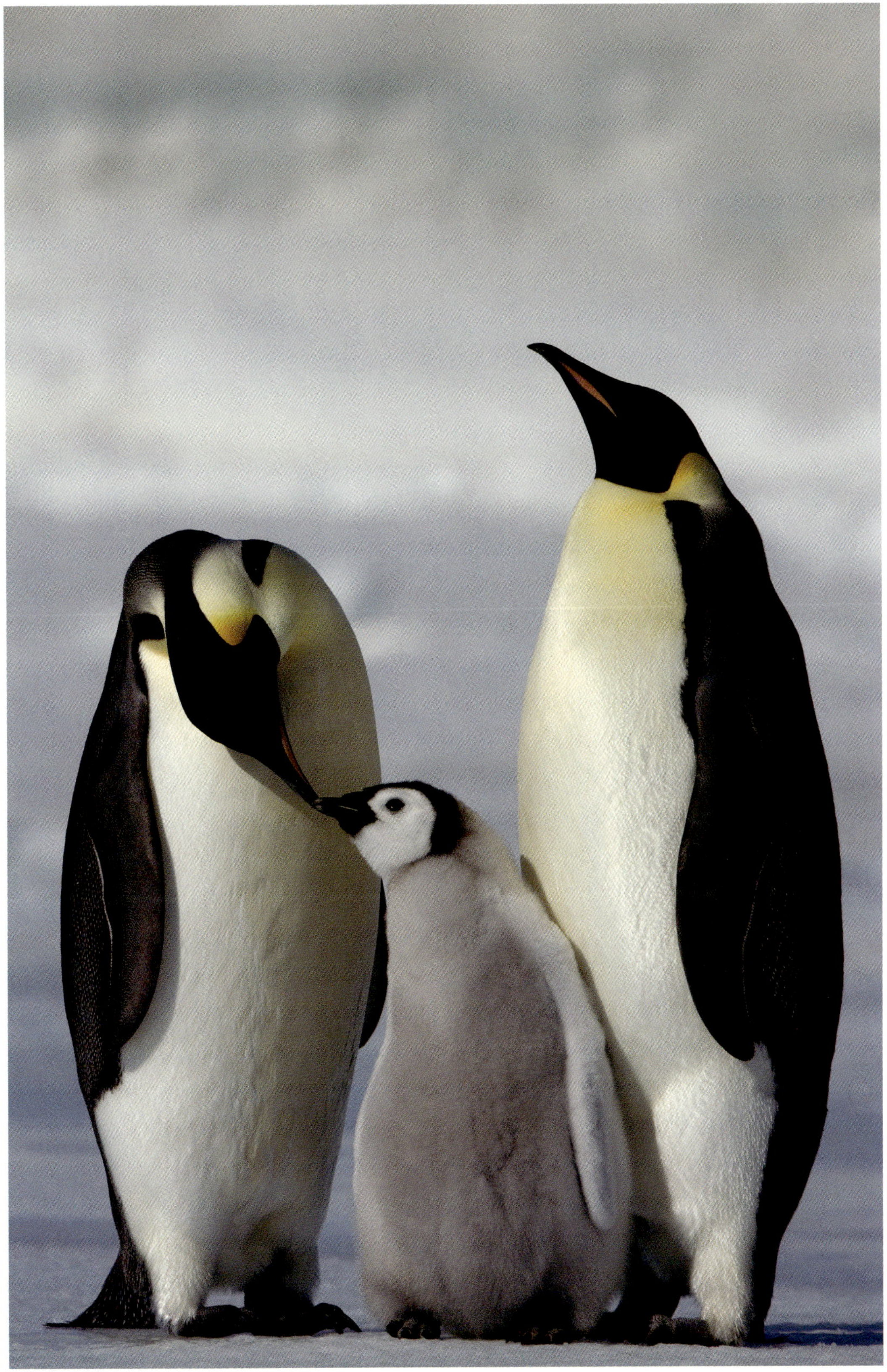

Despite the care lavished on these emperor penguin chicks, 25 to 50 percent of the young birds die. They die because they are orphaned, because they are snatched by predator gulls or giant petrels, or because they venture too far from the colony and freeze or starve to death in storms. Or because the colony's breeding ground melts from under their feet if the pack ice breaks up too early. If the chicks are still moulting when this happens their feathers are not yet waterproof and all chicks hatched in that year drown – and the parents' toil will have been in vain.

But if all goes to plan, the adolescent birds simply hop onto an ice floe and float out to sea.

None of their childhood lessons is of use to them when they jump into the sea for the first time. When still on the ice, they had no land predators to fear. Now a veritable welcoming committee of predators has assembled at the edge of the ice to await their arrival.

As chicks, the young penguins have never practiced swimming. Yet they are among the deepest divers, and, thanks to their elegant streamlined shape and powerful paddle-like wings, among the fastest. They fly through the element which is their home.

Their chances of catching quantities of krill, fish and squid are excellent; their prospects of outswimming the ocean's sharp teeth, however, only middling. And yet 20 percent of the fully-fledged emperor penguins are still alive and well at the end of their first year of life. ■

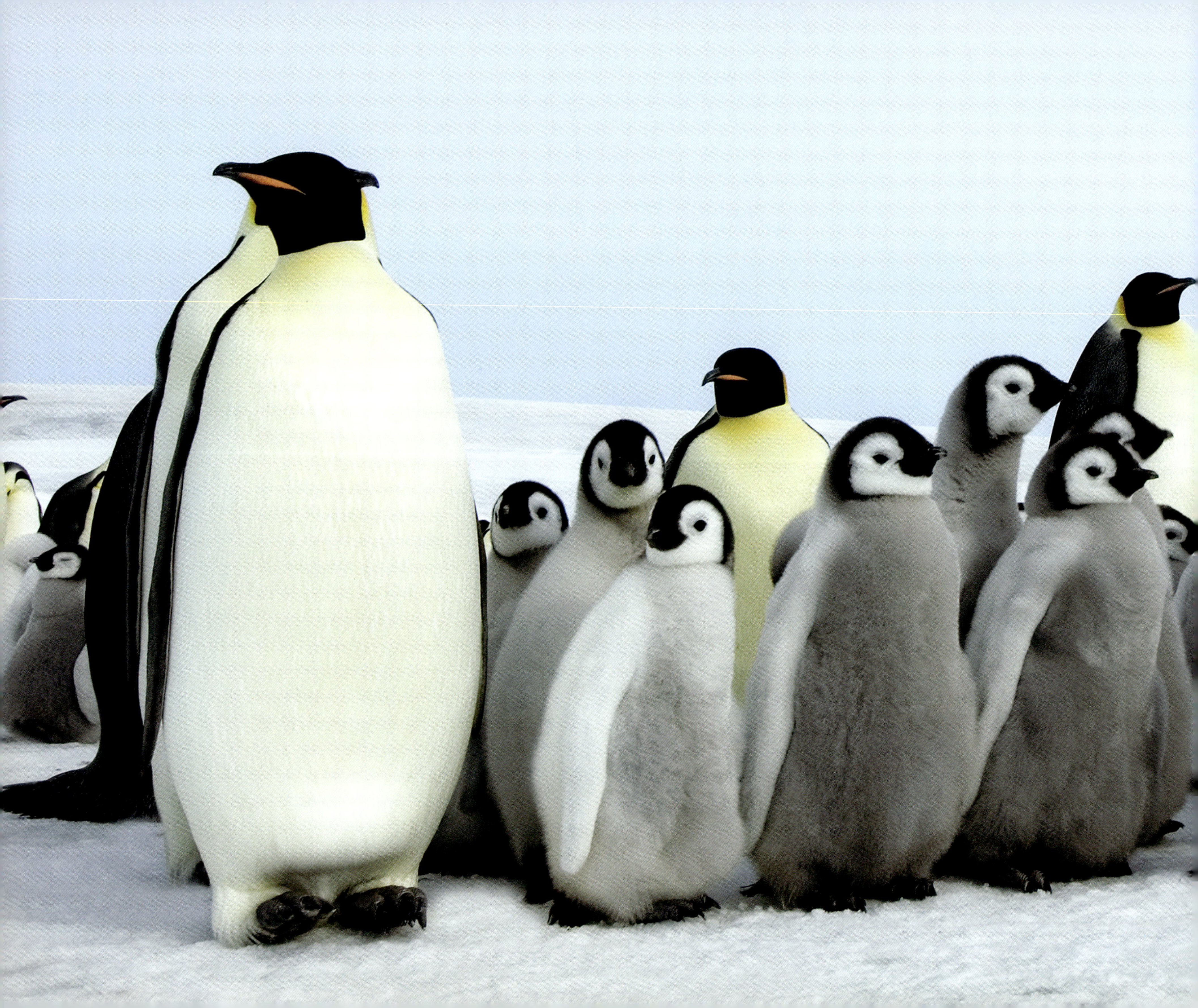

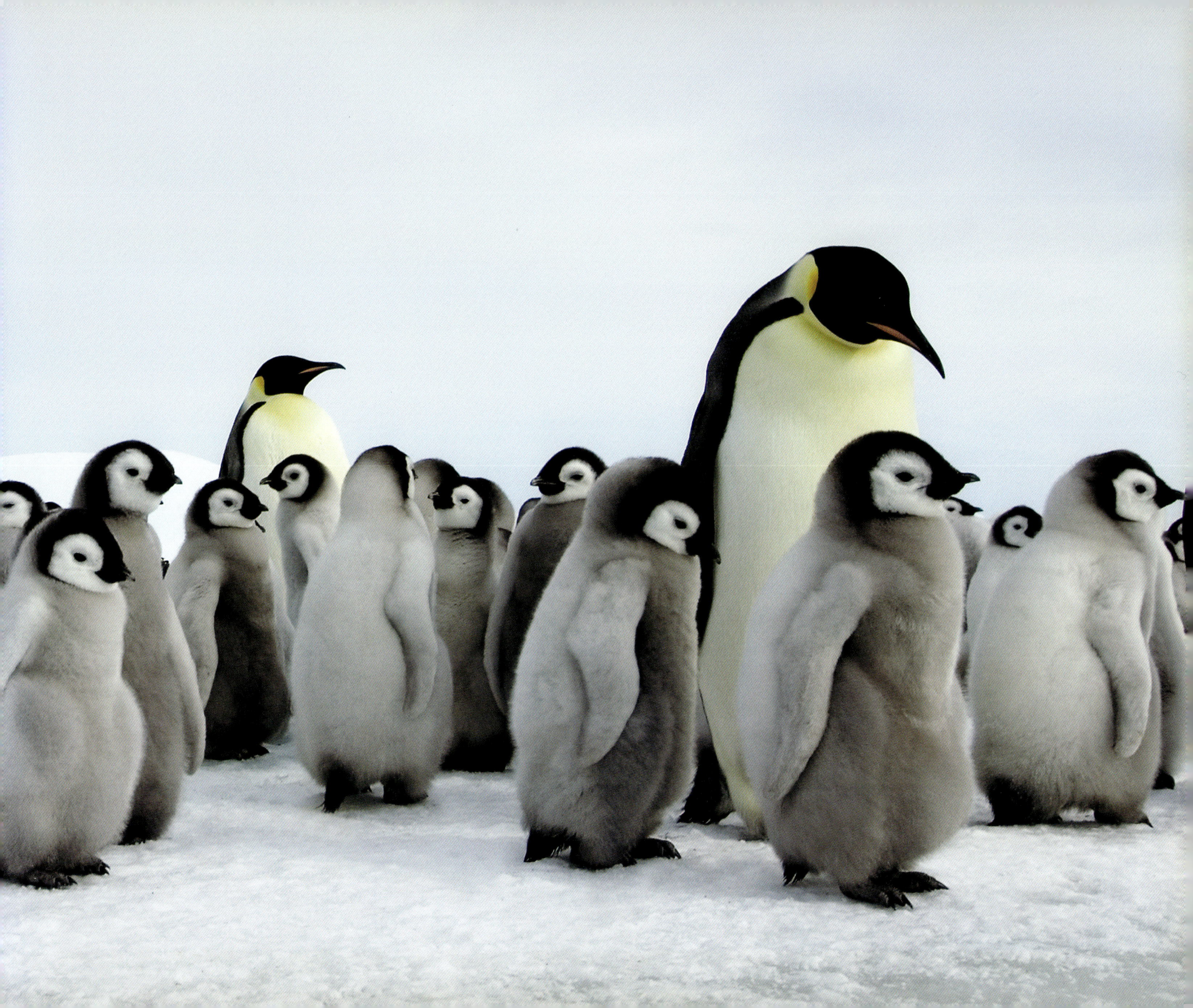

Emperor Penguins – at a glance

Their place in the animal kingdom

- They belong to the phylum of vertebrates
- to the class of birds
- to the order of sphenisciformes
- to the family of penguins

Scientific name

Aptenodytes forsteri

Their closest relatives

There are many indications that penguins are the descendents of flighted birds which evolved 80 million years ago in the New Zealand region. Their nearest living relative which can be traced to this prehistoric line is the albatross. Emperor and royal penguins began to diverge early on from the 15 species of penguin.

Where emperor penguins live (population numbers)

Emperor penguins (200,000 pairs) are aquatic birds, inhabiting the oceans around the Antarctic. They do not take to the land even to lay their eggs, but breed on the firm sea ice in the Weddell and Ross Seas.

Emperor penguins in figures

- The largest of all penguin species, they grow up to 120 centimeters (47 inches) in **height**.
- They **weigh** around 40 kilos.
- They reach **sexual maturity** at the age of five.
- The **gestation period** between mating and egg-laying is 63 days.
- Emperors have a **lifespan** of 40 years.
- Emperor penguins can **dive to a depth** of more than 500 meters (1,640 feet) and remain under water for **20 minutes without drawing breath**.
- They swim at a **constant speed** of 24 kilometers (15 miles) per hour, with **brief spurts** of up to 50 kilometers (31 miles) per hour.

Emperor penguins' characteristic features

Emperor penguins have golden areas around their ear openings and at either side of the throat. They have a black back and white abdomen as protective coloring against ocean predators: seen from below, the birds are indistinguishable from the bright sky, while seen from above they blend in with the darkness of the deep water. Their wings have evolved into paddle-like fins and, like their entire body, are covered with short, overlapping feathers. Emperor penguins have short legs and powerful feet with large claws. They stand upright and cover large distances in their waddling walk.

What emperor penguins eat

Emperor penguins hunt in the cold currents around the Antarctic continent, which are a rich source of nourishment. They may travel up to 1,900 kilometers (1,180 miles) on a single hunting trip for krill, fish and squid, grasping their flapping, slippery prey with their spiny tongue and powerful jaws and swallowing it whole.

Emperor penguins' lifestyle

Emperor penguins spend around 75 percent of their lives in the sea. However, far less is known about this aspect of their lives than about their amazing mating and reproductive behavior. The aquatic birds are extremely social, gathering in colonies of up to 10,000 pairs and beginning to breed around March, when they travel to their traditional breeding grounds. The female penguins choose a mate, taking his yellow markings and girth into consideration. Only well nourished, healthy fathers with flawless feathers can endure the months of fasting and freezing sub-zero temperatures involved in rearing a penguin chick. Occasionally, penguins return to their mate from the previous year.
Mating is preceded by a courtship ritual of bowing, preening and ecstatic song, in which the birds familiarize themselves with their partners and their calls – later vital when they must locate their partner in the colony of several thousand birds.

How emperor penguins raise their young

Male emperor penguins have a legendary reputation as devoted fathers. They take the freshly laid egg from the female and roll it onto their feet below the thick abdominal fold known as the brood pouch. The egg is thus shielded from contact with the ice and is warmed from above. For nine weeks the "male mothers" incubate the eggs, huddled together in a group and enduring extreme temperatures, snowstorms and hunger. They have fasted since they emerged from the ocean and traveled to their breeding ground – 115 days of torment. Around mid-July, when the chicks hatch, the female penguins return, recognizing their partners by their unique call, and take over the task of feeding and keeping the chick warm, while the males in their turn travel to the sea to feed. For months the parents alternate in their duties, and finally both move constantly between ocean and breeding ground until December, when their chick has finally grown a full coat of feathers and is ready to begin life as an aquatic bird.

Dangers to emperor penguins

South polar skuas, sheathbills and giant petrels all attack penguin chicks which have been abandoned when their father or mother fails to return to the colony. Fully-grown adolescents diving for the first time may fall prey to leopard seals, orcas or sharks.

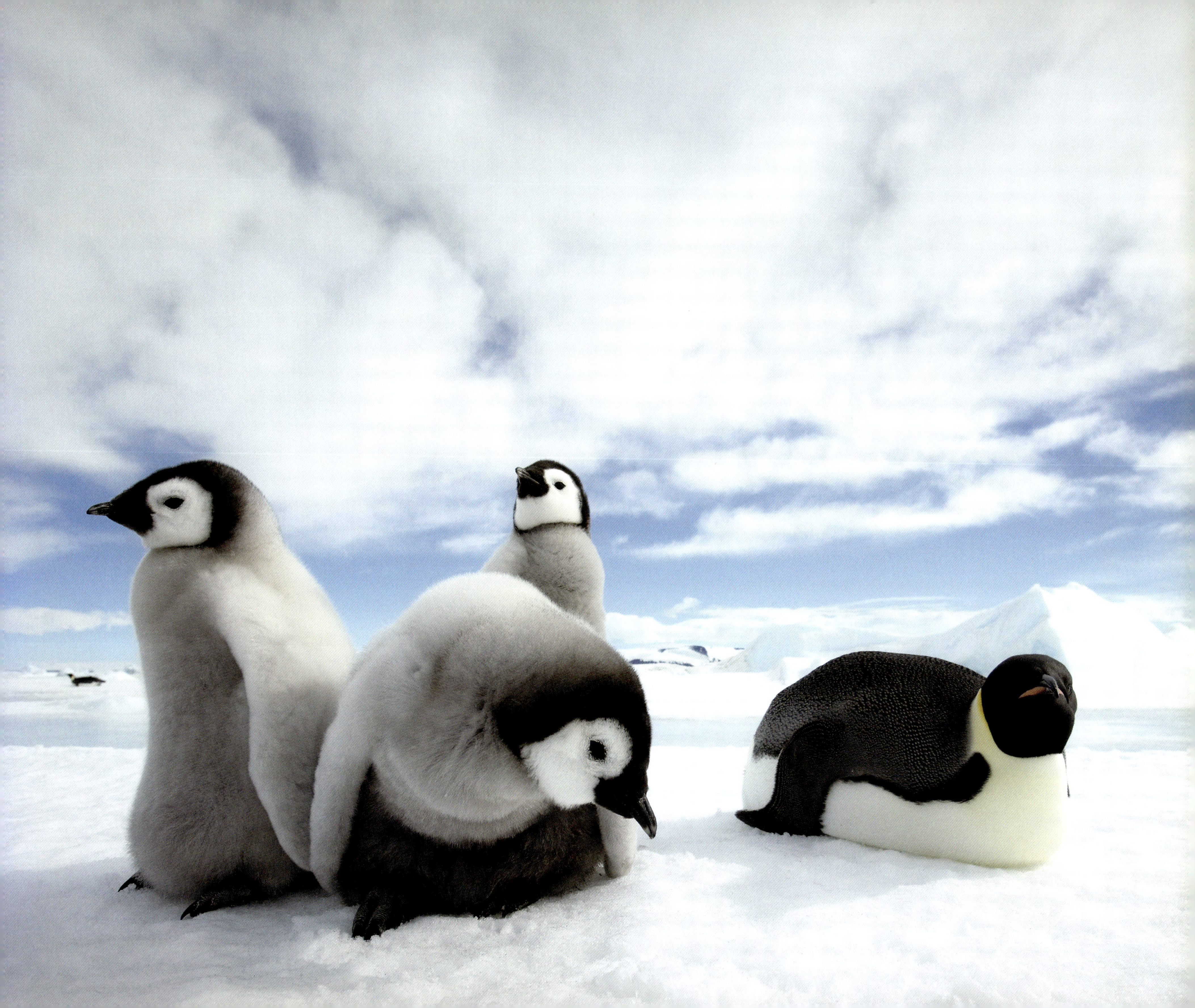

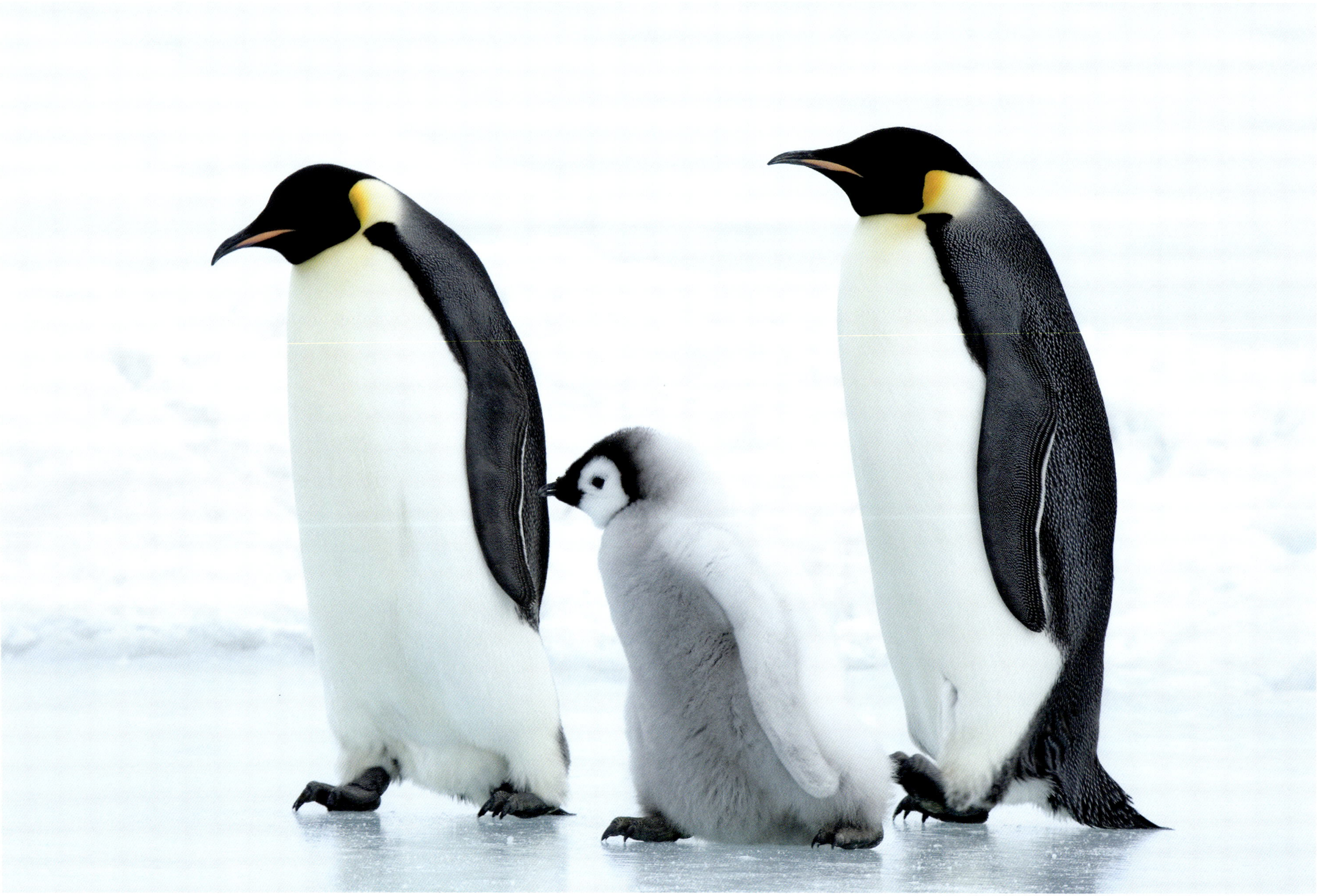

Young penguins grow a thick layer of down protecting them against wind and weather.
As soon as they emerge from their parent's cozy brood pouch, they head off to explore their surroundings.
A visible layer of subcutaneous blubber keeps the chicks warm in the icy chill of their polar playground.

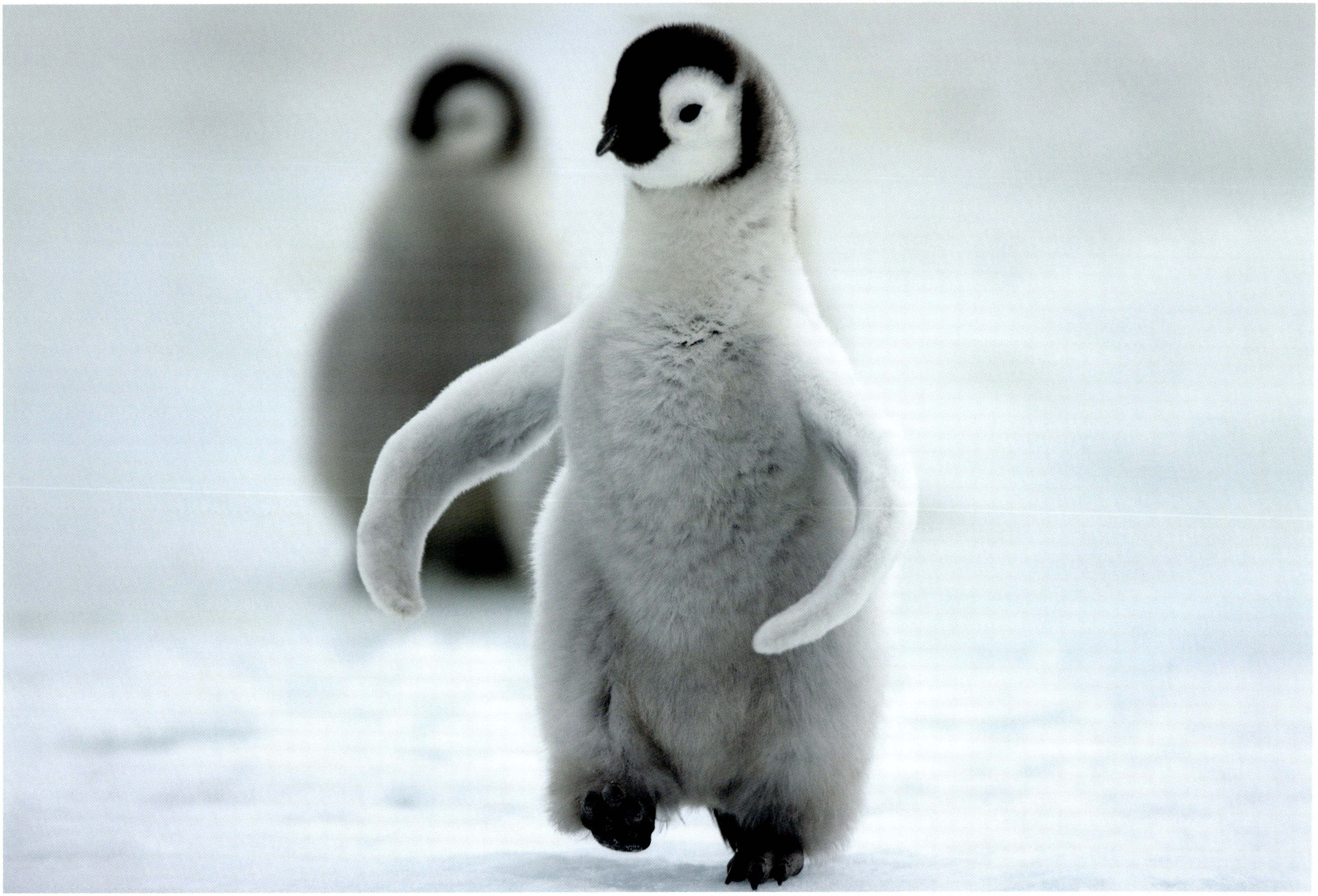

The upright posture typical of penguins is tricky for the lively chicks to master.
They need practice to achieve the waddling gait, rocking from one foot to the other.
As if walking a tightrope, they flap their wings wildly to maintain their balance.

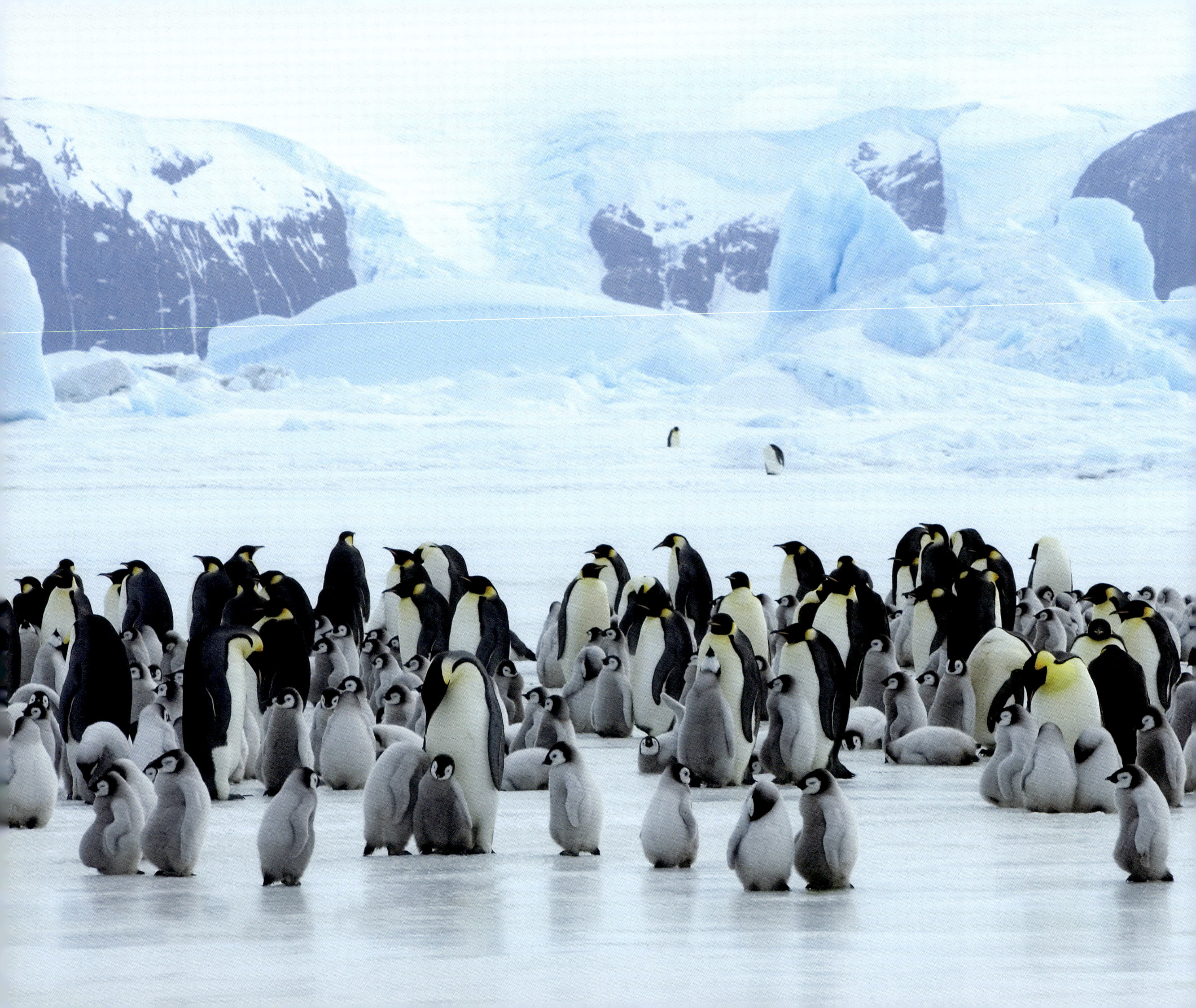

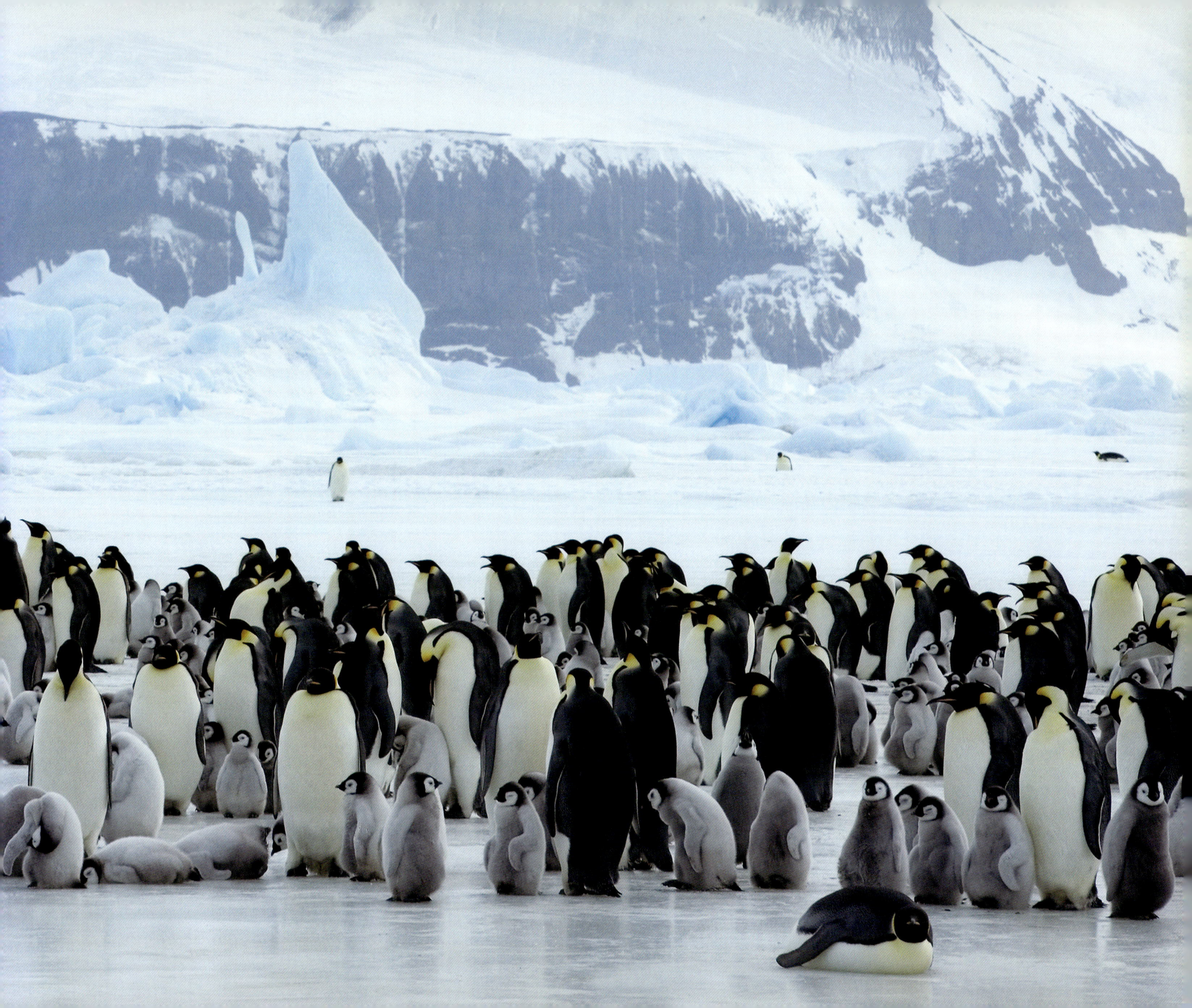

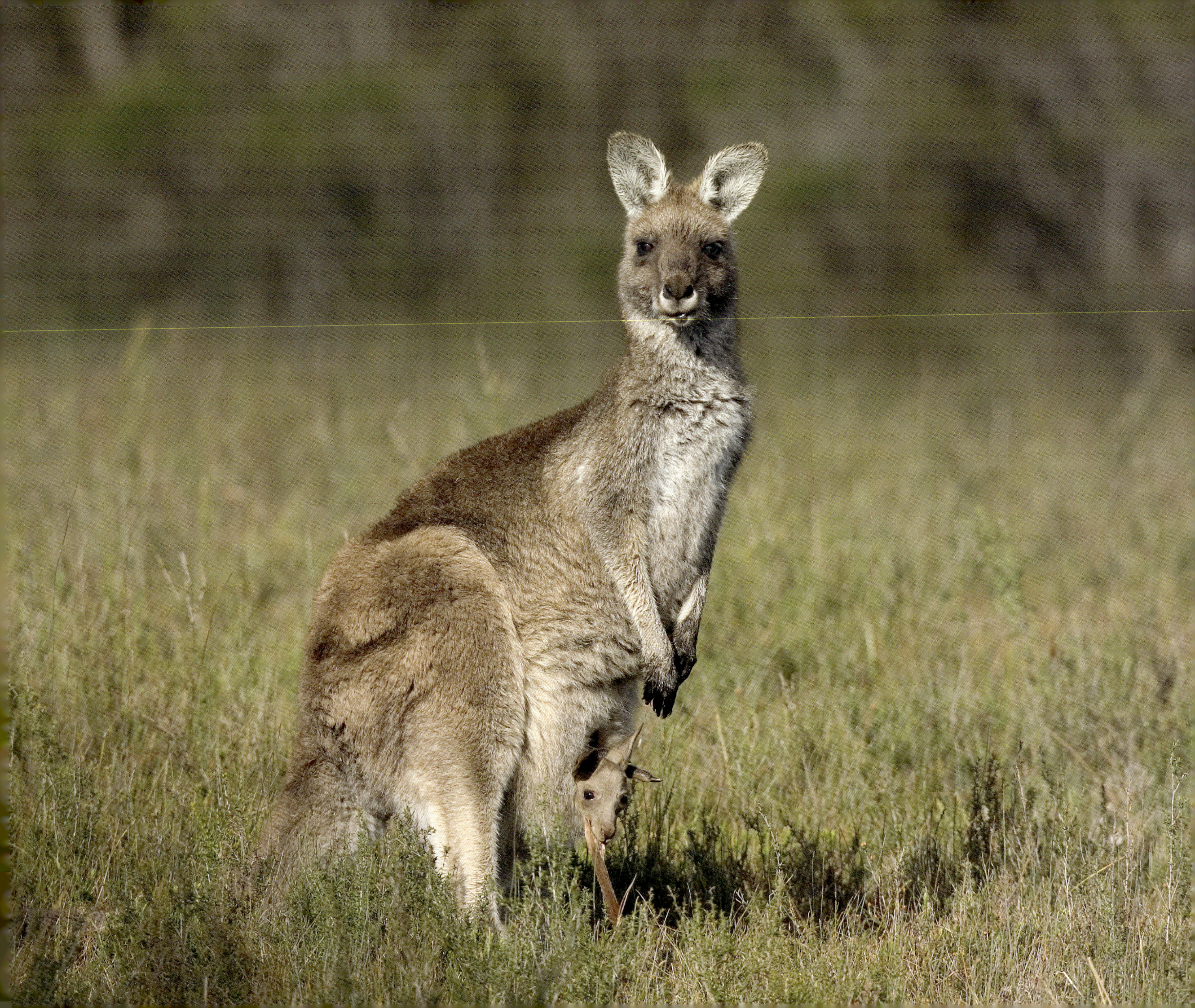

Grey Kangaroos

Safe in the Pouch

Today is a special day in the life of the female kangaroo. It's one of the very few days in her life when she is not pregnant. She is resting in the dappled shade of an acacia grove, a good ten meters (33 feet) away from the rest of her group or "mob." The large, liquid eyes in her slim, deer-like face seem to be looking inward, unaware of her surroundings. Nothing moves except her ears, constantly perked to catch the slightest suspicious noise, but nothing disturbs her except for the rather too close proximity of an alpha male.
The male has been hard on her heels for days, appearing in exhilaration after wrestling matches with neighboring mobs, even sniffing at her.

Kangaroos keep their distance from each other, avoiding competition over grazing space and staying off each other's patch. Likewise, they require their personal space when resting. When in the mood for play and contact, a not infrequent occurrence, they simply bound over to their neighbor. The mob is held together and its boundaries marked by loose ties that primarily constitute a feeling of belonging. There are no visible features of demarcation.

Fifteen eastern grey kangaroos – young males and mothers with young – are dozing in the grass, stretched out or casually leaning on one arm, jaws rotating as they chew. The desiccated ground is smothered under the day's heat, a vast blanket that crushes everything under its weight.

Everything, that is, except the leader of the mob, the dominant "boomer." Despite the heat, he guards his females, for other mobs have settled not far away, and boomers meeting when on patrol emit coughing or clucking warnings if the other approaches their harem too closely.

This female kangaroo has adopted a position that is clearly different from that of the others

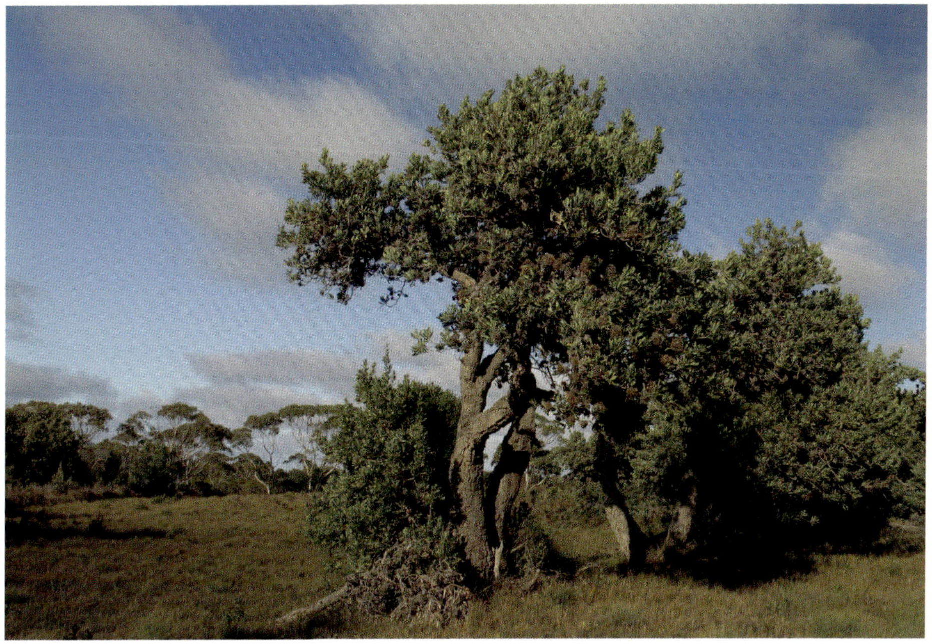

in the mob. She is lying on her back propped against a tree, her pelvis facing upwards, her powerful tail tucked under her, between her spread thighs. She leans far enough forward to enable her to hold the edges of her pouch apart with her paws and lick it clean with her tongue. Between bouts of cleaning, she deposits a trail of saliva on her fur, a slippery trail between her cloacal opening and her pouch. This will be the landing-strip to guide her newborn young.

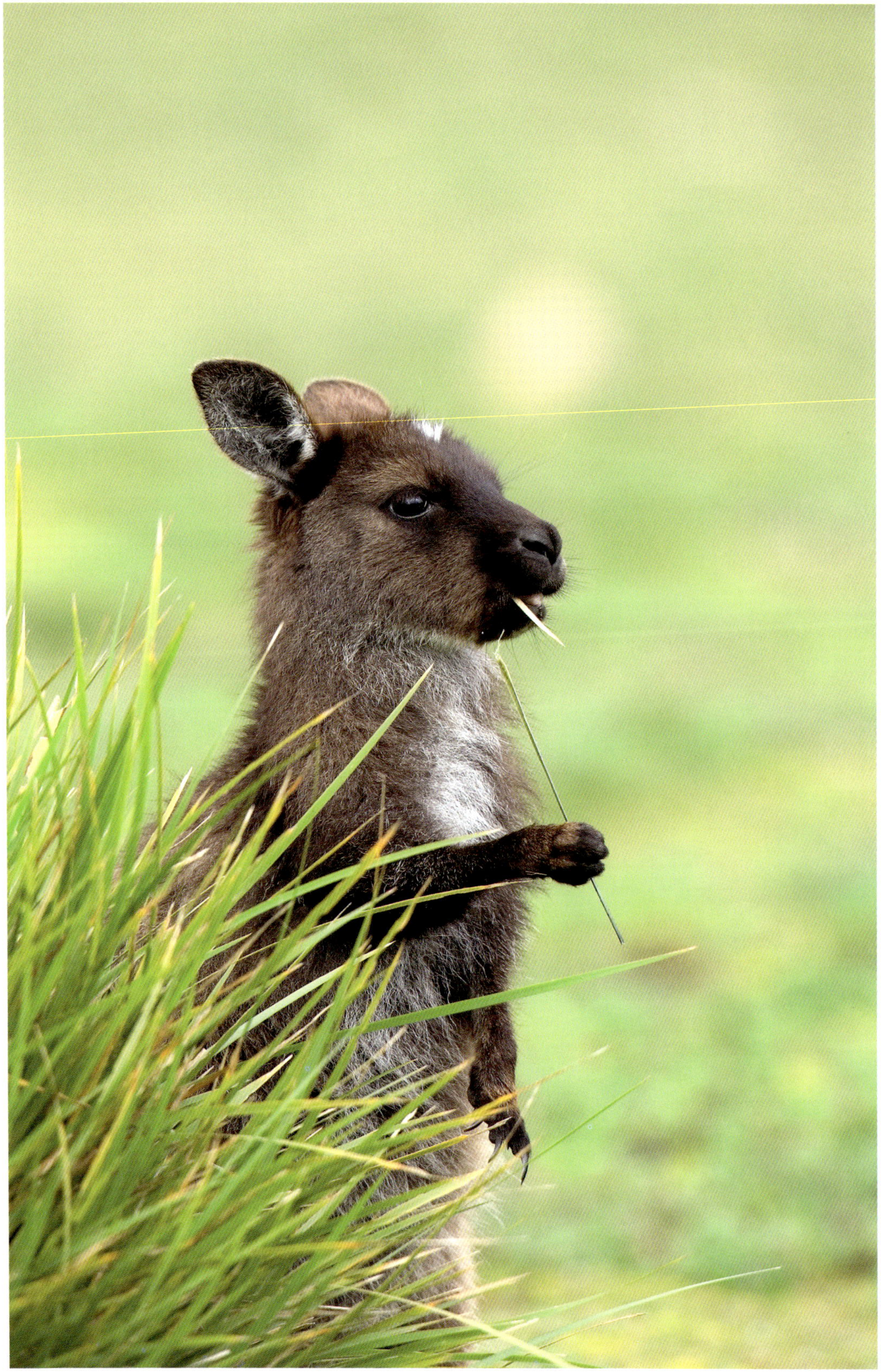

Around six weeks ago, her youngest joey, a daughter aged nine months at the time, was finally ejected from her pouch. Every time that the young kangaroo tried to enter her mother's pouch, head first as usual, her mother tensed her muscles and firmly closed the pouch. For the first time, the daughter realizes it takes two to be carried. And that her mother is evidently sick and tired of carrying a pretty heavy youngster around in her pouch. Particularly since space in there is now at a premium, and the daughter's long back legs generally protrude from the mouth of the pouch.

Overnight, the young kangaroo's life has changed completely. No more cosy hiding place in the mother's pouch, no longer the feeling of being sheltered and shielded. Suddenly the joey finds herself in a new world, in Australia's endless grassy plains. The mother must stand firm for a while, even using her paws to push her uncooperative daughter away. The adolescent is now permitted only occasional nursing sessions at "her" teat, putting her head in the pouch to do so.

The ejection of a joey from the pouch, compelling it to take its first steps towards independence, is a drastic step – and not only for the young kangaroo itself. The mother, too, notices that her pouch is strangely light. However, her pituitary gland has registered a change which will have more momentous consequences. This small gland, located at the base of the brain, has registered that the regular sucking reflex of the little kangaroo's mouth has been diminishing since the young joey was banned from the pouch. The adolescent now hopping about outside no longer rules the roost; she can no longer nurse whenever she feels like it, but has to negotiate the right moment with the pouch's owner. When the mother moves on to new pastures, flees from a dingo in great sweeping leaps or draws herself up to her full height of 170 centimeters (5.5 feet) to nibble on leaves growing in high places, her milk source is temporarily unavailable. To her pituitary gland, the waning of the sucking signal has the effect of a biochemical command. The pituitary promptly curbs the production of prolactin, thus saving milk.

In a highly developed system such as that of a large marsupial, metabolic swings of this kind do not go unnoticed – and certainly not when an egg fertilized nine months ago is waiting in the wings to be awakened from its Sleeping Beauty slumber. As long as prolactin levels remain high, they act on the egg like a sedative. When prolactin drops, the blob of cells awakens and rapidly begins to grow. After an amazingly short gestation period of 36 days, the embryo is born.

It is blind, naked, weighs not even one gram and is still fully immature. Mere buds indicate the points where its hind legs, with their powerful thighs, will later develop. Nevertheless, while still inside its mother's body this baby kangaroo has already conducted a small orchestra of chemical messengers to pave the way for its own birth and future nourishment. Hormones ensure that the mother adopts the correct birthing position, and induce the start of labor. Hormones ensure that milk production resumes. And hormones order the mother's pituitary gland to produce oxytocin – a "wonder drug" that awakens the doe's powerful motherly instincts for the tiny mite that now slips out of her body and lands on her stomach.

Once there, the fetus – all of 25 millimeters (1 inch) long – rests for a while, but only a mere 15 seconds or so. It then grasps its mother's fur with its well-developed, but gossamer-fine front limbs and clambers up to the entrance of the pouch. The scent of the mother's trail of saliva guides him, for his nostrils are already highly developed. The wet fur protects him from drying out.

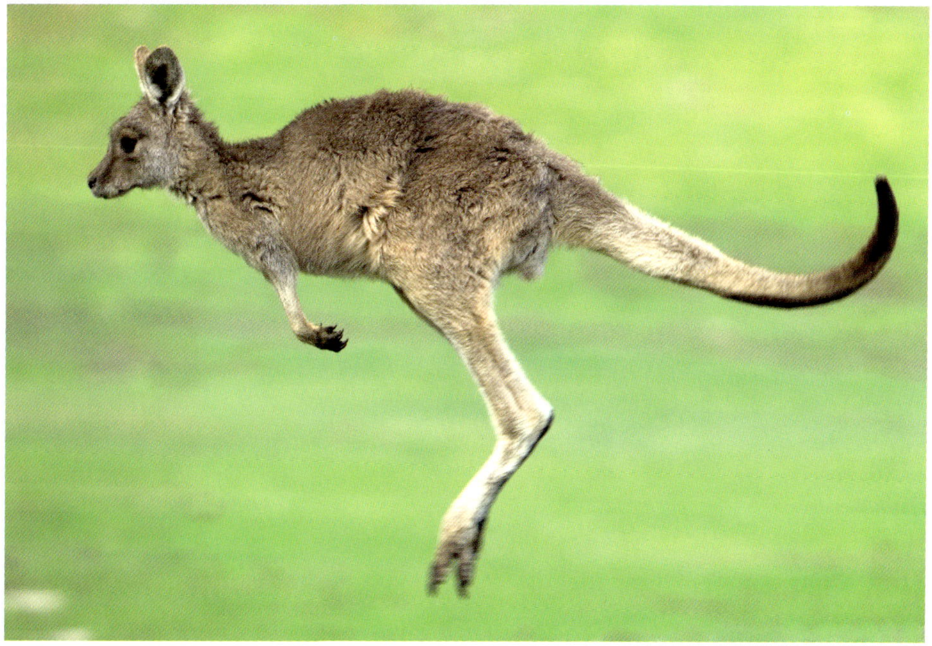

His mother watches these efforts without intervening, offering no assistance as he climbs into the pouch. Evidently these few moments represent a vital proficiency test; the joey must demonstrate his ability and his dauntless will to live in order to win his mother's affection.

The tiny athlete takes three minutes to scale the pouch, his sense of smell leading him to the four teats. He keeps well clear of his sister's milk fount, quite simply because of its comparatively enormous size. Selecting one of the other nipples two millimeters (0.08 inch) long, he

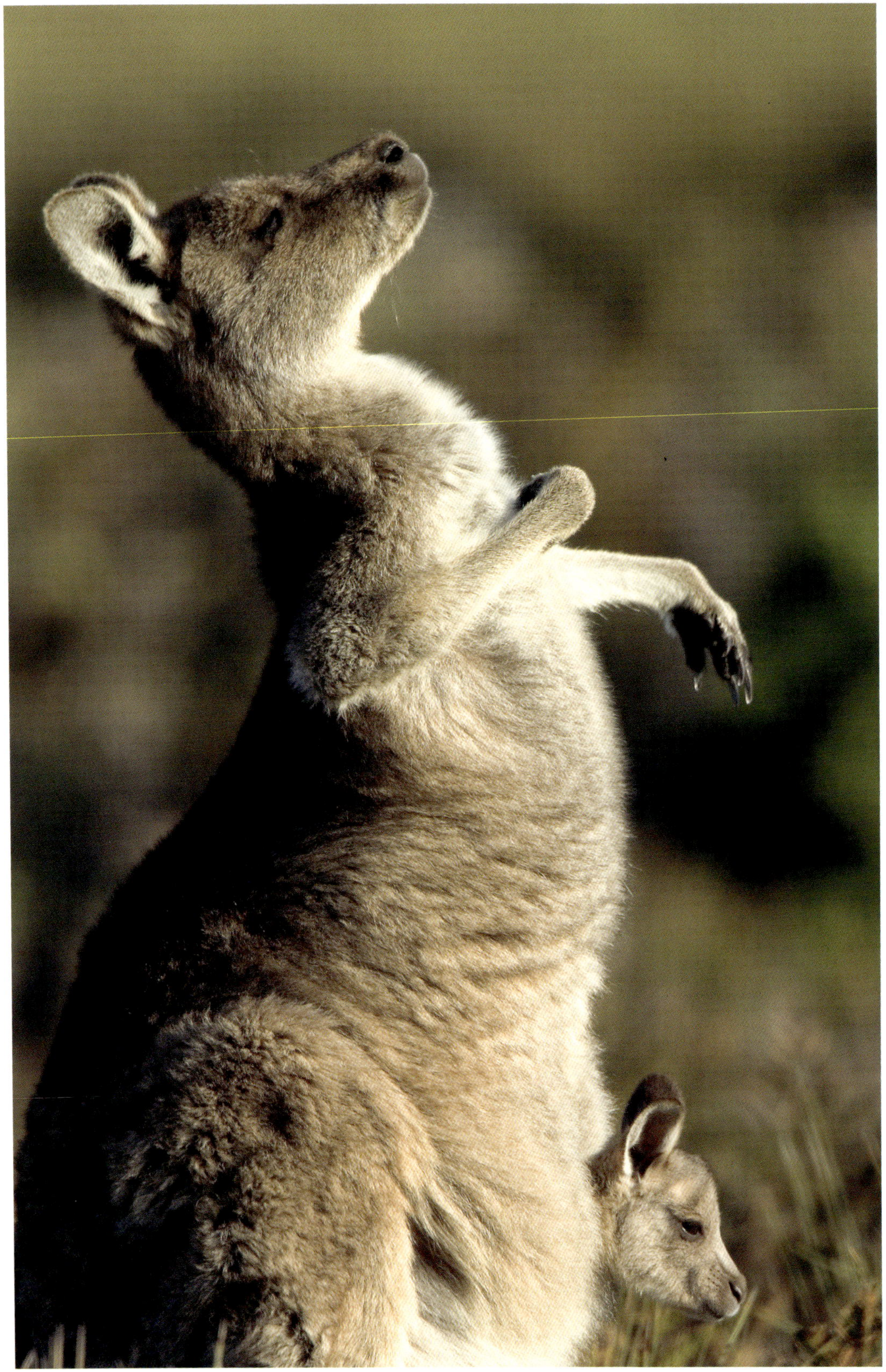

places his tiny mouth over it and clamps it in his jaws. For the next 100 days, he will dangle there as if he were a part of the teat.

At first, newborn kangaroos are too weak to suckle. The muscles in the teats take over the task of feeding them, contracting regularly to force the milk directly into the tiny mouth. As the weeks and months pass and the baby grows, the teat, nipple and lactiferous gland keep pace, ensuring that the composition of the milk is always aligned to the needs of the baby.

The first milk is watery and contains primarily carbohydrates, the building blocks that help to speed the development of the brain cells. These cells form an interconnected network with the developing sensory organs and the nervous system responsible for controlling movement. After three months the fetus is able to lift its head, and to find and release the teat on its own. At four months it opens its eyes; at five months it can stand.

From now on the little fellow is hungry for energy to grow. His organs, bones and muscles all clamour for substantial nourishment, and the composition of the life-giving fluid changes dramatically to accommodate these needs. The proportion of carbohydrates all but vanishes, while the fat content rises to more than 60 percent.

But the milk bar in the kangaroo's pouch is capable of doing far more than merely shake up the perfect nutritional cocktail for each growth phase of her young. The mother is generally feeding two young at any one time: her newborn joey, and the daughter hopping at her side. Each of her babies receives its own special formula, since each teat secretes a different type of milk in a quantity and composition exactly corresponding to their individual needs.

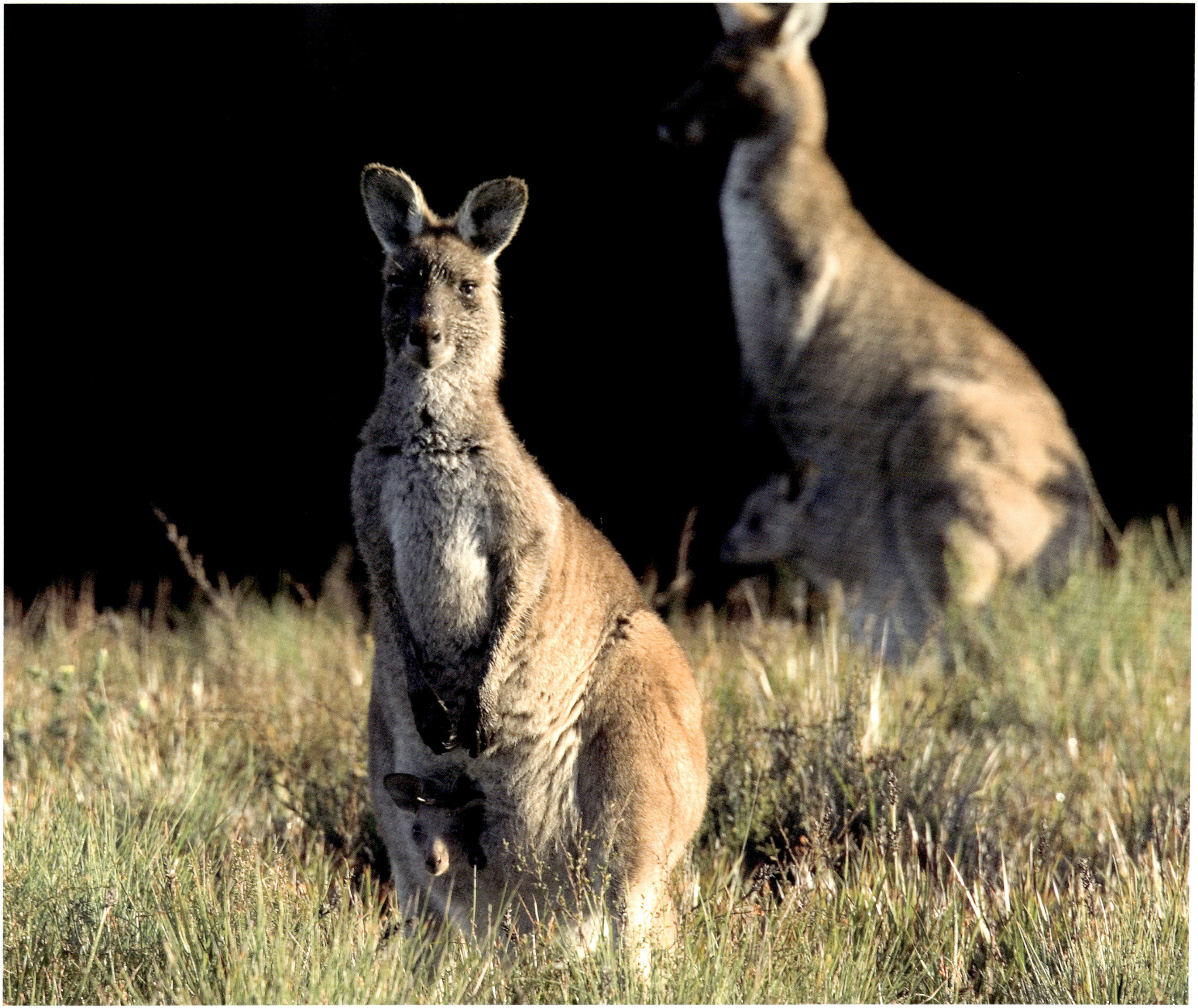

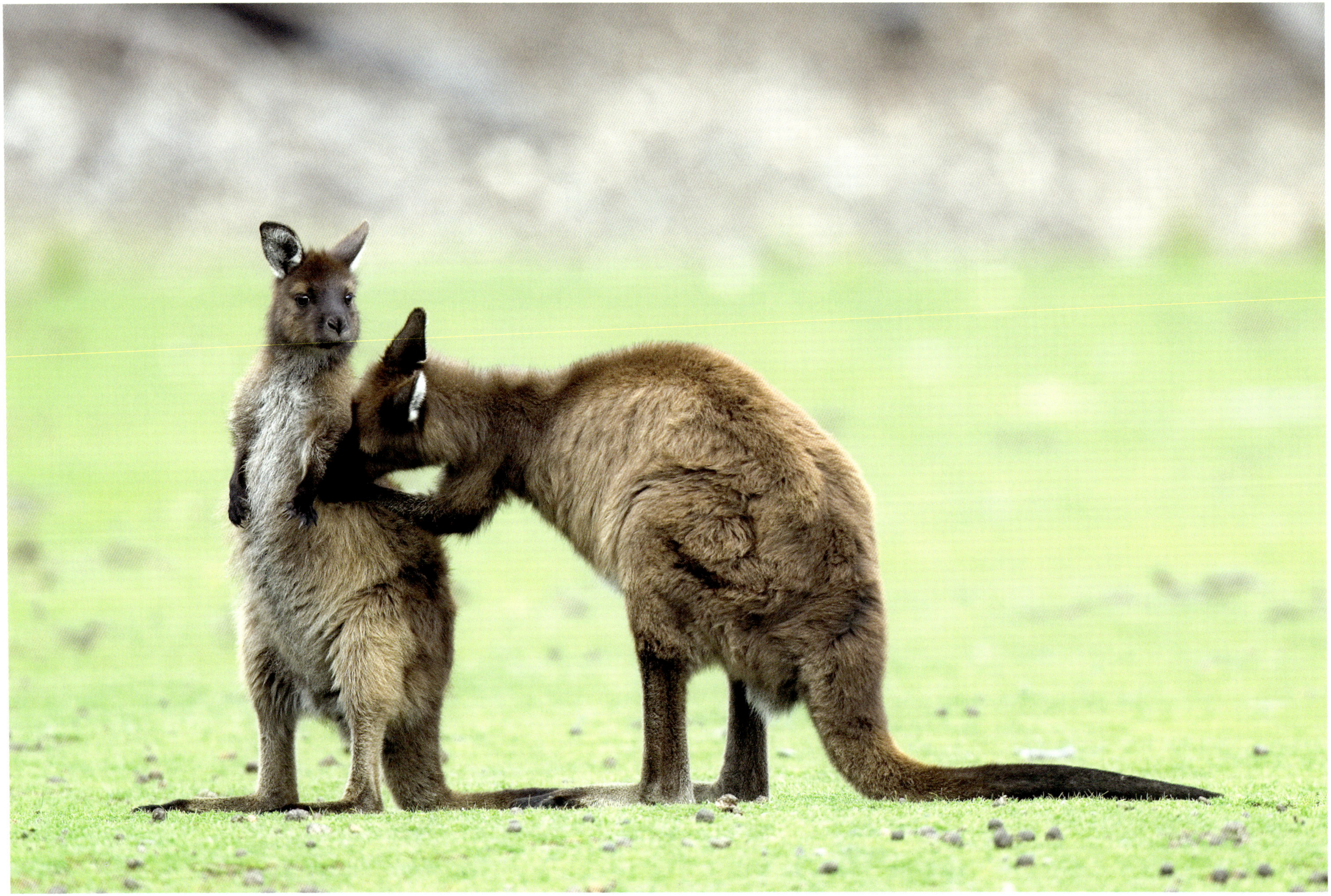

Mother kangaroos painstakingly groom their young ones' fur, using the delicate finger-like claws on their front paws. If their baby's fine fur is knotted, the mothers apply their powerful ruminant's tongue.

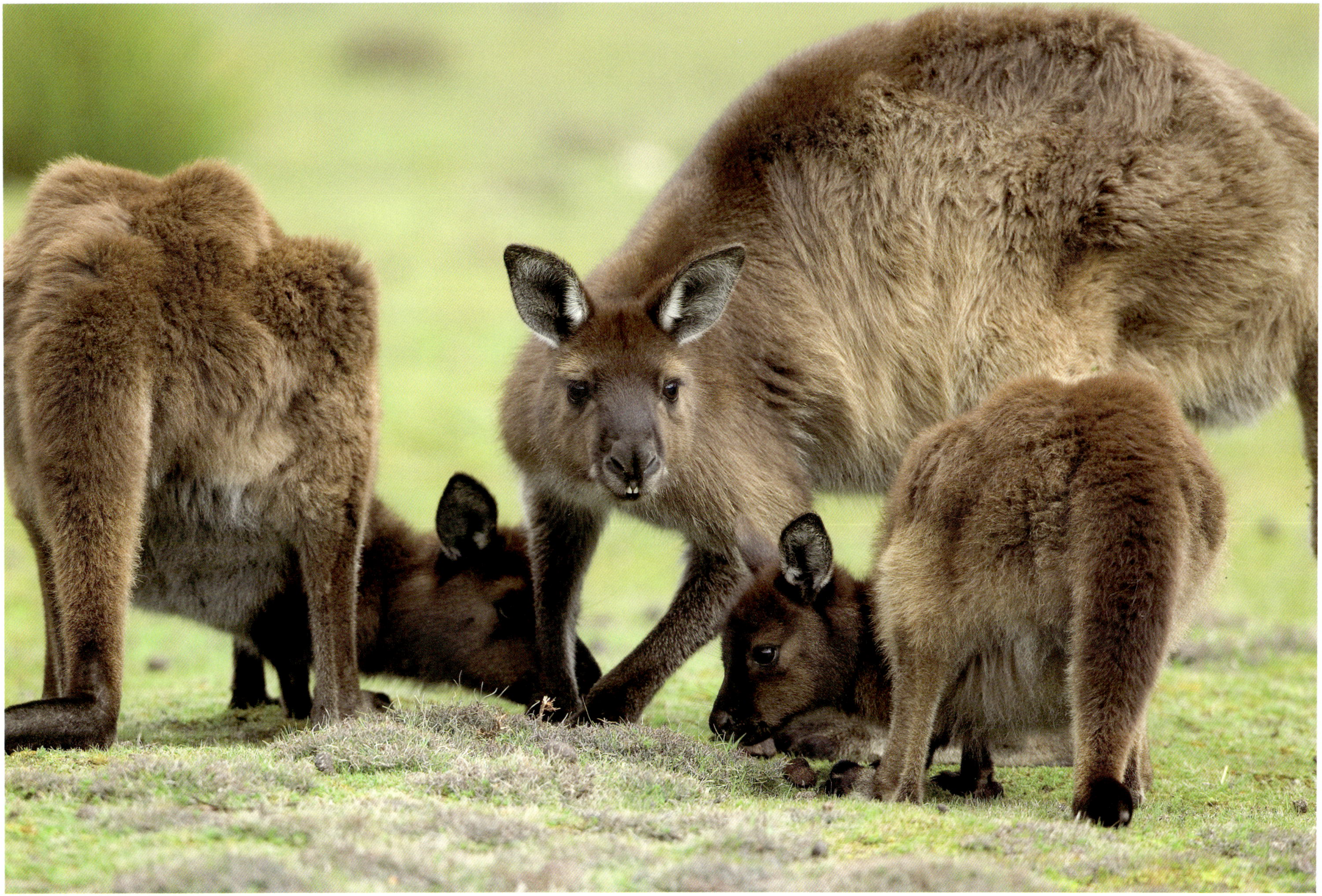

Eastern grey kangaroos live in harem groups with a male alpha kangaroo, the sole father of all of the group's young.
This "boomer" weighs more than twice as much as the females in the mob.
When he shadows one of his females closely, he is usually checking whether she is ready for mating.

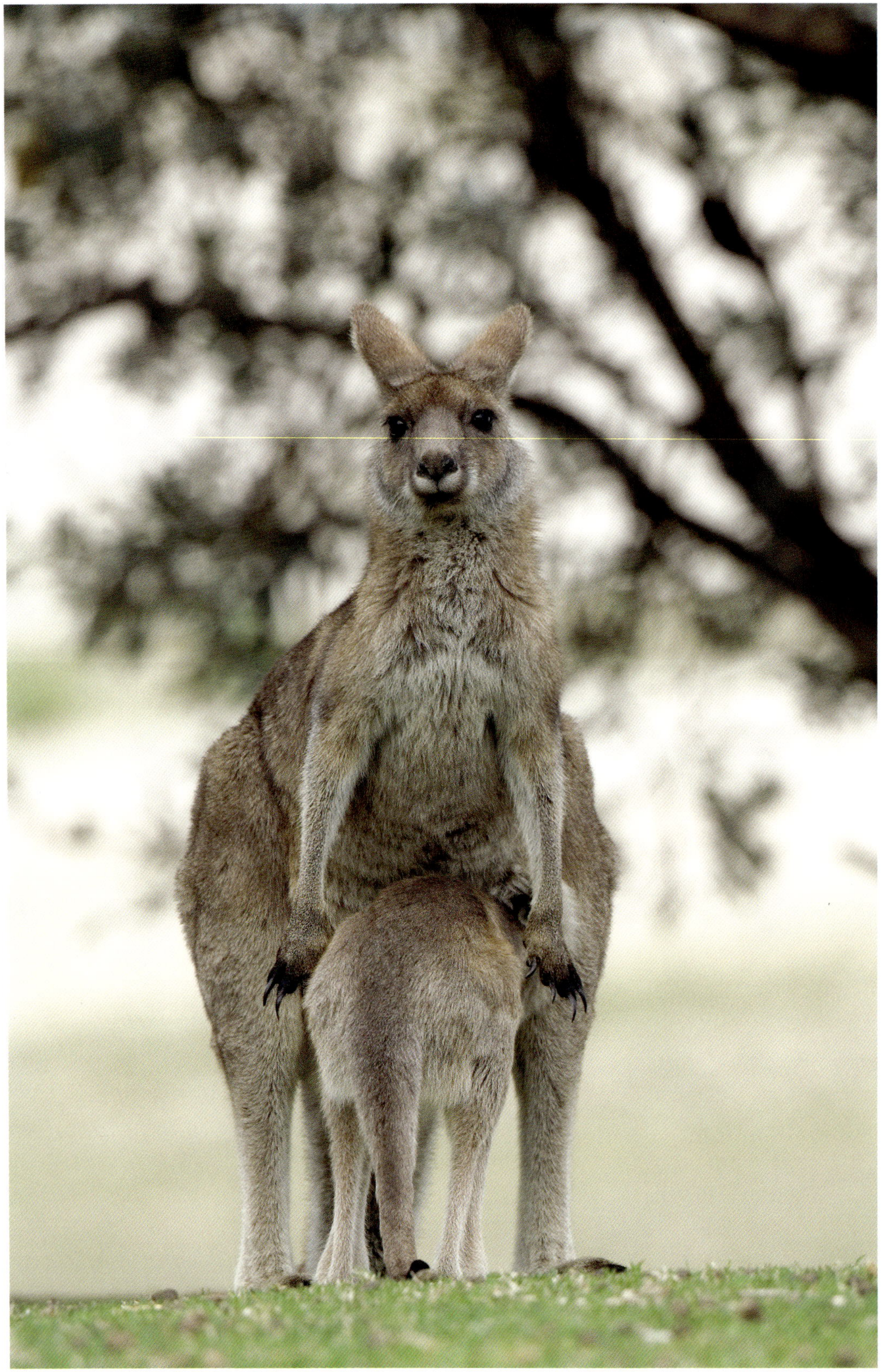

At seven months, marsupial babies have grown a thick coat of fur. Inquisitively observing the daily routine of life from their pouch, they experience the equanimity that is characteristic of grazing animals, the rhythm of migrations dictated by the seasons of fresh grasses, herbs and leaves, and the ecstasy of flight when the mother bounds through the air, shaking the baby in her pouch up and down. When it rains, the joeys seek shelter deep inside the pouch; the mother flexes her abdominal muscles, closing the pouch into a watertight haven. When the mother grazes, the joeys swing just above the ground as if in a hammock, nibbling at whatever vegetation is within their reach, sampling what their mother is eating and avoiding what she avoids.

From their elastic grandstand, the young kangaroos familiarize themselves with the social structure of the mob, follow the tussles and trials of strength of the young males, and marvel at the leaps and pirouettes of the frolicsome young. For months they are mere spectators, secure within their mother's skin.

That is, until the day when their mothers decide to eject them. Before the event, the does inspect their surroundings carefully, listening and sniffing the air. If everything seems calm, they relax their abdominal muscles and catapult the little one a few centimeters into the grass. This is obviously quite a shock, since most of the joeys immediately climb straight back in. But each time their expeditions last longer, and the babies grow in confidence and independence.

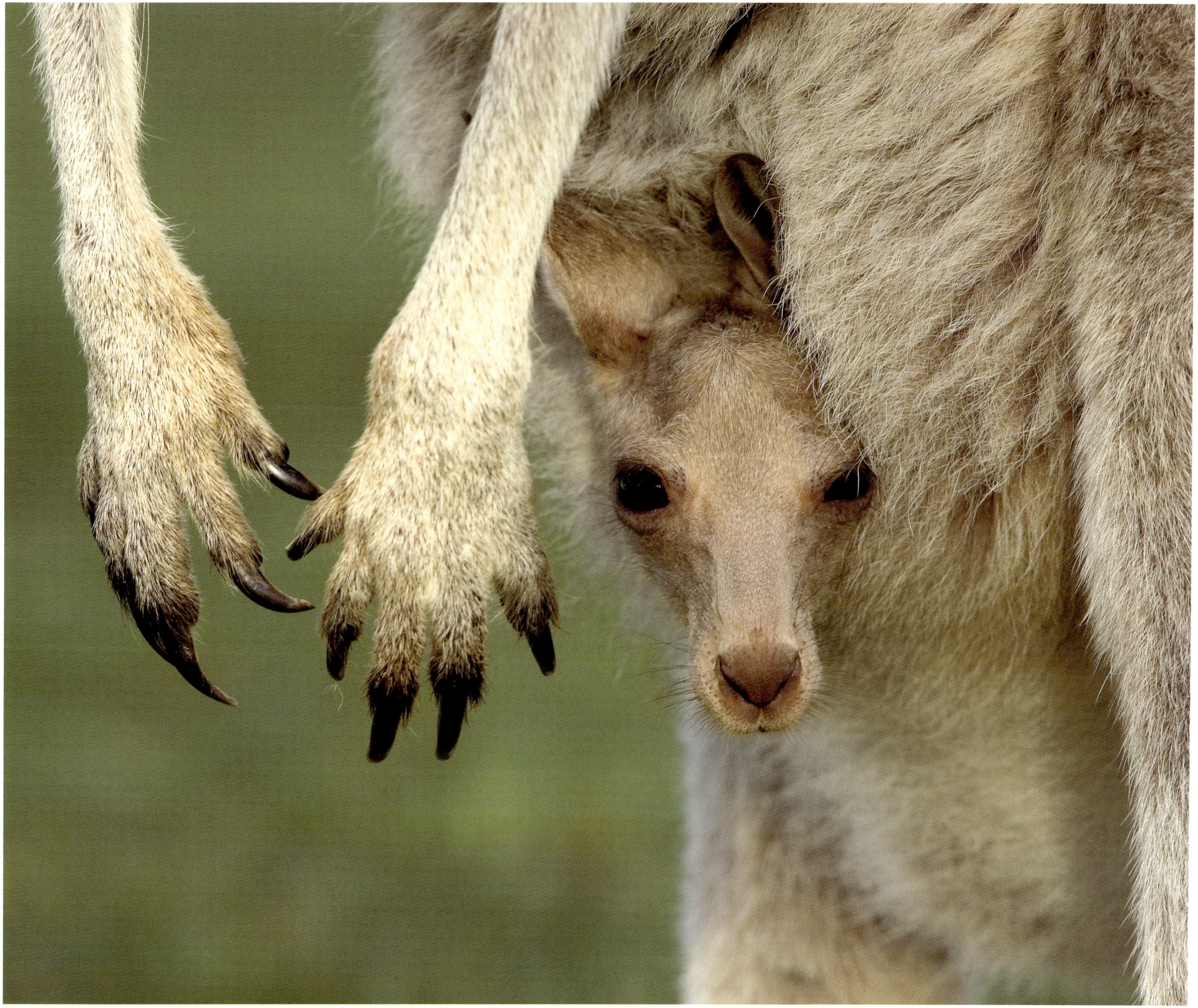

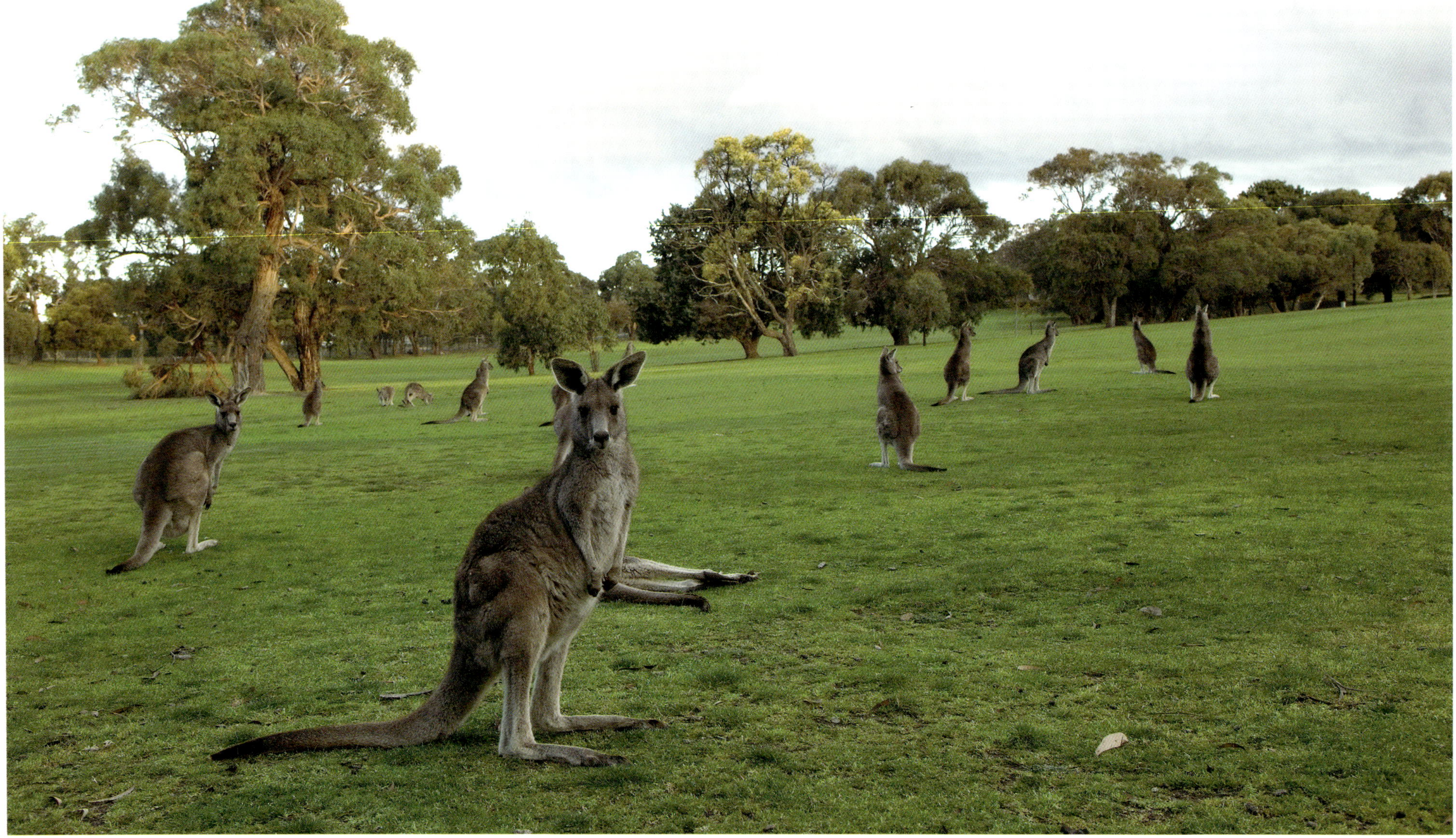

Golf courses with well-fertilized and irrigated grass are a delicacy for kangaroos.
200 of the ruminants are permanent residents at the golf course at Anglesea, a small town on the south coast of the state of Victoria. The marsupials are now a tourist attraction and feature in the town's advertising.

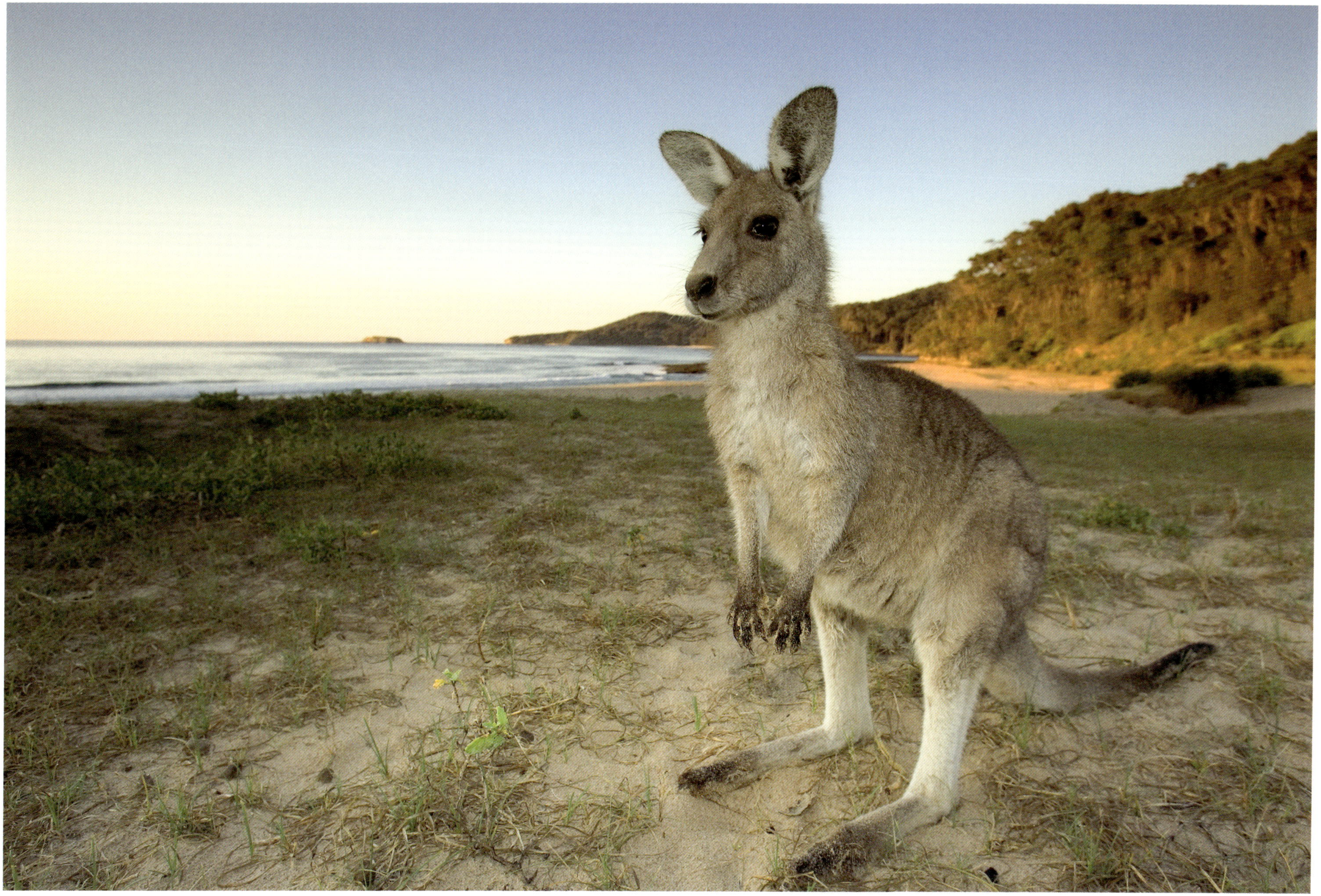

In Murramarang National Park, on the coast of New South Wales, around 20 kangaroos have found juicy pastures. The salty tang of the beach grass appeals to the animals. Kangaroos support themselves on their short front paws when grazing and use their powerful tails as a third leg when upright.

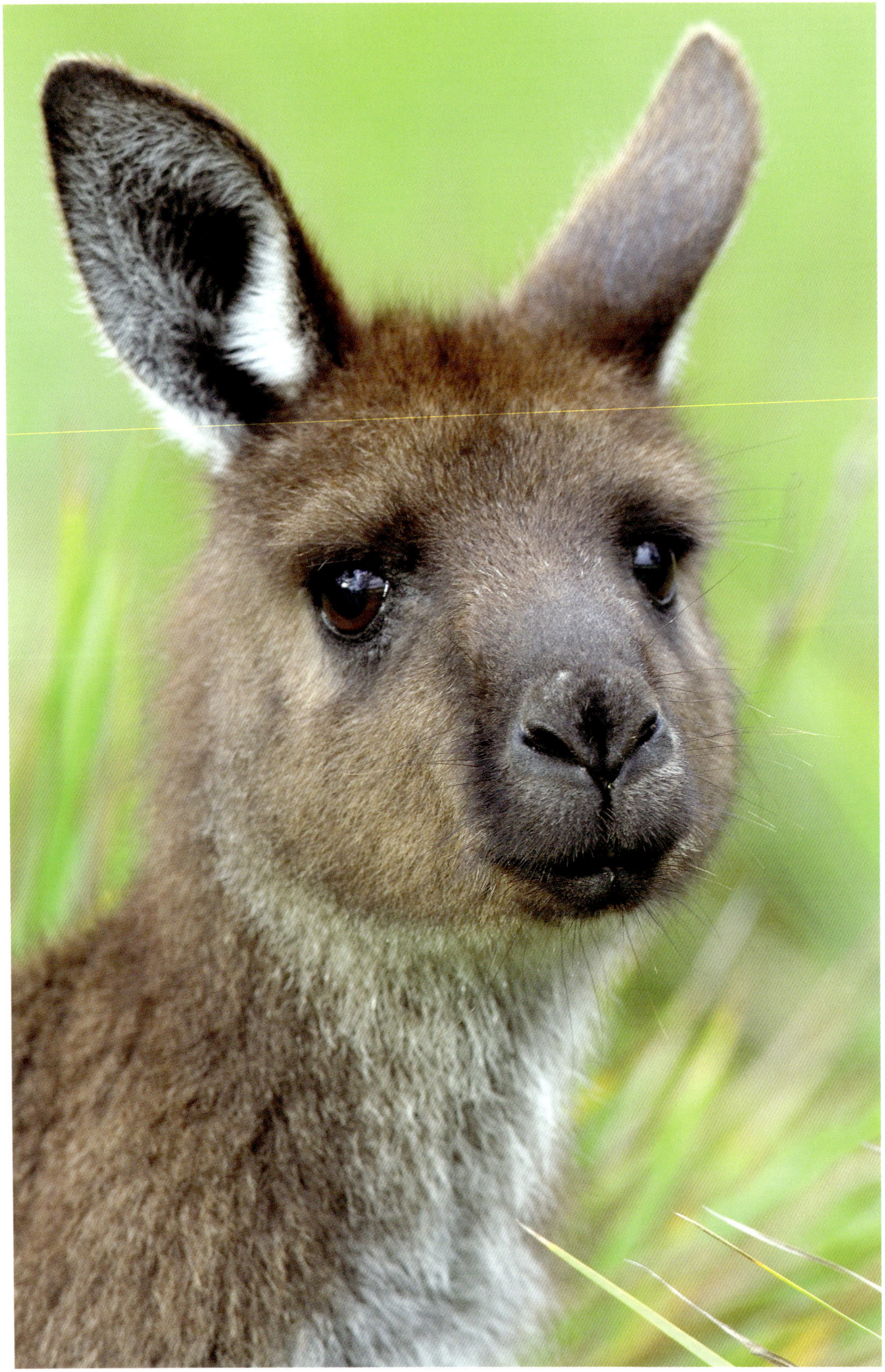

The relationship between mother kangaroos and their young is particularly close. They can often be seen embracing their joeys, resting their heads against those of their babies, or playfully boxing with them. If a young kangaroo is lost, mother and baby call each other until they are reunited, drawn by the familiar sound of their voices.

Yet this idyllic time inevitably nears its close. Every joey must face its moment of crisis – when the pouch no longer opens, the Open Sesame magic no longer works – because its mother is expecting a new tenant for the living quarters in her pouch.

Like a baby conveyor belt, the older children move one place along. The joey newly banned from the pouch is permitted to nurse at its mother's teat for a further nine months. The adolescent daughter ejected from the pouch eighteen months previously to make way for the newborn is now reaching adulthood and will be weaned; its teat in the mother's pouch begins to shrink.

But where did the youngest joey, the immature little mite, actually come from? When was he conceived? The answer is that special day when the doe was not pregnant for once, but had just given birth to her youngest and begun to nurse it.

The boomer spotted her weeks ago. Her empty pouch and the nine-month-old daughter at her side signaled to him that she would soon be ready to mate with him. He regularly sniffed at her cloacal opening, shadowed her everywhere, keeping a distance of two meters (6.5 feet), and occasionally even neglected his guard duties as head of the harem – all in order to ensure he would not miss the opportunity of fathering young.

When the mob arrives at a eucalyptus grove in the early morning hours, the boomer grazes at the side of his chosen female. He sniffs the scent of her urine and, with the accuracy of a biochemical laboratory analysis, ascertains that the time has come. She has ovulated and is now ready to conceive. He rubs his paws over her shoulders, rears up and touches her nose with his. As the doe accommodatingly bends forward, he mounts her and sires the next baby in waiting. ■

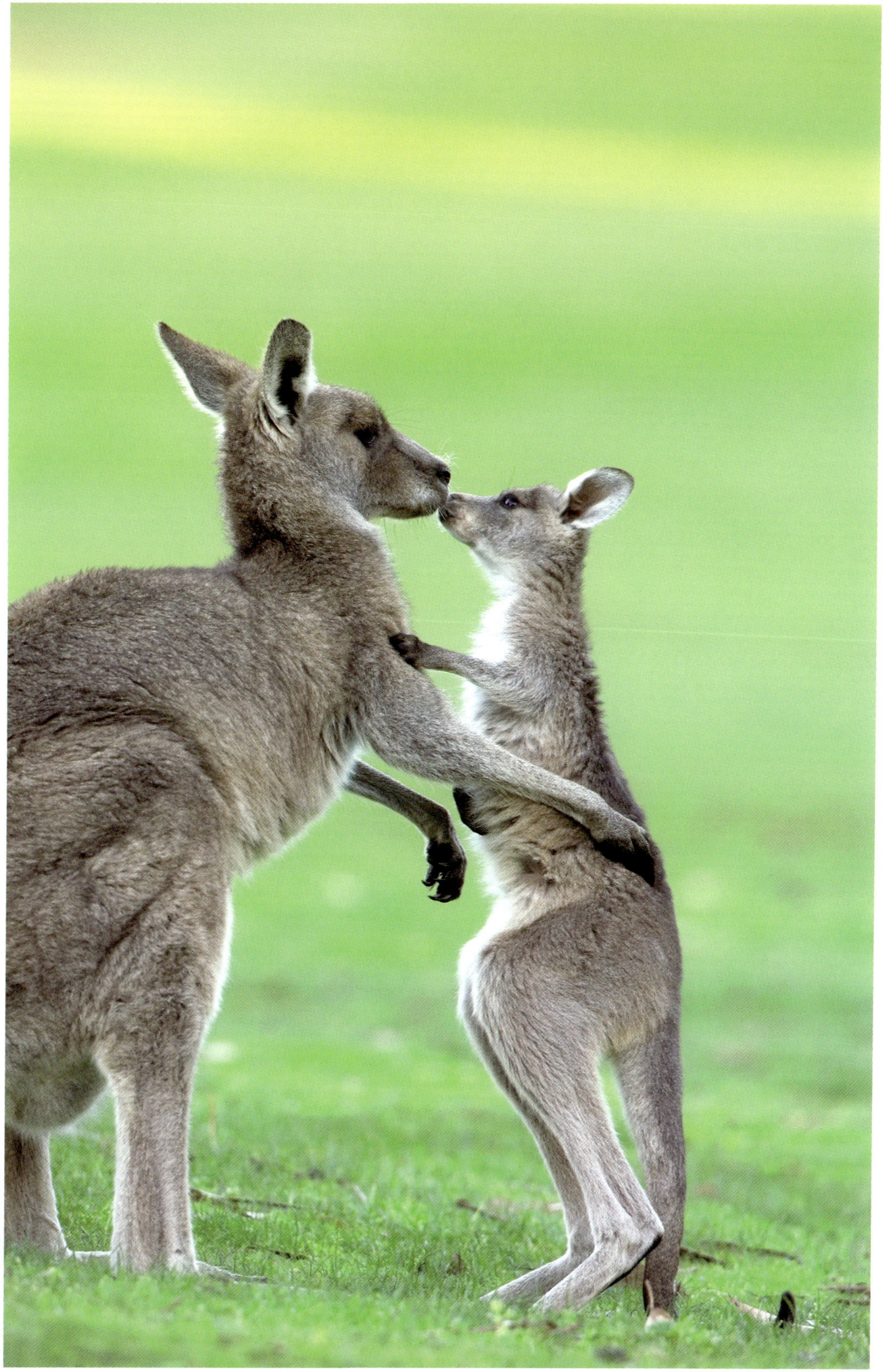

Eastern Grey Kangaroos – at a glance

Their place in the animal kingdom

- They belong to the phylum of vertebrates
- to the class of mammals
- to the order of diprotodontia (animals with "two front teeth")
- to the family of kangaroos

Their scientific name

Macropus giganteus

Their closest relatives

All young mammals undergo an extremely long period of development. Many grow inside the mother's body; others are born in an immature state and grow to maturity in the mother's pouch. These two strategies have been in existence for over 150 million years. Marsupials reached Australia 50 million years ago and developed into around 170 different species, including the various species of large kangaroos. The eastern grey kangaroo is less closely related to the red kangaroo than to the western grey kangaroo.

Where they live (population numbers)

As the name implies, eastern grey kangaroos live in Australia's eastern regions including Tasmania (population: many millions). They are frugal creatures and can survive on sparse vegetation.
They prefer thinly wooded regions.

Eastern grey kangaroos in figures

- From head to rump, eastern grey kangaroos reach a **length** of 140 centimeters (4.6 feet). The powerful **tail** grows to a length of 100 centimeters (3.3 feet).
- Males **weigh** 90 kilos, around twice as much as females.
- Eastern grey kangaroos are superlative **leapers**, and can reach lengths of 13.5 meters (44 feet), heights of 2.5 meters (8 feet) and a speed of 50 kilometers (31 miles) per hour.
- They reach **sexual maturity** at 20 months.
- Their **young** are born after a gestation period of 36 days, weigh just under one gram and are 2.5 centimeters (1 inch) long.
- Female kangaroos have **two uteri and vaginas**; male animals have two penises, with the testicles in front of the penis, not behind.
- The **lifespan** of the eastern grey kangaroo is around 18 years.

Eastern grey kangaroos' characteristic features

The most prominent feature of kangaroos is their muscular back legs, which enable them to leap extraordinary distances, yet use very little energy to do so thanks to their elastic sinews. Like rubber bands, the sinews always spring back to their normal length, and the faster the kangaroo moves, the more nimbly the sinew stretches. The kangaroo's best-known feature is its pouch, in which it carries and nurses its young. Kangaroos can do more than merely box with their short front paws; the five delicate claws on each paw are as skilful as a hand, and are used to grip objects and clean their fur.

What eastern grey kangaroos eat

While kangaroos may not resemble cows, like cows their principal food is grass. Marsupials too have a multi-chambered stomach, enabling them to digest their cellulose-rich fodder and break down its nutrients. They have further adapted to better process the tough stalks of their primary source of nourishment by developing wedge-shaped molars formed to deal effectively with the vegetation, although only the two front teeth are used to actually grind the food. When these teeth wear down they fall out and are replaced by the next pair.

Eastern grey kangaroos' lifestyle

During the day, kangaroos generally rest in the shade of bushes and trees, becoming active in the twilight and night hours. Marsupials are social creatures. Several does, their young and one adult male live in a group known as a mob. The head of the mob, the "boomer", attempts to mate with all the females and defends his position against rivals within the mob and from other mobs. The size of the group's territory depends on the climate in the region; where food is scarce, territories are necessarily more extensive, while in areas where food is abundant, kangaroos live in close proximity to one another.

How eastern grey kangaroos raise their young

If grass is plentiful, mother kangaroos will raise three children more or less simultaneously. One is nine months old and still permitted to nurse, but has been ejected from the pouch. One is born after a gestation period of five weeks and is completing its development in the pouch. And one was conceived immediately after the pouch dweller was born, but will not begin to develop until the pouch is empty. That will take about nine months.

Dangers to eastern grey kangaroos

Dingos are the kangaroo's only natural enemy. Human beings are far more deadly opponents. In 2006, the Australian government designated 1.6 million eastern grey kangaroos as fair game for hunters.

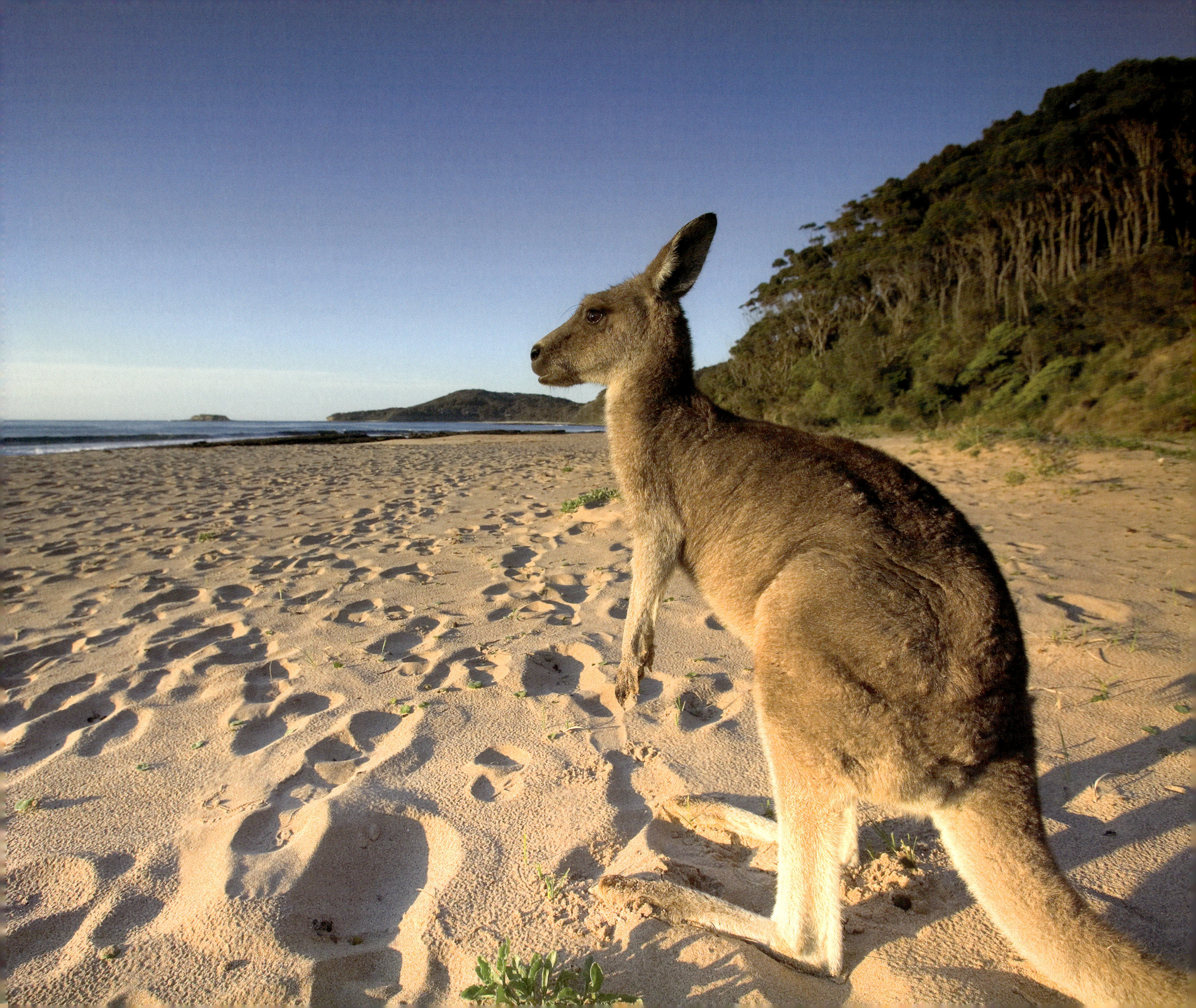

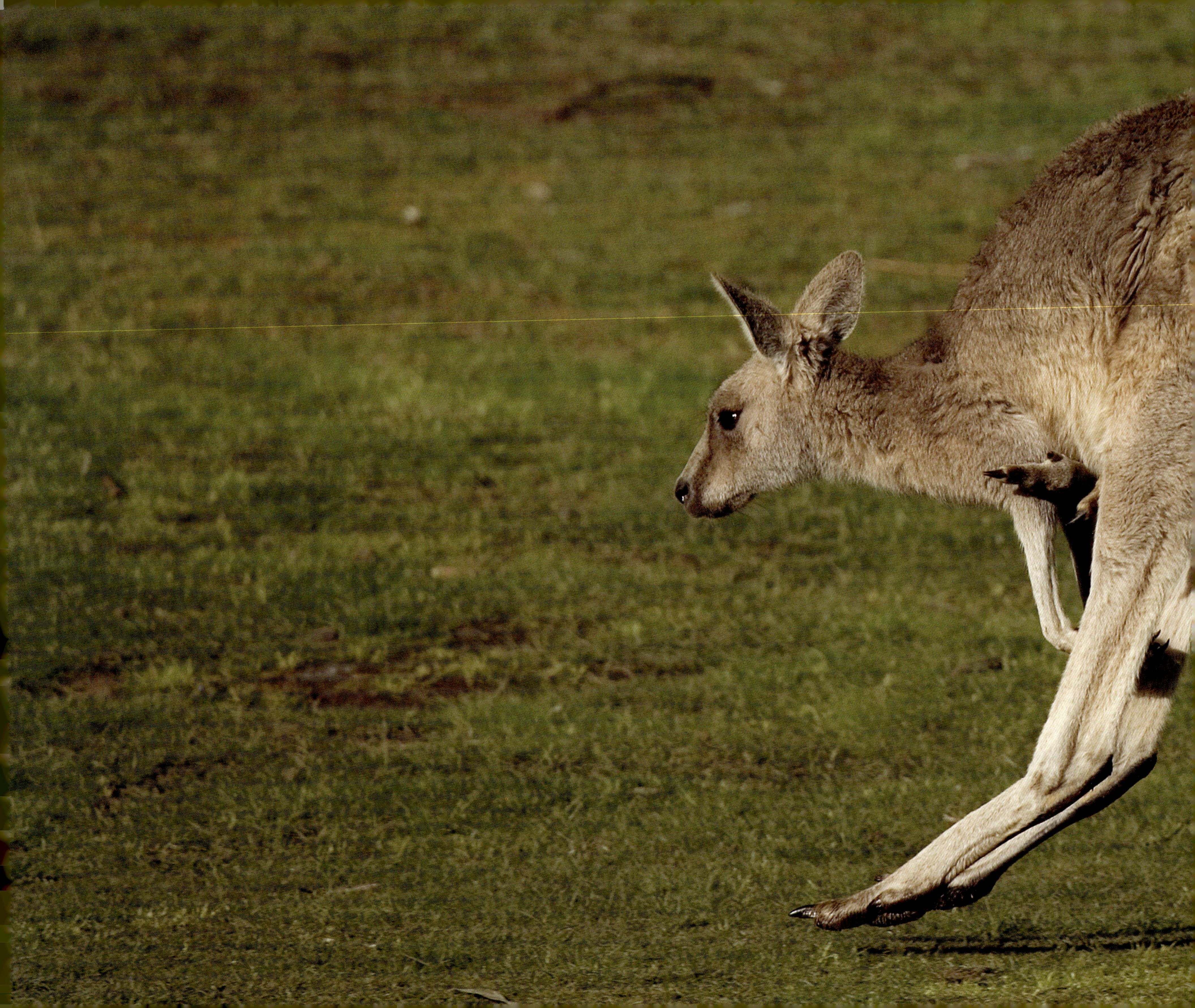

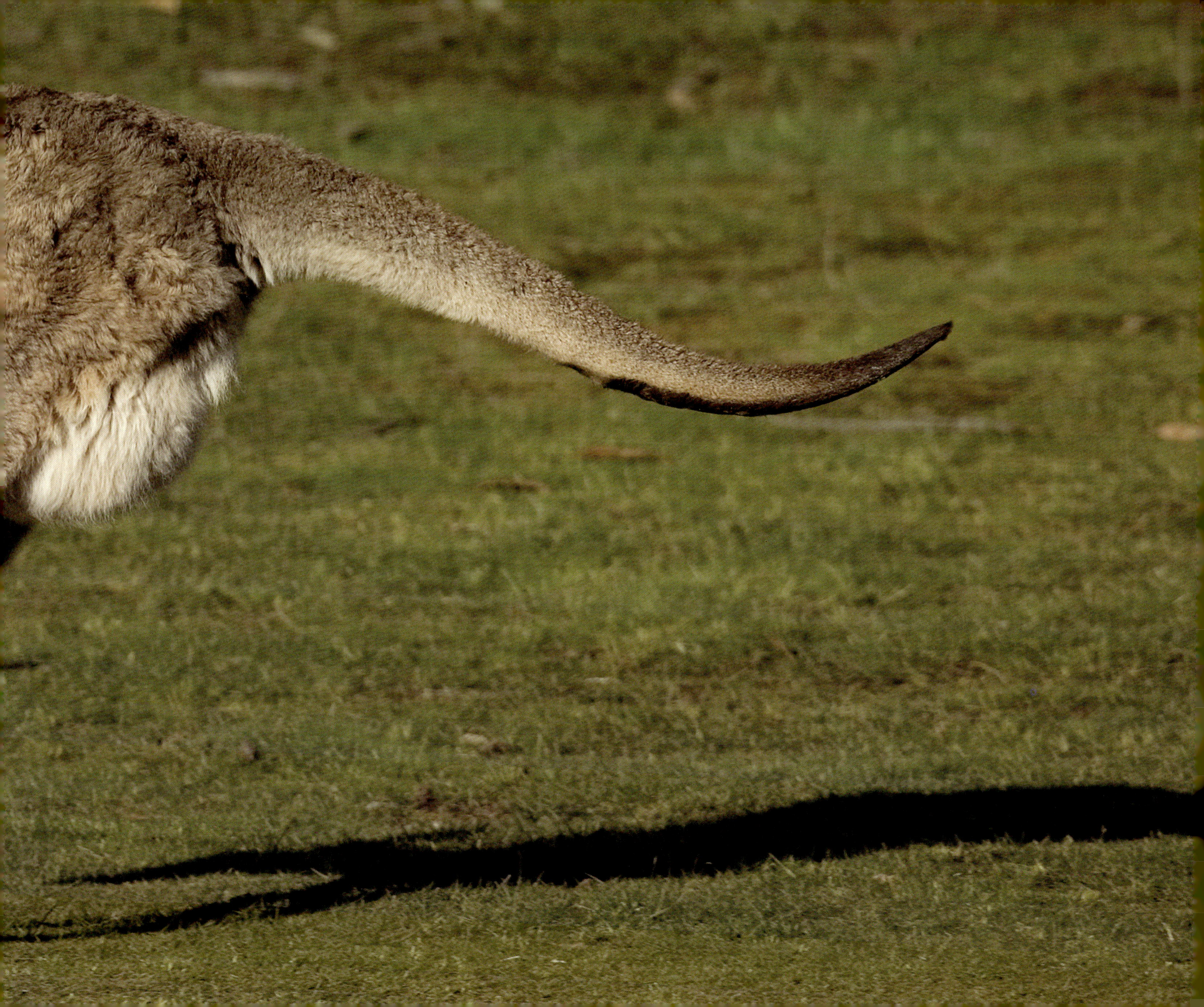

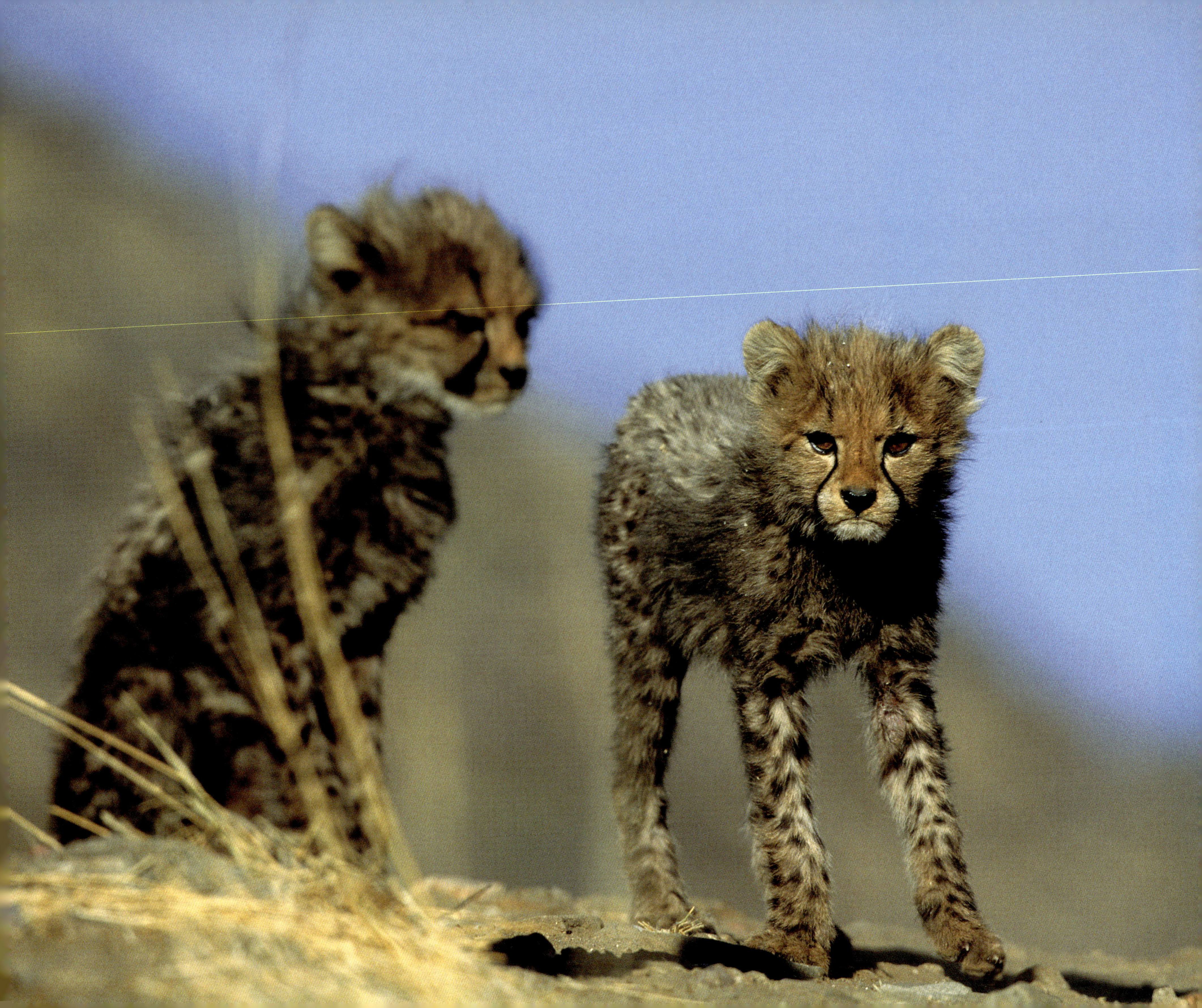

Cheetahs

The Hunted Hunters

After the hunt is over, the female cheetah sits bolt upright and inspects her surroundings. The black lines with which nature has marked her round cat's face give her an expression of stern vigilance. All appears peaceful on the plains. As if no harm could ever come to the inhabitants of this pastoral landscape stretching out under a flat blue sky. A few wildebeest and springboks become visible against the horizon, emerging from the grey dawn. The warm glow of the morning washes over bushes, termite mounds, low dips in the ground, the crowns of the acacia trees and embankments created by river erosion. The thick forests of stems projecting from the green blanket of grass are transmuted into sparkling gold, and the last veils of dew evaporate in the hollows.

Only the breathing of the big cat, the rapid pulse of her flanks indicate the extent of her recent exertions. From her throat comes a bird-like twitter. Again and again it sounds, becoming more urgent, more pressing with every repetition. Finally a chorus of twittering rises in reply from a disheveled bush around one hundred meters away. And as if this was the signal they had been waiting for, four young male cheetahs burst out of their hiding-place and charge forward. The six-month-old cubs bound excitedly around their mother and around the kill lying at her feet. They press forward towards the feast, greedy yet uncertain where to start.

The amber gaze of the female cheetah still scours the grassy plains. Her sharp alertness unsettles a herd of springboks. Feeling the eyes of the huntress resting upon them, almost like a physical touch, the antelopes nervously jostle together, seeking protection in the throng, in the indistinguishable brown of the coats, the white bellies and the coordinated trot of 60 hooves. They slowly retreat, all heads turned toward the deadly menace that has just carried off a member of their herd.

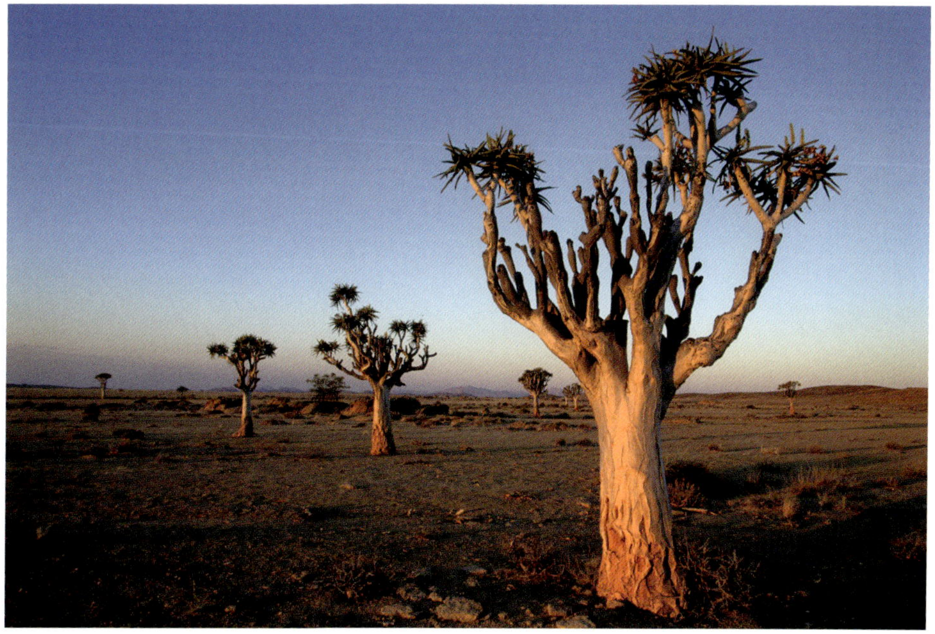

The cubs notice nothing of this. They stretch purring next to the lolling body of springbok, victim of only a moment's lapse in vigilance, and begin tearing at its fur.

A moment ago, the springbok had been grazing unsuspectingly, lulled into a false sense of security in the cover afforded by a low copse. So when his herd moved on, he was slow to catch up. A fatal mistake, which the female cheetah spotted from a distance and immediately exploited. She rapidly approached her prey from a distance of 300 meters (984 feet), her cubs behind her.

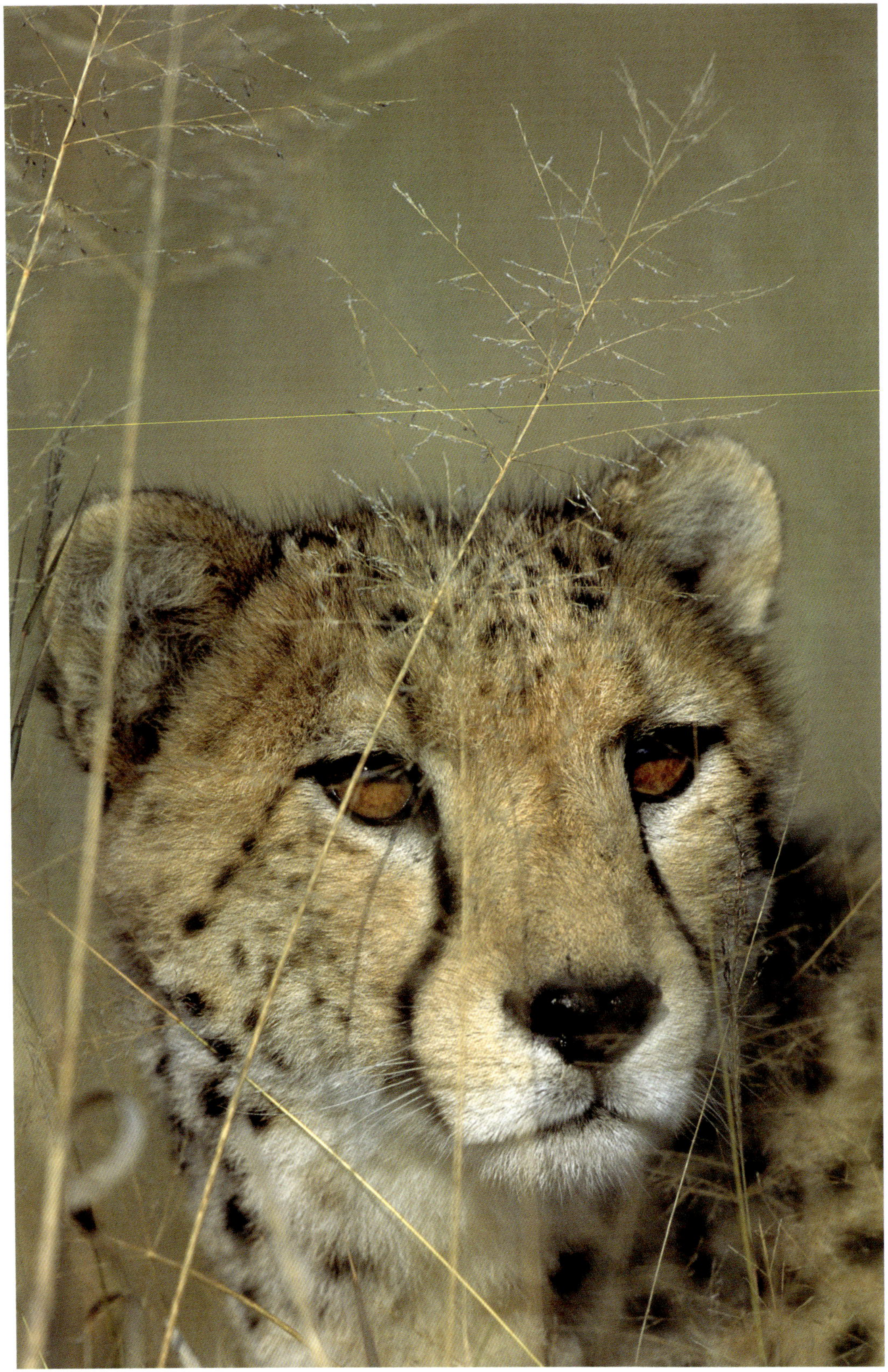

As soon as cheetah cubs have developed enough strength for longer expeditions, they accompany their mother on hunting expeditions. The babies open their eyes roughly twelve days after birth, and begin to walk at about the same time. Tottering and weak at first, they are introduced to their first taste of prey by their mother at the age of only six weeks.

Cheetahs are naturally endowed with the build and keen senses of the predatory big cats, but their slumbering talents must be awakened and honed by training and practice. They need around two years of learning, eighteen months of which are under the supervision of their mother, before they are self-sufficient.

Although already six months old, the quartet of brothers is still playful. The cubs romp around their mother, sometimes even forging ahead of her, and have still not grasped the principle of stalking, the necessity of remaining in hiding until the moment to pounce arrives.

As the behavior of the happy-go-lucky cubs threatened to betray their presence to the antelope, the female cheetah sat down. Her cubs immediately joined her and threw themselves into the grass next to her. After five minutes she stood up again and ran on, crouching low. This time, the cubs followed slowly. The springbok had now disappeared behind a few tree trunks. The huntress was able to stalk her prey unobserved up to a distance of 100 meters (328 feet); then she broke into a sprint, halving the distance between them in a few bounds before the antelope raised its head, recognized the danger it was in and fled.

Cheetahs are less effectively armed with deadly weapons and strength than lions or leopards; these graceful, light big cats have shorter teeth and weaker jaws than their relatives. Their claws, which are not retractable like those of other cats and which therefore wear down as they run, do not have curved points to lacerate or tear open their prey. The print of their delicate paws is more similar to that of a wolf. If cheetahs were not so fast, their success as carnivores would be seriously threatened.

But they are most certainly fast. Unrivalled, in fact, because they have every physical feature they need to achieve top speeds. Thanks to their extremely long legs they can leap a distance of seven meters (23 feet), their flexible spine bending and relaxing like a spring as they bound forward with the speed of an arrow. Flared nostrils, an extensive network of bronchial tubes and capacious lungs supply the high levels of oxygen a cheetah needs when mobilizing its entire energy reserves for short sprints, in which it can reach up to 120 kilometers (74.5 miles) per hour. *Acinonyx jubatus* is born to run. A cheetah can maintain this speed over a good 300 meters (984 feet). Once it has overtaken its prey, it lowers its speed to adjust to-the zig-zag course of the fleeing antelope.

The springbok doubles back three times attempting to shake off its pursuer. The cheetah reacts instantly, using her tough claws to brake, changing direction herself in a whirl of dust and grass tufts, so that she is suddenly hard on the antelope's heels.

At this point, the cheetah launches a risky maneuvre. Still traveling at a breakneck 70 kilometers (43 miles) per hour, she lifts a claw and deals the antelope a blow – all that is needed to turn the delicate balance of flight into a stumble. The springbok somersaults through the air, landing heavily. The cheetah shoots past, turns back, grasps her victim by the throat and bites firmly until all struggling ceases. After two minutes the animal has suffocated, and the drama is at an end. Since 50 per cent of all attacks are successful, the cheetah's cubs are supplied with around eight kilos of meat per day.

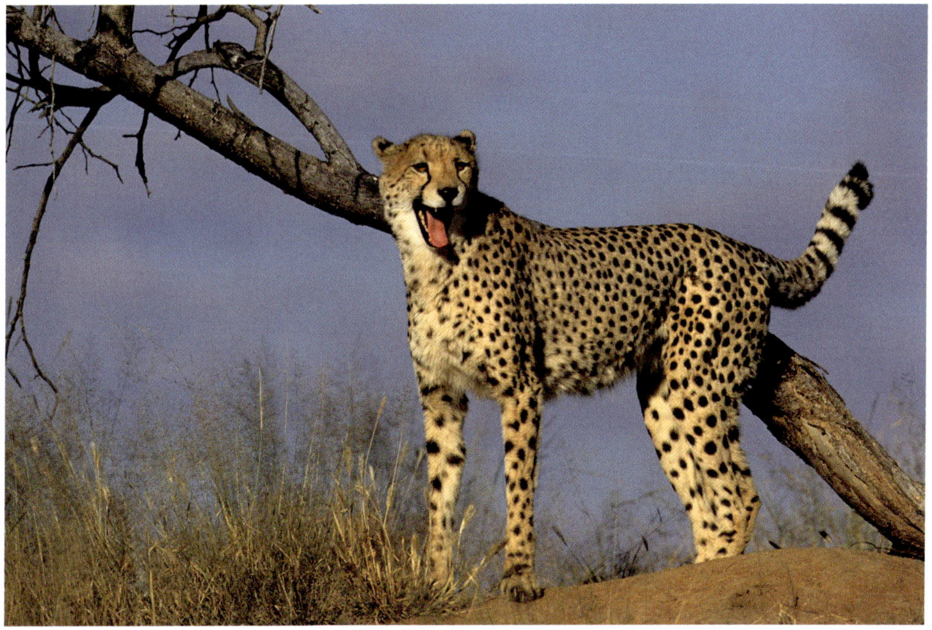

The cheetah grabs the springbok by the thigh and drags her kill around 200 meters (656 feet) to a small hill, depositing the 50-kilo load under a group of small trees. The cubs can eat in the dappled shade of the sparse vegetation.

The mood among the four male cubs is peaceable – unlike a pride of lions, where each begrudges the other his share. A cheetah cub may snatch a meaty bone from his brother, but placidly suffers its return a short time later. Their mother constantly breaks off her meal to keep watch. After half an hour, a pile of entrails, bones and fur is all that is left of the antelope.

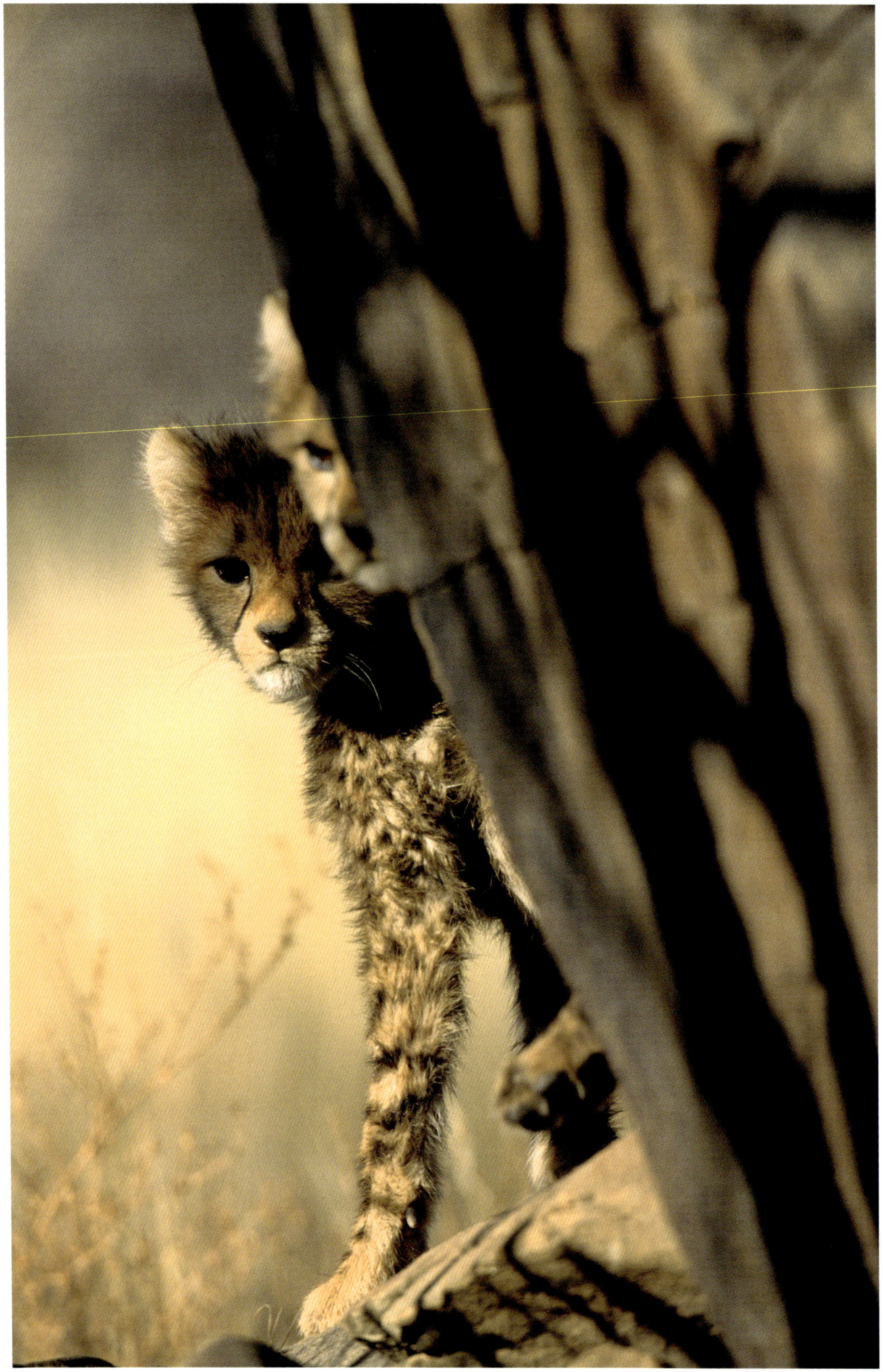

Relaxed and replete, the five cheetahs sink into the grass. Their spotted coats are absorbed by the colors of the vegetation, the soil and the flecks of light dancing in the wind. The big cats lie close together, one even snuggling against its mother's belly, and lick each other's stained faces.

As if imitating what their mother has just demonstrated, the four cubs begin to stalk each other, prowling, hunting and knocking each other over with the characteristic blow to the flank or rump. They become familiar with each other, with their own strengths and weaknesses and with those of their siblings. Male cheetahs forge these bonds at an early age and sustain them throughout their lives. Later, it will be easier for a group to lay claim to a territory of around 40 square kilometers (15 square miles) and hunt down large prey such as wildebeest and even buffalo.

Female cheetahs, however, roam alone before giving birth to their first litter at the age of two. Their territories are far more extensive, and may be anything up to 830 square kilometers (320 square miles) in area.

The most powerful of the four cubs zigzags exuberantly around their resting place at top speed, with his tail vertical. One of the others takes up the chase, and is hunted in turn by his two brothers. The cubs switch roles frequently, each given the opportunity to play both the hunter and the hunted.

In real life, the adolescent cubs are still very far from successful hunters. Not even when their mother occasionally brings a live kid to practice on. Although the cubs pursue the kid eagerly as soon as it tries to flee, even managing to bring it down after a few attempts, they do not know what to do next. In the end it is their mother who finally takes action and finishes off the victim.

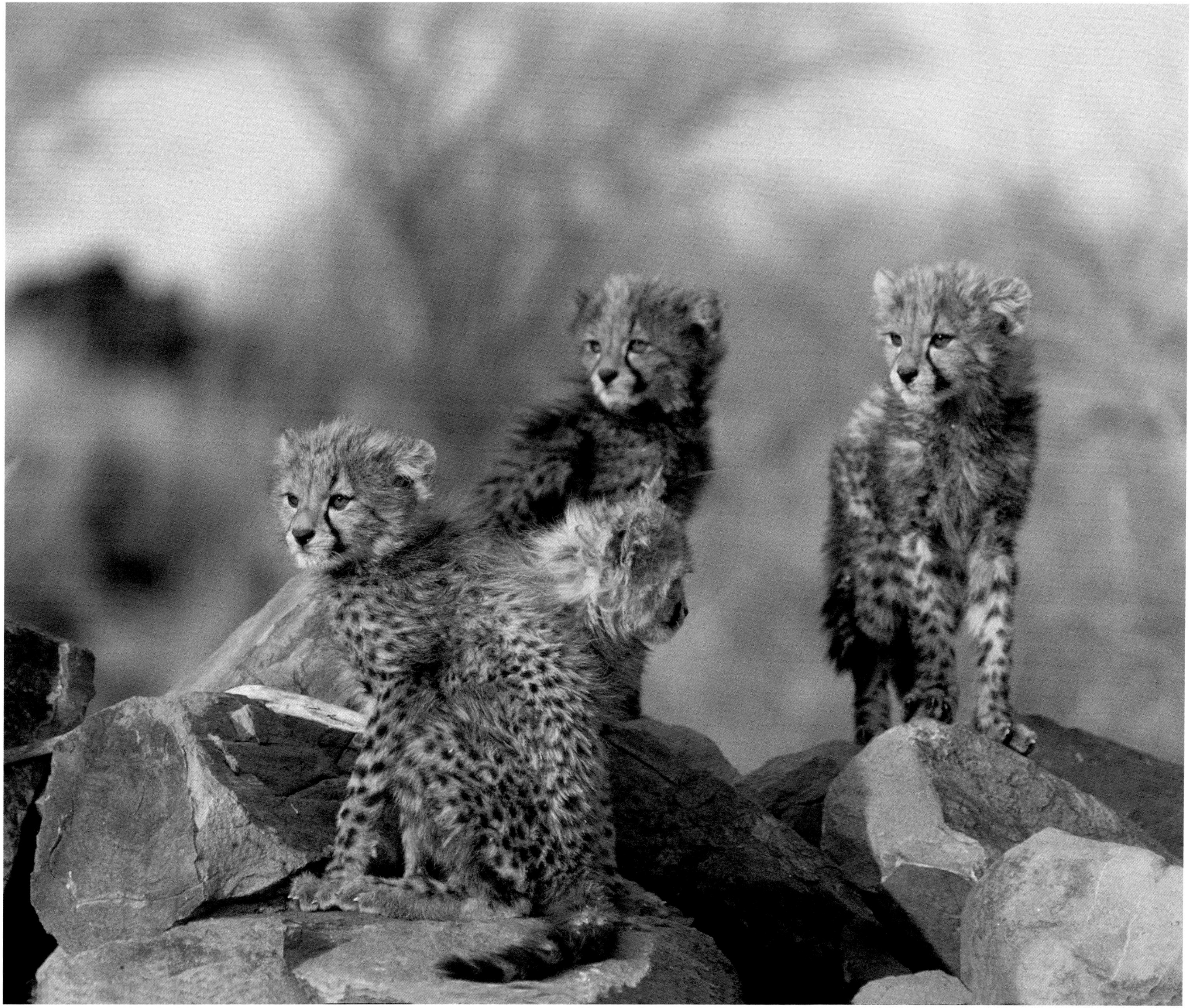

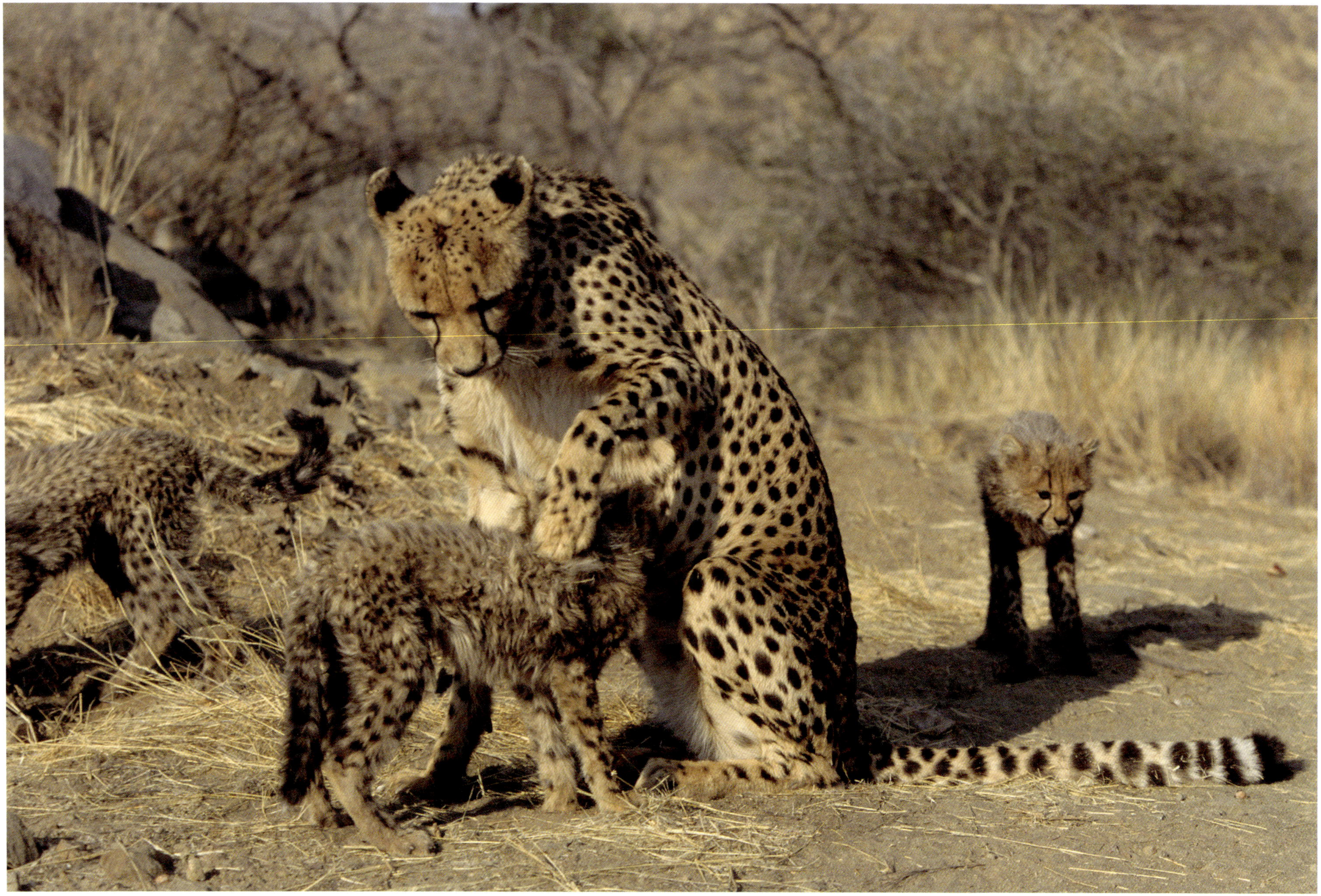

Although the three-month-old cheetah cubs have recently started to eat meat, they are still nursed by their mother. She generally lies on her side, enabling all the cubs to drink at once. This one needed a reviving snack.

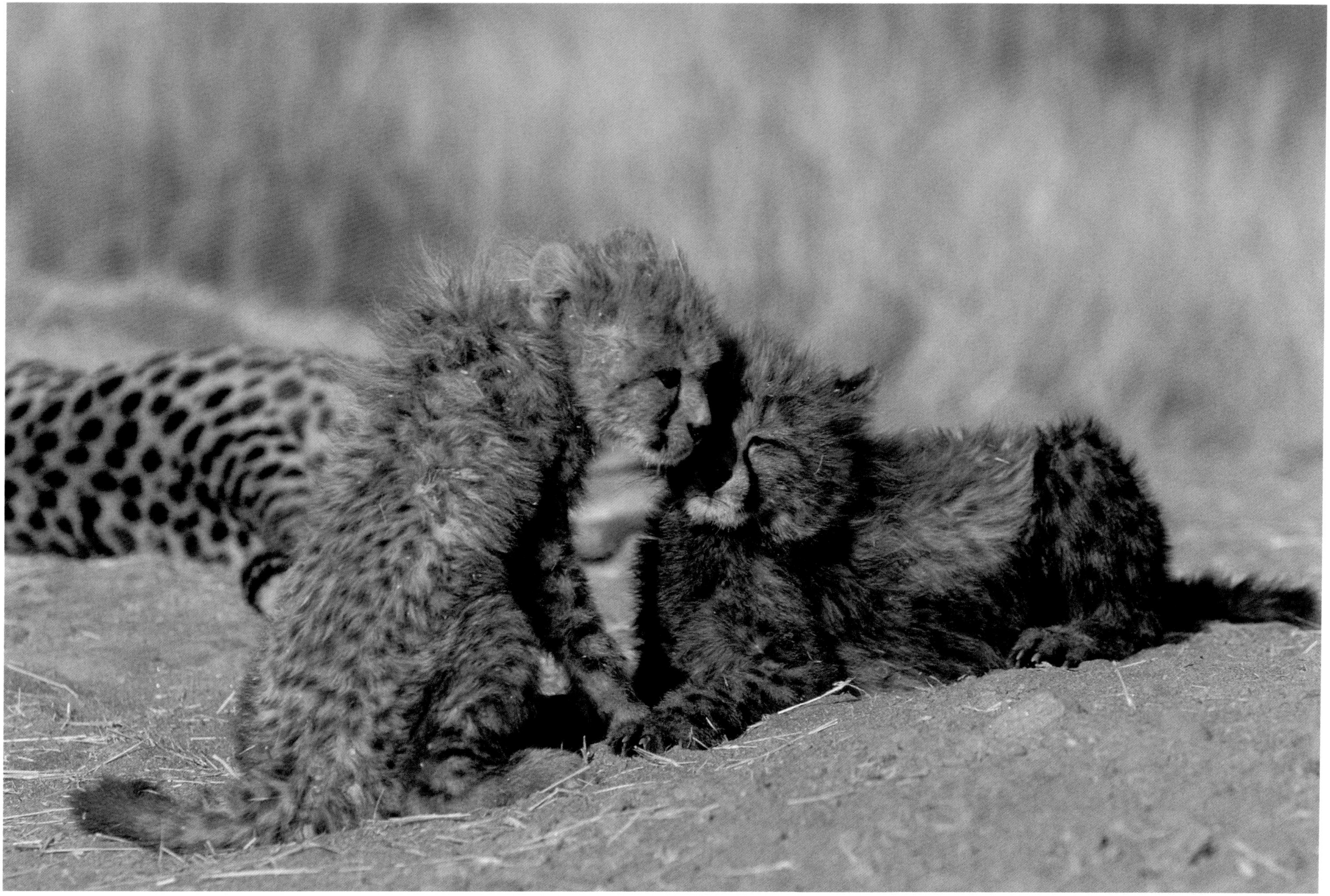

Young cheetahs have a mane of fur which blurs their outlines, effectively camouflaging them from the sharp eyes of hyenas and lions in Africa's grassy savannahs. This fluffy mane begins to disappear only when the cubs are almost grown.

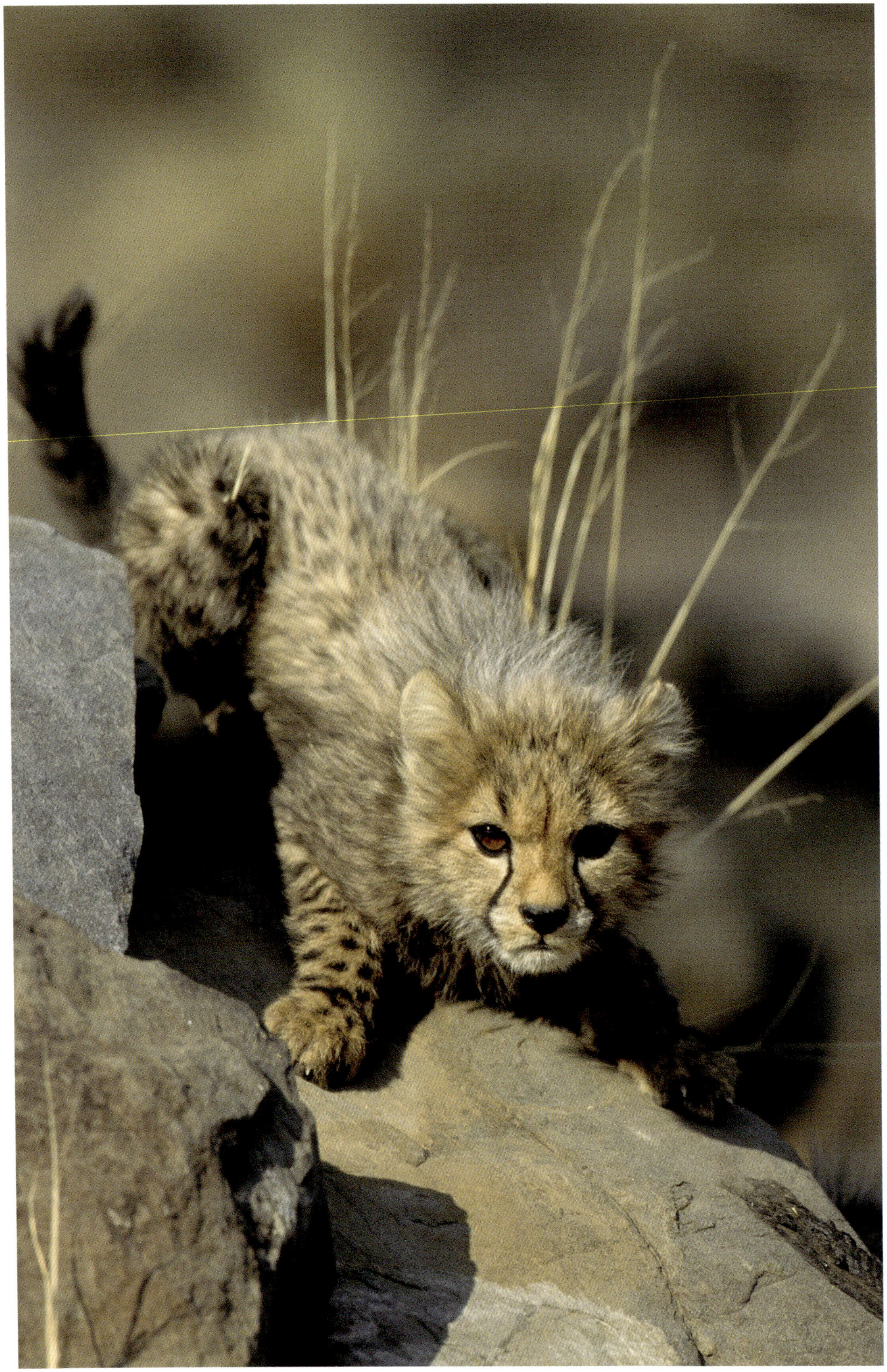

Before the phase of protection is over and the four cubs are abandoned to their own resources, they have almost a year to benefit from their mother's knowledge. They must learn what it means to enter the fray against the survival instincts of swift antelopes, armed only with the most fragile of weapons and a few sophisticated tactics.

But they also need to learn what is involved in competing with more powerful predators. The issue is not want of food; the problem is not that the base of the food chain is too meager to feed all the members of the predatory top level. Instead, it's all about convenience. Whenever the opportunity arises, carnivorous consumers such as lions, leopards and hyenas let the swift, successful cheetahs do the hunting. The kill has hardly been brought down when the scroungers appear and appropriate the still-warm feast. However much the injured party spits and hisses in rage, a cheetah cannot assert itself against the brutal power of these thieves.

A far bitterer lesson is that less than five per cent of all cheetah cubs survive. In the pastoral landscape of the African savannah, they are not only hunters, but also the hunted. 78 per cent of all young cheetahs are killed by lions, 12.2 per cent by hyenas and 1.5 per cent by leopards and birds of prey respectively. Of the fourteen litters borne by a female cheetah during her life, only a single one will survive.

For this reason, the predatory society of Africa's ecosystems is home to a large number of hyenas, lions and leopards – but far less cheetahs.

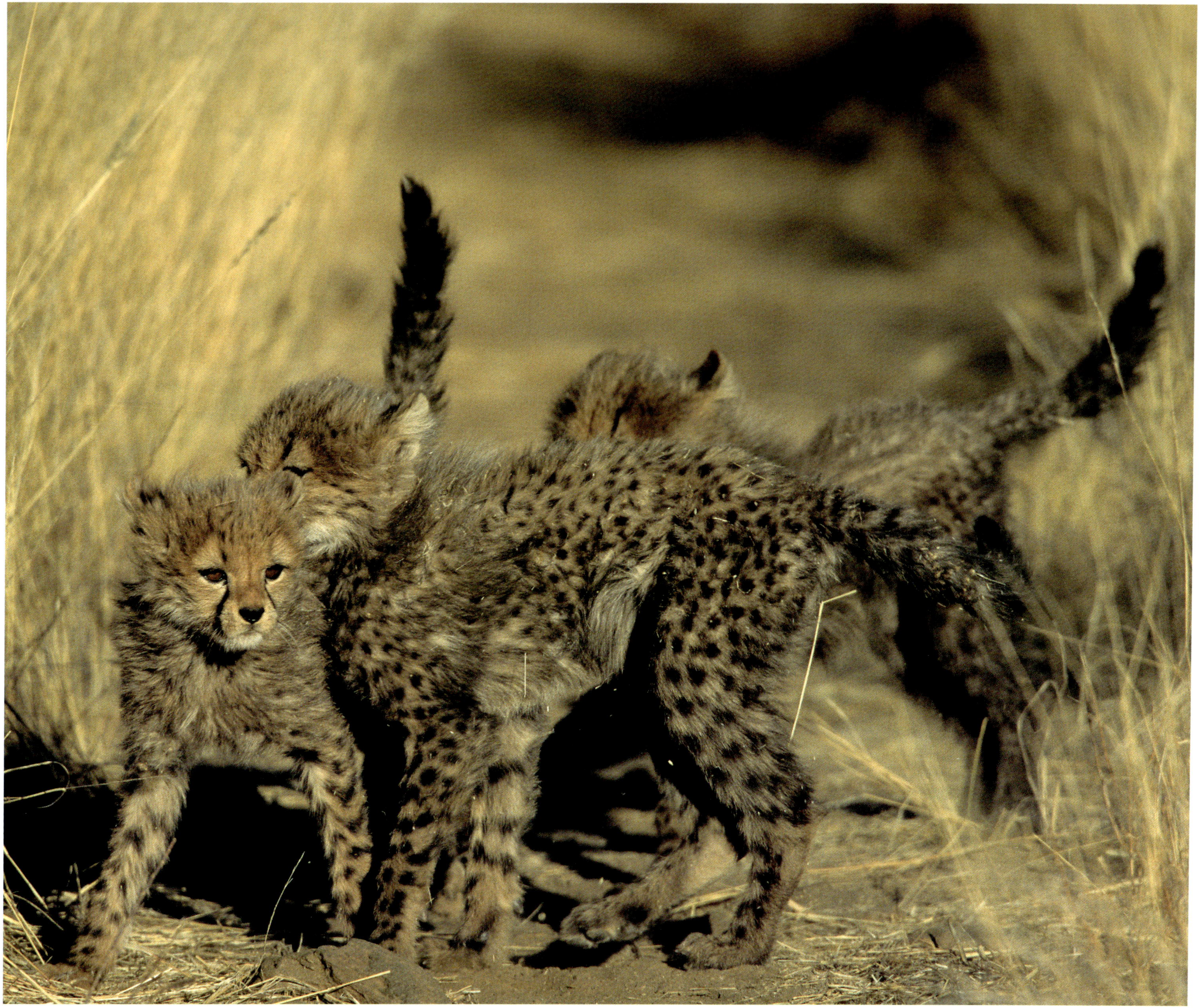

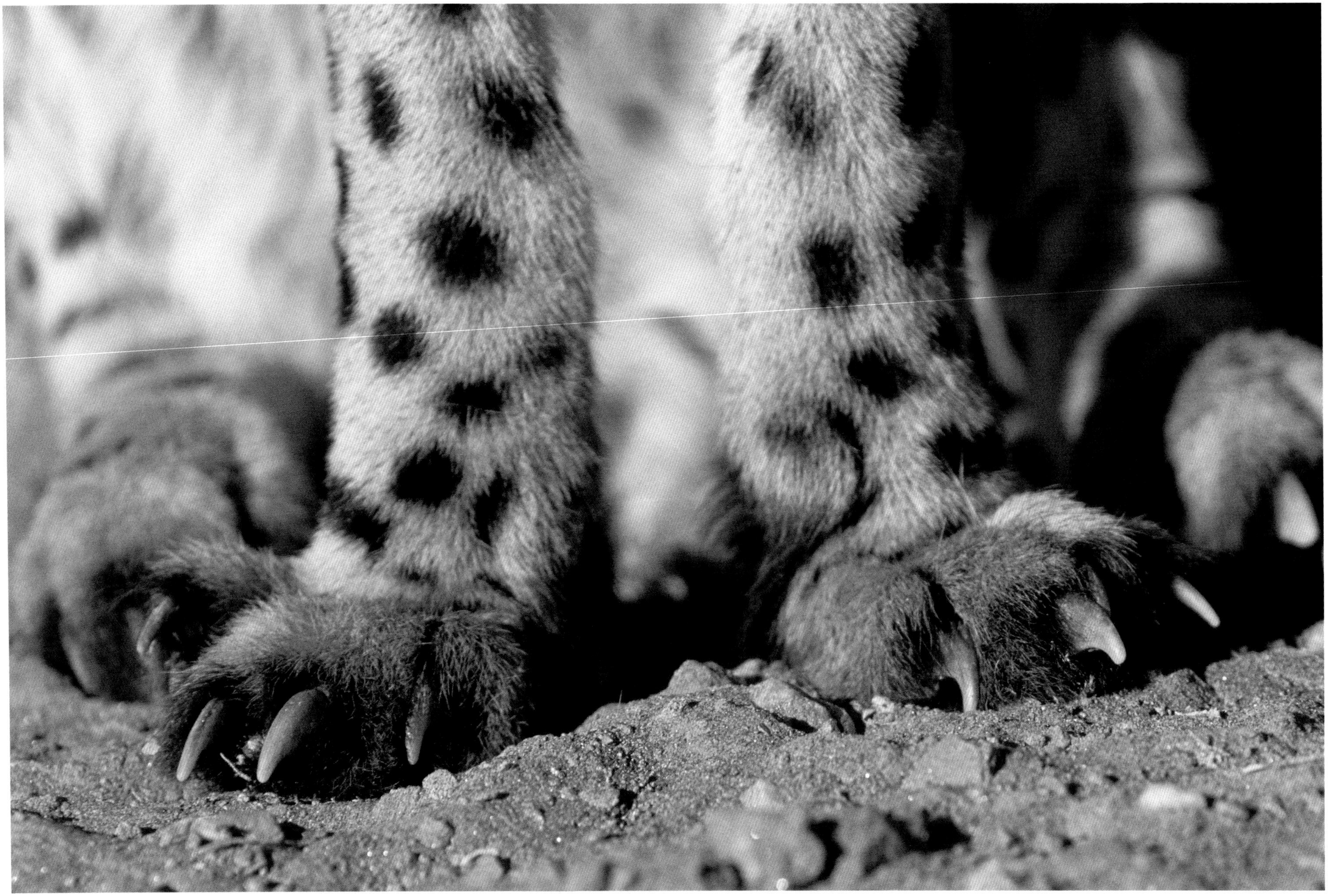

Cheetahs have slim legs and delicate paws, unlike the mighty pads of lions and tigers. These sprinters of the cat family are unable to retract their sharp claws – another feature that distinguishes them from other felidae.

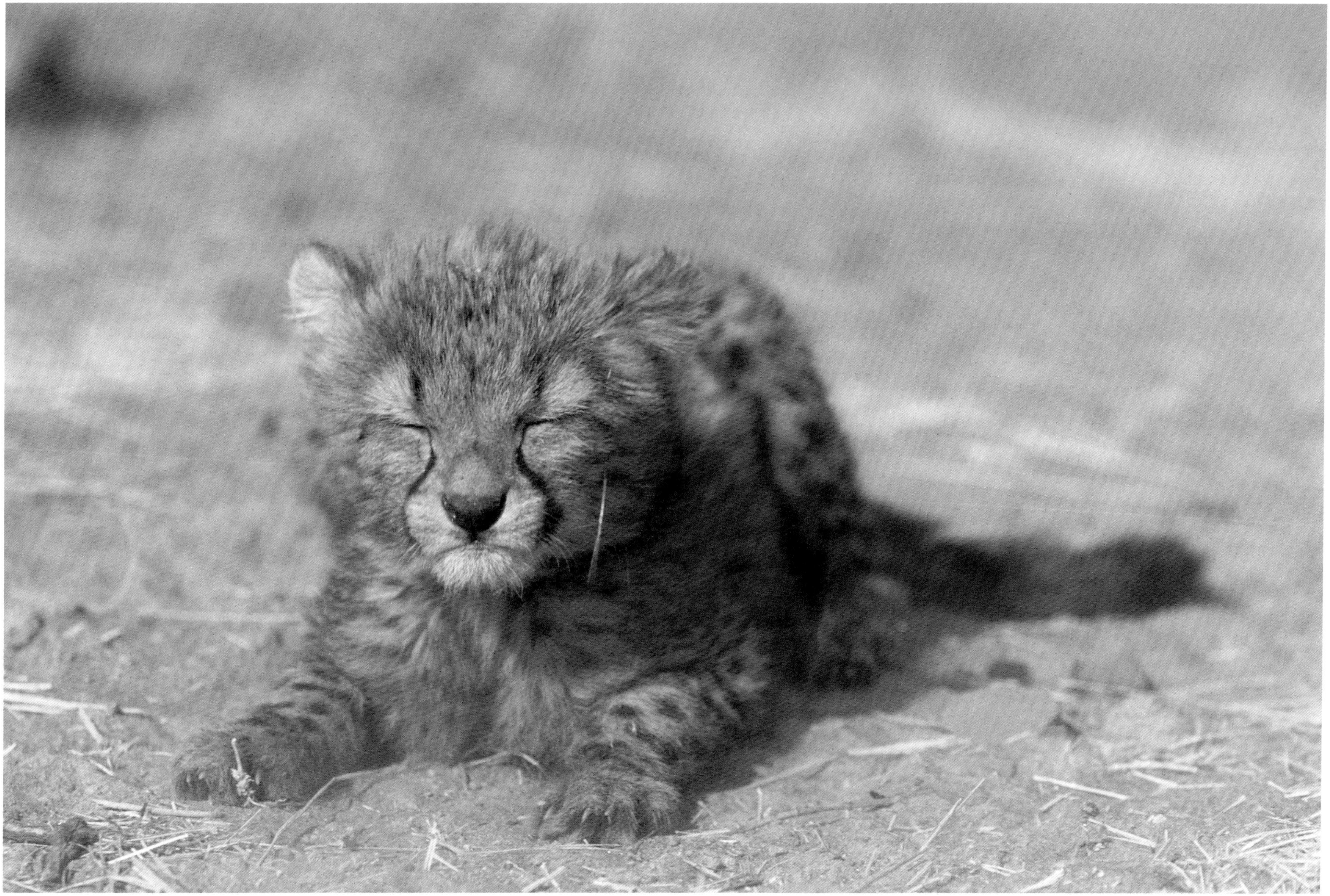

*A gust of wind blows sand into the little cheetah's eyes.
The black lines running from the inner corners of his eyes to his chin add a severe,
even slightly menacing expression to the cat's soft head.*

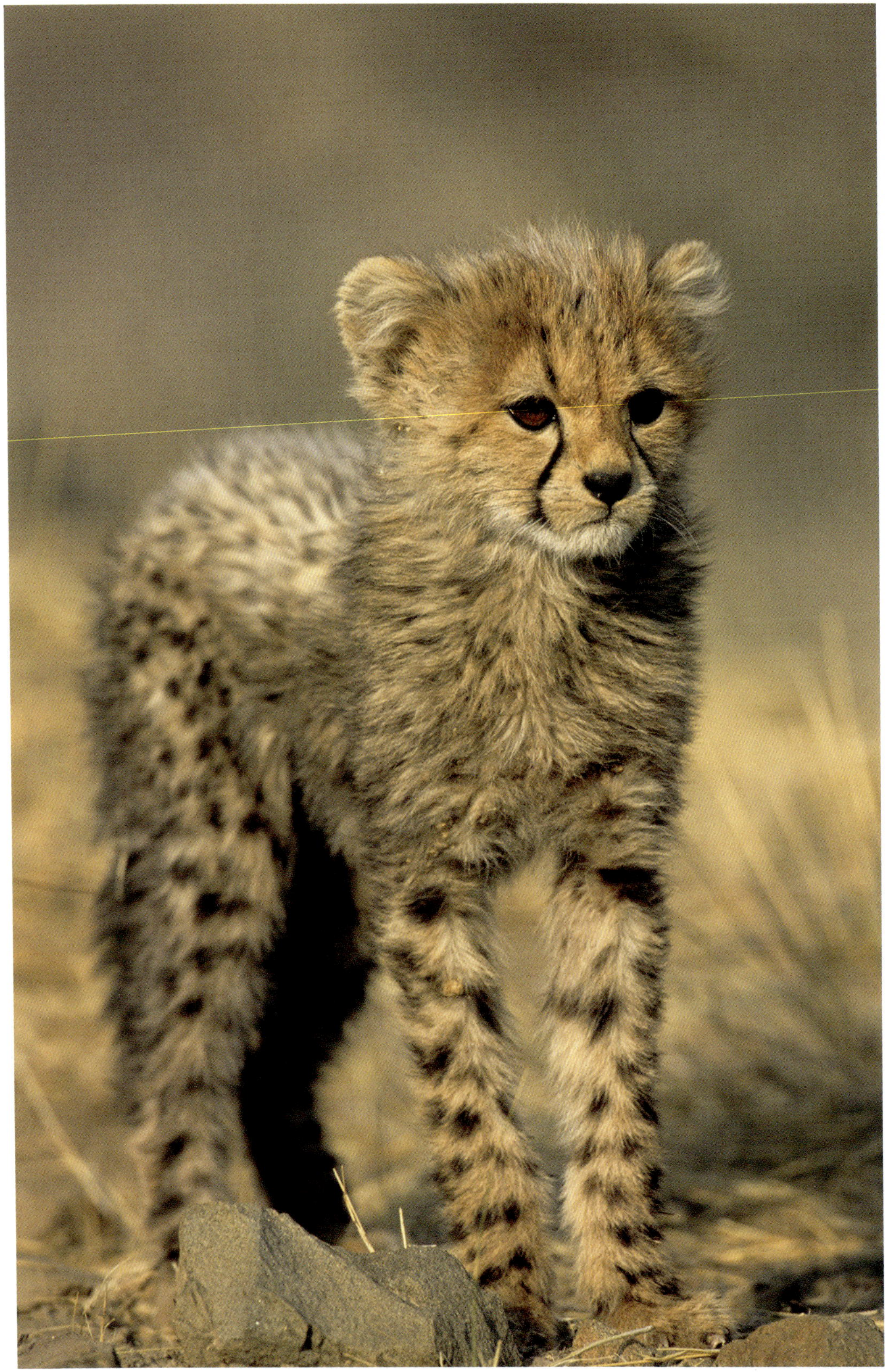

Only by being as inventive as they are flexible can these hunted hunters manage to eke out a living. For example, they hunt by day when other predators are asleep. Or choose territory with a smaller antelope population that does not awaken lions and hyenas' hunting instincts. Or drag their kill under cover as fast as possible to avoid its discovery by vultures, betraying the news as they hover. Cheetahs devour their food within minutes. And mother cheetahs seek out a different hiding place for their new-born cubs every day, condemning the young to a restless, footloose existence as soon as they are born.

A brief sound from the mother cheetah warns the frolicking cubs. She has noticed something on the plains that makes her uneasy, and makes ready to move on. The cubs trot after her at a leisurely pace. As each hour and each day passes, their grasp of the important issues in life increases. Always on the move, familiar with the habits of their enemies and taking care to avoid them: such are the rules of survival for cheetahs. ■

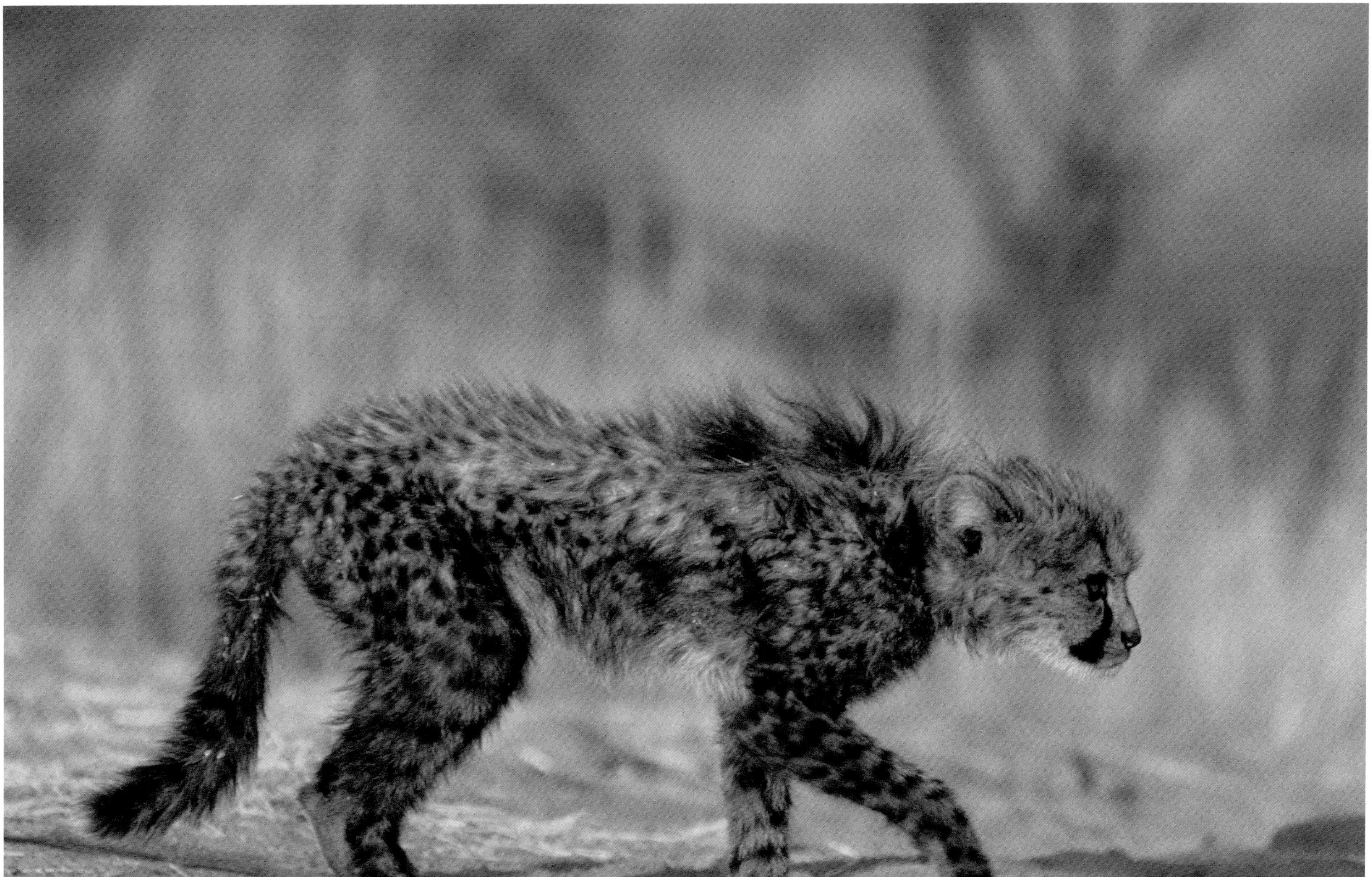

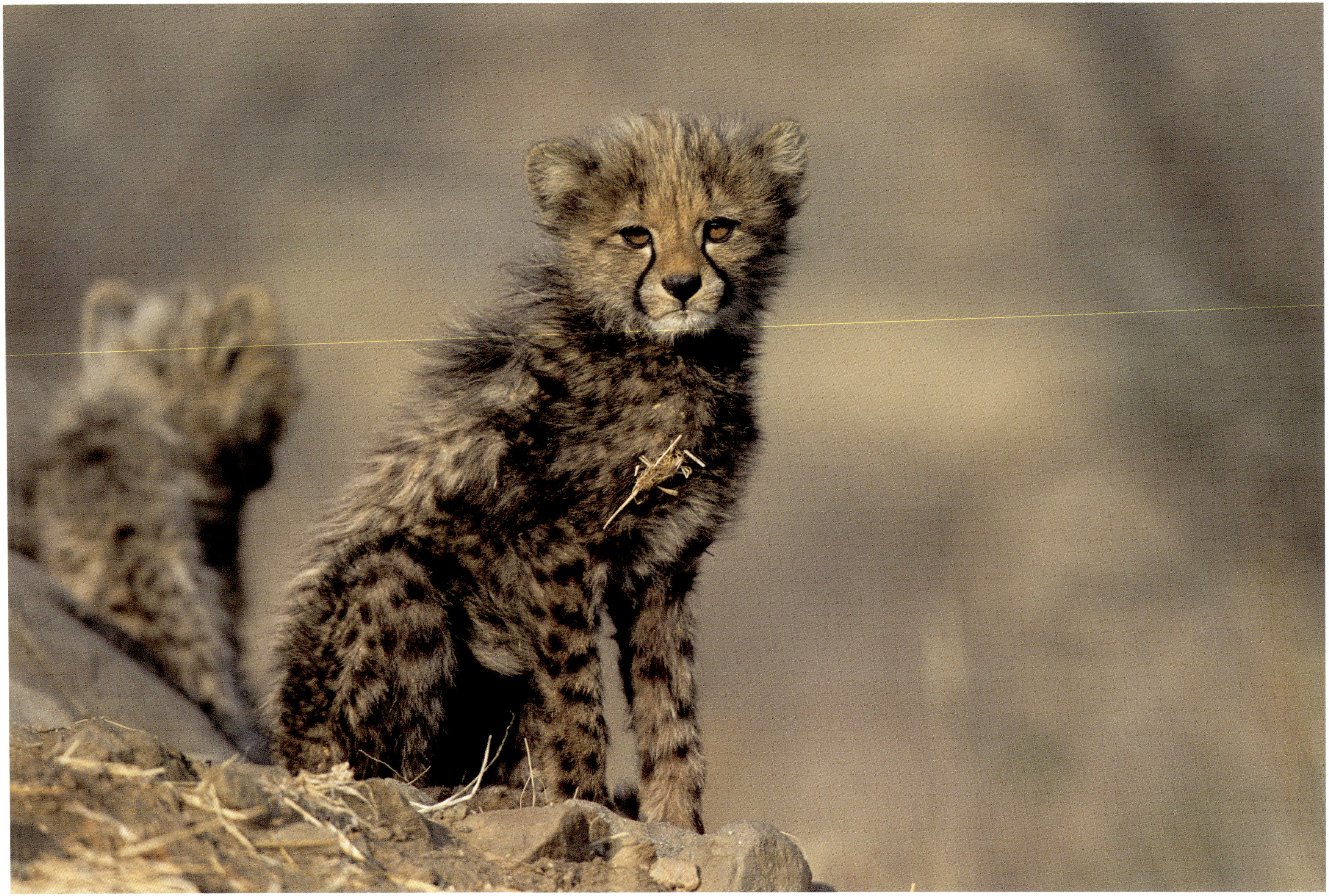

Even siblings have differently colored coats.
At an early age, the little ones learn to use every hill, climbing up to spy out prey or watching for enemies to enable them to take cover in time.

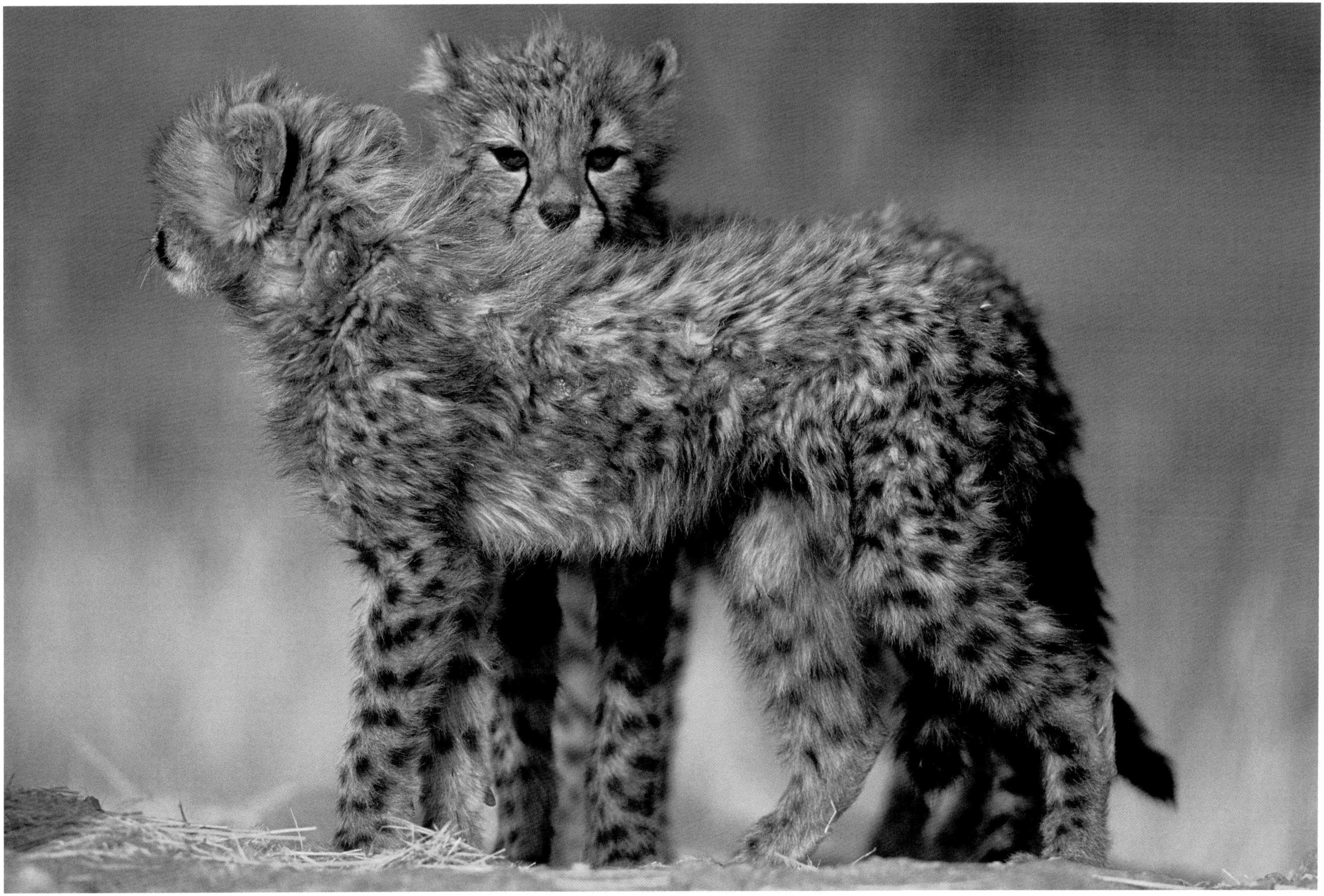

Cheetahs hunt at daybreak. From an early age the cubs accompany their mother on hunting expeditions, initially learning from observation. Left to their own resources at the age of 18 months, they will still have to work on their hunting technique for a long time yet.

Cheetahs – at a glance

Their place in the animal kingdom

- Cheetahs belong to the phylum of vertebrates
- to the class of mammals
- to the order of predators
- to the cat family

Their scientific name

Acinonyx jubatus

Their closest relatives

Cheetahs are members of the panther family, which includes servals, golden cats, clouded leopards and pumas. This family divided again around two million years ago, when one strain evolved into the "great cats", such as lions, tigers, leopards and jaguars.

Where they live (population numbers)

Cheetahs live in Iran (200?), Egypt (40?), northwest Africa (500?), Namibia (2,500), East Africa (1,000) and South Africa (10,000). They are adaptable, surviving easily in semi-desert, open grassland and thick underbrush, providing their habitat offers sufficient cover for them to stalk prey and conceal themselves.

Cheetahs in figures

- These slim cats have a total **body length** of 2 to 2.5 meters (6 to 7.7 feet) including tail.
- They **weigh** 40 kilos (females) to 65 kilos (males).
- Females reach **sexual maturity** in their second year, males not until the age of three.
- The **territory** of mother cheetahs, like that of lone males, may extend from more than 500 to 1,500 square kilometers (190 to as much as 580 square miles); groups of male cheetahs, however, generally occupy 15 to 35 square kilometers (6 to 13 square miles).
- A cheetah's **lifespan** is between seven and 15 years.
- Over short stretches, cheetahs can reach **speeds** in excess of 100 kilometers (62 miles) per hour, making them the fastest of all land mammals.

Cheetahs' characteristic features

Cheetahs are slimly built big cats with sandy fur covered in small spots. Their claws are dull, like those of dogs, and are non-retractable, delivering additional momentum to these fast sprinters. Their long, slim legs have delicate paws, unlike the large pads of lions and tigers.
Cheetahs have small, round heads with short ears. Their characteristic facial markings feature two dark "teardrop" stripes from the inner corner of the eyes down the nose and under the chin, giving them a serious, even menacing expression. Male cheetahs are considerably larger and heavier than females.

What cheetahs eat

Cheetahs hunt their prey, overpowering medium-sized ungulates such as gazelles, impalas and springboks and the young of larger animals such as wildebeest and buffalos. However, they also hunt hares and other smaller mammals, and may even catch an occasional bird. Unlike the majority of big cats, they hunt by day, avoiding the fierce competition of lions, leopards and hyenas. Cheetahs stalk their prey and launch into a sprint as soon as they are closer than 300 feet to their chosen victim. Around half their attempts at a kill fail. Cheetahs can maintain their high speed for only 20 seconds or so. Their teeth are short and can inflict only skin wounds on their prey, so that they usually hurl their prey to the ground and suffocate it by compressing its throat in their jaws.

Cheetahs' lifestyle

Cheetahs do not have a definite pattern of life. While females may occasionally live alone, they generally live with their cubs. Males, however, frequently roam around as loners, although some, primarily male siblings, may form coalitions to occupy, defend and hunt in their territory together.

How cheetahs raise their young

Bringing up the cubs is solely the province of the females. The gestation period is three months. A litter seldom comprises more than five cubs, which weigh up to 300 grams each at birth. The cubs open their eyes at the age of roughly ten days. They are nursed by their mother for up to six months, but are able to follow her on hunting expeditions from the age of six weeks. The family of mother and cubs seeks new hiding places almost daily. The cubs are self-sufficient at 18 months, by which time they have learnt the basics of hunting from their mother. Cheetahs are fully adult at the age of just under two.

Dangers to cheetahs

Adult cheetahs are relatively safe from other predators, but their cubs are not: up to 95 percent of all cheetah cubs are killed by lions, leopards, baboons or hyenas. In many areas of Africa farmers still shoot cheetahs to protect their livestock.

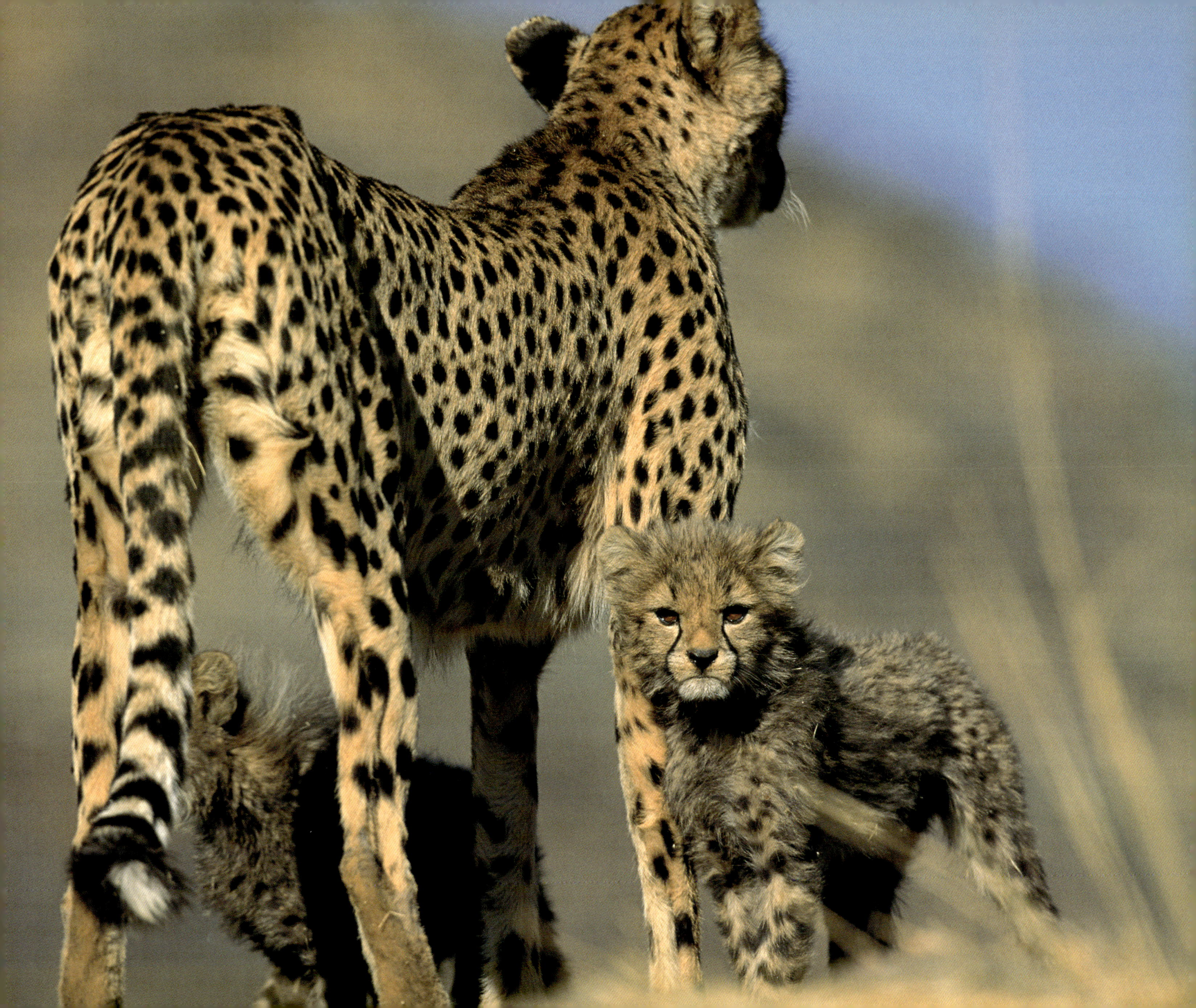

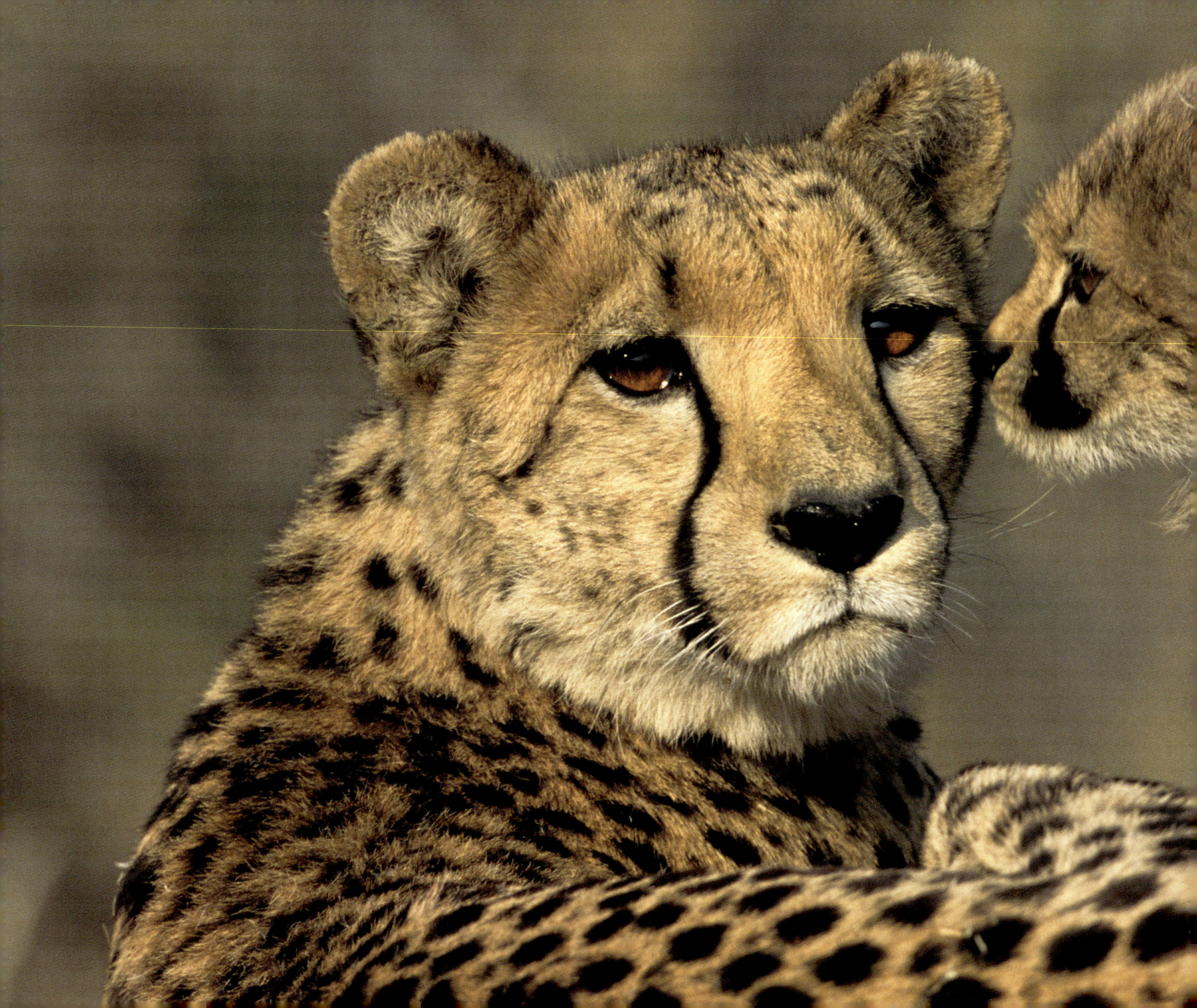

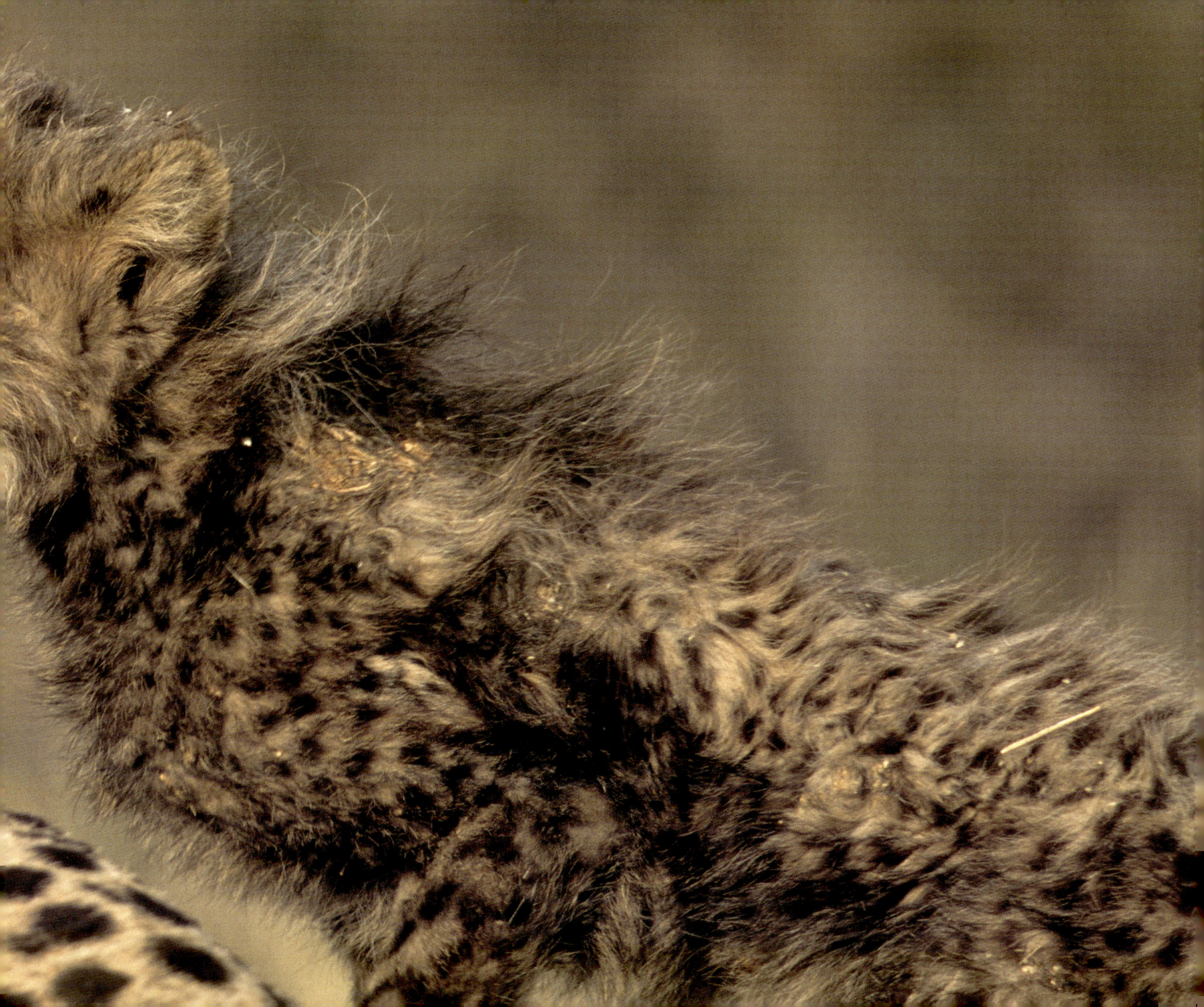

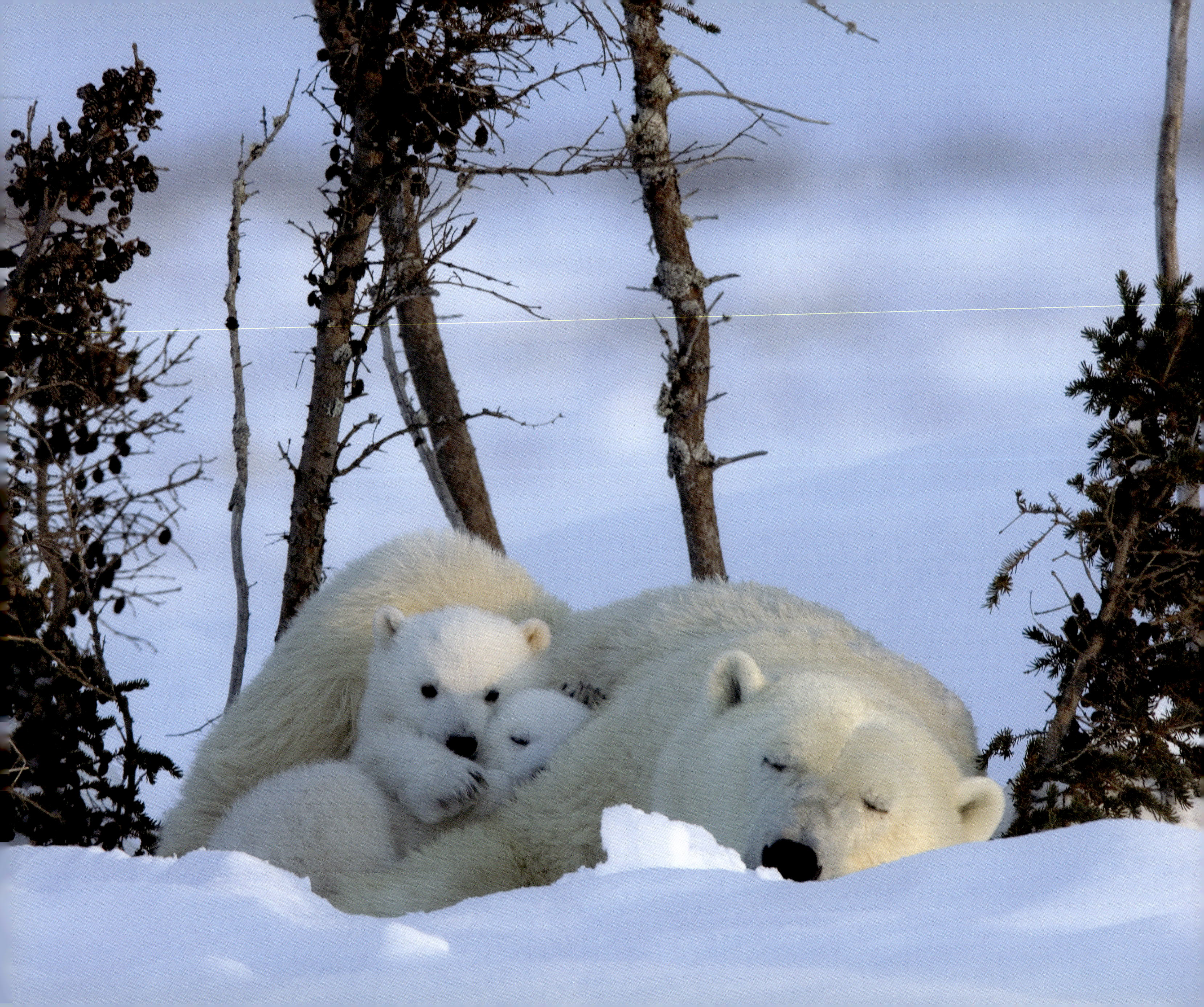

Polar Bears

Hunting is Child's Play

It's the light that startles them most. Brightness cascades through a great blazing hole in the ceiling of the den, penetrating the familiar twilight and boring into the black eyes of the little polar bears. They immediately screw up their eyes – but just as quickly they squint up to the opening carved out by their mother's front paws through which she has just vanished. In addition to the light pouring into the den under its two-meter blanket of snow, a fresh, icy draught bursts in, grips the three cubs by their fine fur and impels them to move.

They clamber somewhat clumsily up the snowy slope their mother has shoveled into the den, the strongest leading the way. Reaching the top, they poke their heads over the edge and first spot what they have so urgently been hoping for: their mother. The little bears have never been separated from her for even a moment since their birth around four months ago. The sudden absence of the great warm body, the soft fur, the feeling of security is unendurable. And so the baby bears totter towards their mother, snuggle up to her legs under the shaggy canopy of her belly, and recreate their sensation of being part of a unit. Only then, from this safest of all places, do the little ones begin to examine the world of glittering whiteness now spreading out before their eyes.

It is March, in the western reaches of Hudson Bay. Every year, up to 180 female polar bears heave themselves out of their dens in the 11,475 square kilometers (4,590 square miles) of Canada's Wapusk National Park and entice their young into the open. The white dunes of driven snow conceal the tundra, which is locked in permafrost. Around 70 kilometers (43.4 miles) south of the town of Churchill countless lakes, rivers and streams have washed away up to four meters of peaty subsoil and have created what is probably the largest birthing community of Ursus maritimus: 1,200 dens, many over five meters long and several meters wide, riddle the steep banks of the waterways in the hinterland to the west of the bay. Their entrances face south or east, where the snow piles up first at the beginning of winter, and away from the prevailing winds.

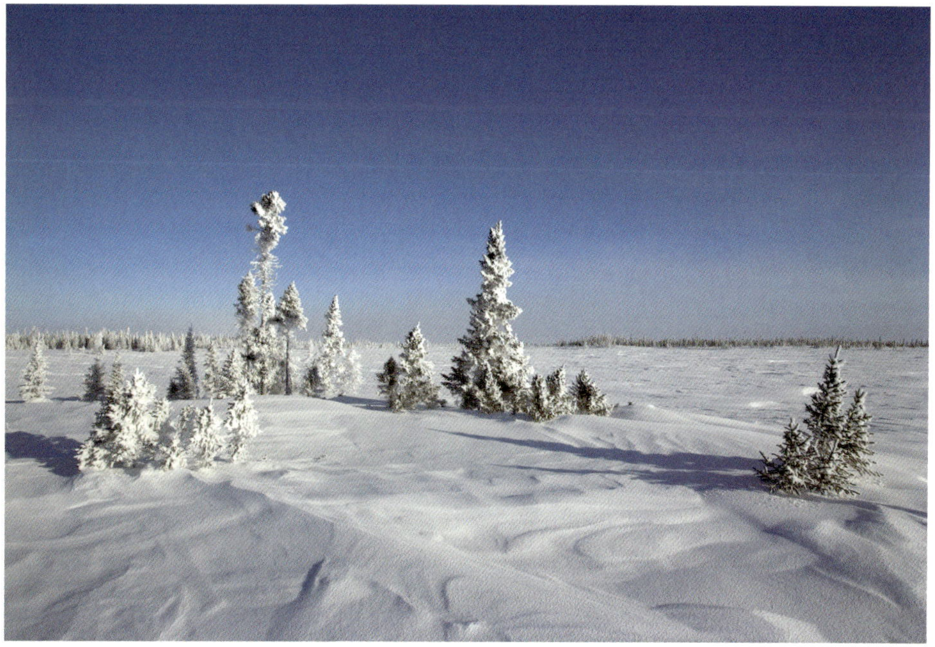

The mother of the triplets was born in one of these dens herself. And years later, when her time came to give birth, she did what pregnant bears do, moving into one of the dens in the fall, cleaning it up a little whilst waiting for her young to be born. She had probably visited the den area previously, to investigate one or other of the subterranean dwellings and to live there for a few days before making her final decision.

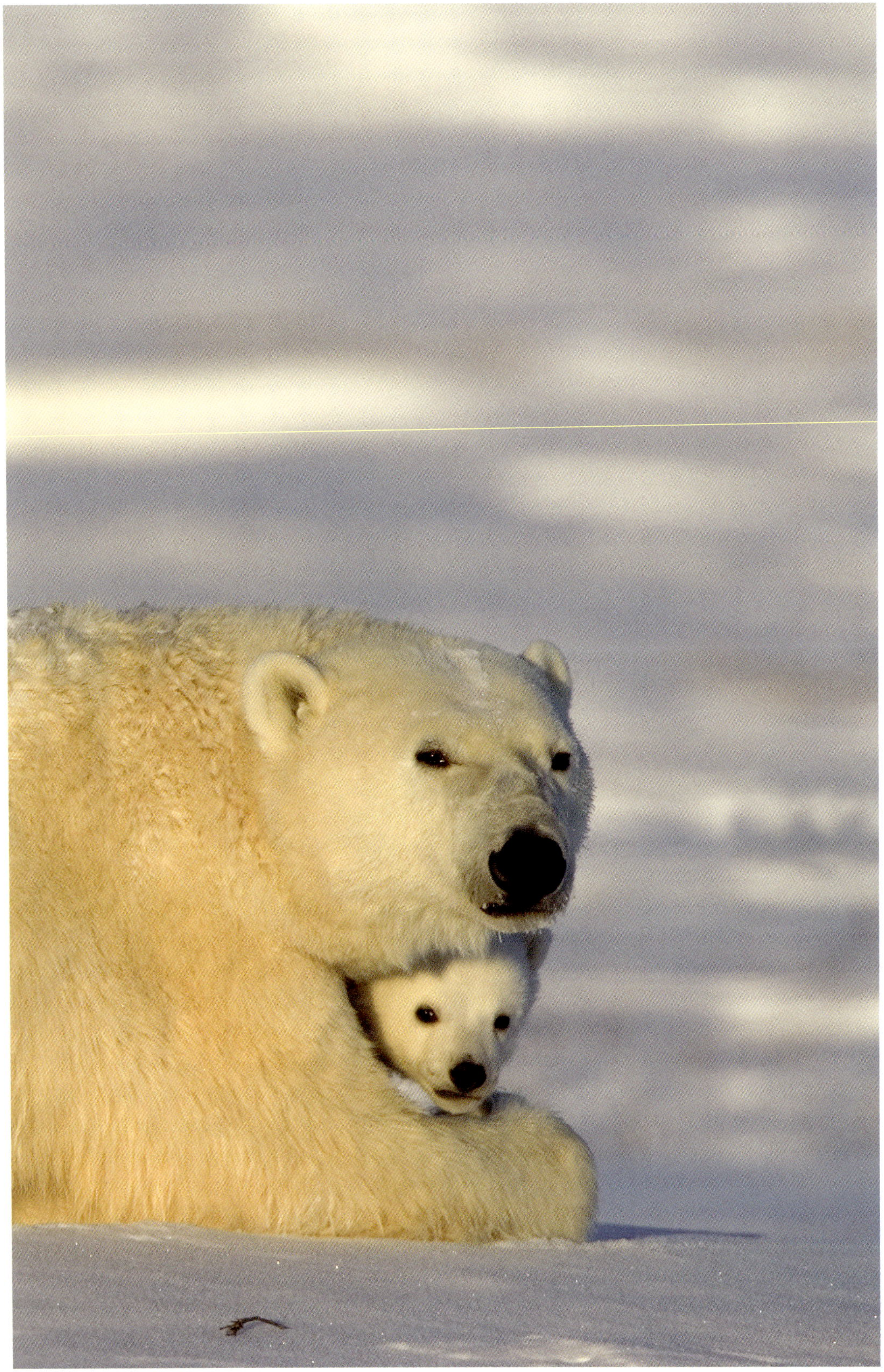

She was joined by other females – and males, too. Male bears also think highly of such hollows, for they make ideal resting places in which to cool off during the summer.

From July, during the warm period of the Arctic year, the bears find themselves literally treading on thin ice in Hudson Bay, and are forced to seek food on the mainland. Unlike their cousins, the brown bears and grizzlies, these snow-white newcomers to the family eat hardly any vegetation, but live almost wholly as carnivores. Their success is due more to their tactics of lurking and waiting than to their endurance when pursuing their prey on foot.

While they are capable of brief sprints of 50 kilometers (31 miles) per hour in the tundra, most of the polar bears' prey is hardly worth the effort that goes into catching it, and they would expend more energy in hunting than they would gain from consuming their catch. For this reason, polar bears prefer to stroll along the coast in their dozens, keeping a lookout for any carcasses of stranded marine mammals. Finally, they wander into the hinterland, crawl into a cool hollow near a lake or river and doze away the ice-free months, their metabolism slowing. Most of the time is spent fasting.

Polar bears can afford to live off their enormous fat stores for a while. Two thirds of the year, from November to July, they hunt on the ice and fatten up on ringed and bearded seals, and walrus, as well as the occasional beluga whale, or even orcas, trapped in the pack ice. Excess calories are stored by polar bears in layers of fat, subcutaneous storage chambers over ten centimeters thick that form the perfect insulation against icy water temperatures.

While still single, the mother of the three little cubs had also acquired a considerable paunch on the floating islands of pack ice. Her favorite delicacy was the proteinladen layer of blubber padding the bodies of her prey. In April, as she roamed, hunting and feasting across the ocean, she met the father of her young, the second male in her life, and spent a passionate week with him under the flaring Northern Lights. In July, when the sea swallowed her hunting grounds and she was forced onto the mainland with hundreds of her kind, she was slightly pregnant.

This condition is not uncommon among female polar bears. After fertilization, the eggs begin to divide and form spherical clusters of cells, the usual procedure in mammals. But then growth ceases. The blastocysts containing the genetic code for young polar bears float freely in the uterus, but do not implant.

This does not happen until about four months after conception, and only in females with a minimum weight of 200 kilos. The delay in implantation of the egg is a kind of biological insurance. Like a soloist awaiting his cue at the right moment to play a melody that harmonizes with the orchestra, the fragile cells of these future polar bear cubs align their development period to the rhythms of polar life. Embryos grow only when their mother is in a position not only to give birth, but also to nurse her young for an extended period.

The chances of survival of the little white bears are pegged to their mother's increasing body weight. The heavier she is, the more food reserves she can mobilize and the stronger her litter will grow. A well-nourished mother bear produces so much fat-rich milk that her cubs grow rapidly. A mere 600 grams at birth, they weigh 10 kilos by the time they leave the den for the first time – around four months later, during which the mother bear has eaten nothing at all. These four months of fasting whilst giving birth and suckling her young are in addition to four lean summer months which, we remember, she also spent primarily fasting, like the rest of her kind in the west of Hudson Bay when the pack ice melts.

Mother bears and their cubs are tucked away around two meters underground, covered by a further two to three meters (6.56 feet) of snow. Motherhood, the most natural thing in the

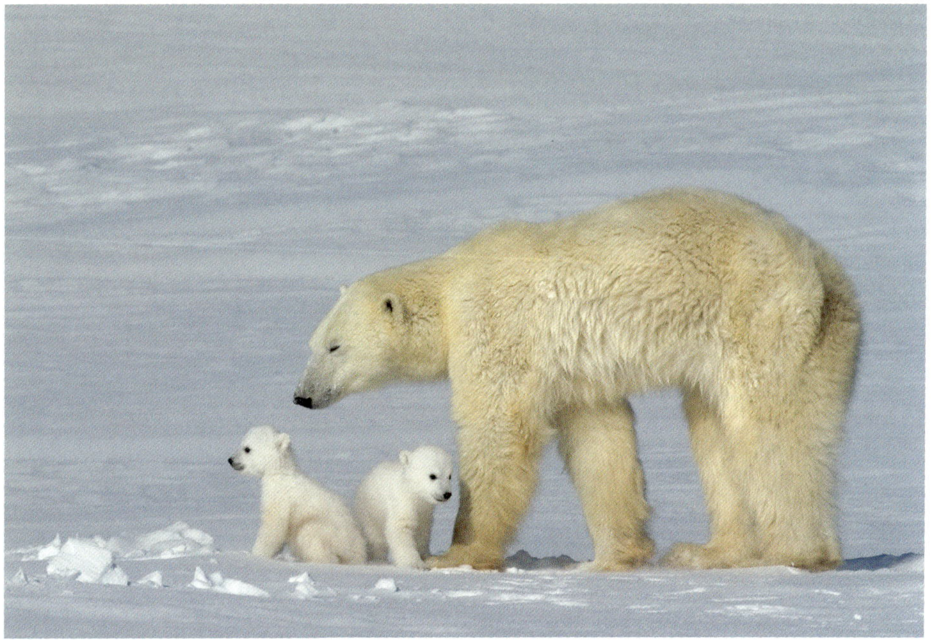

world, means a complete change of lifestyle for the female polar bear. Gone are the times when she could roam freely, swimming, diving, hunting and eating as the fancy took her. In the birthing den she is transformed into a devoted, watchful, broody, nurturing, self-sacrificing environment, existing solely for her young – the only way to ensure her cubs survive the winter.

While storms rage outside and temperatures plummet to minus 50 degrees Celsius, the climate in the birthing den is around freezing point, thanks to the mighty bear's body heat. But for the cubs, new-born in November or December, the temperature is still too cold. Compared with other mammalian young, not only polar bears, but bears in general, are tiny when born, hardly more than a handful of life. And they are as unformed as larvae, blind, deaf and all but naked. Their mother sits on the ground and bends forward to make a kind of warm, fur-lined nest out

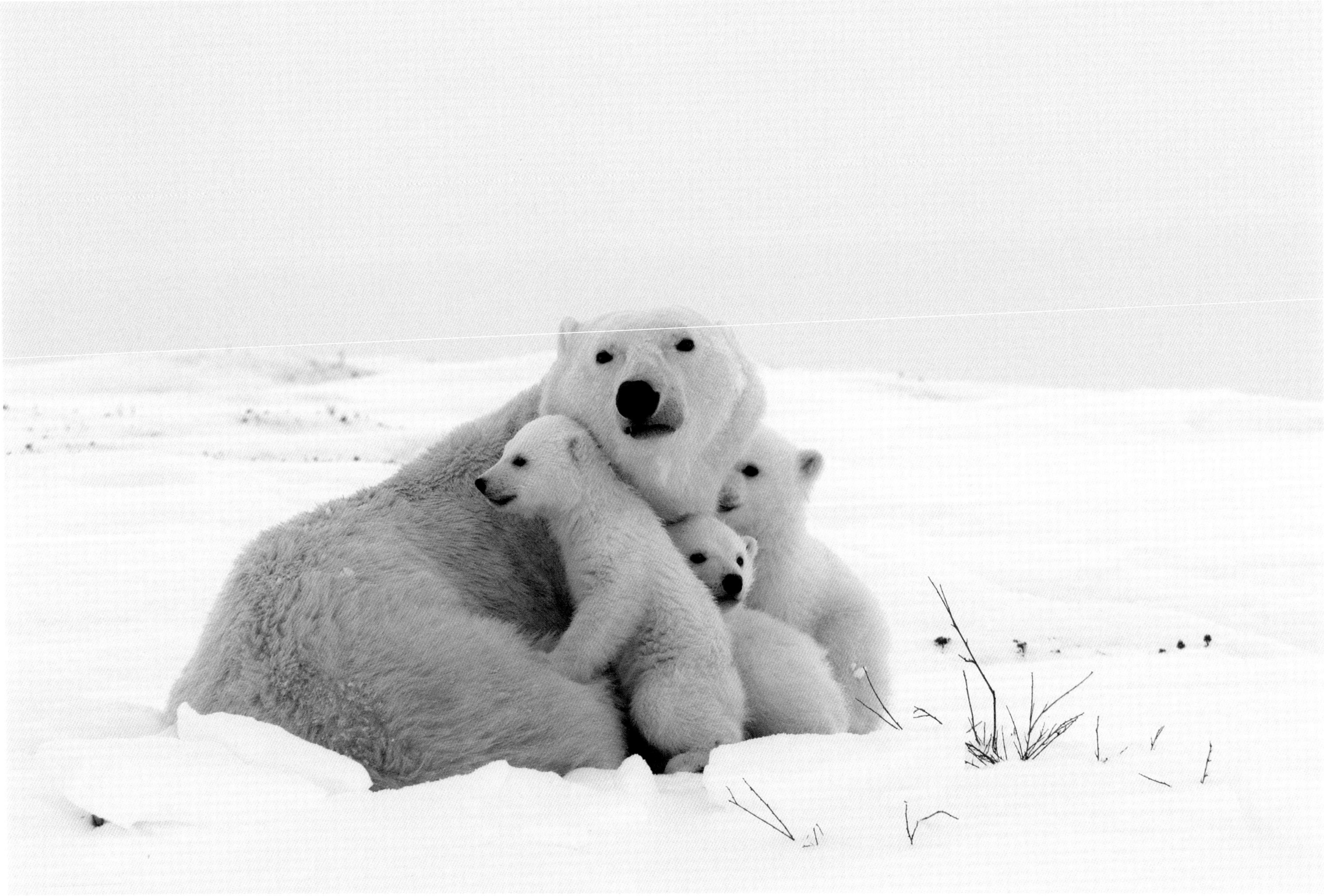

This polar bear mother has left her birthing den together with her well-nourished triplets. This region, used for centuries as a nursery by the female polar bears of the western Hudson Bay area, is in Wapusk National Park.

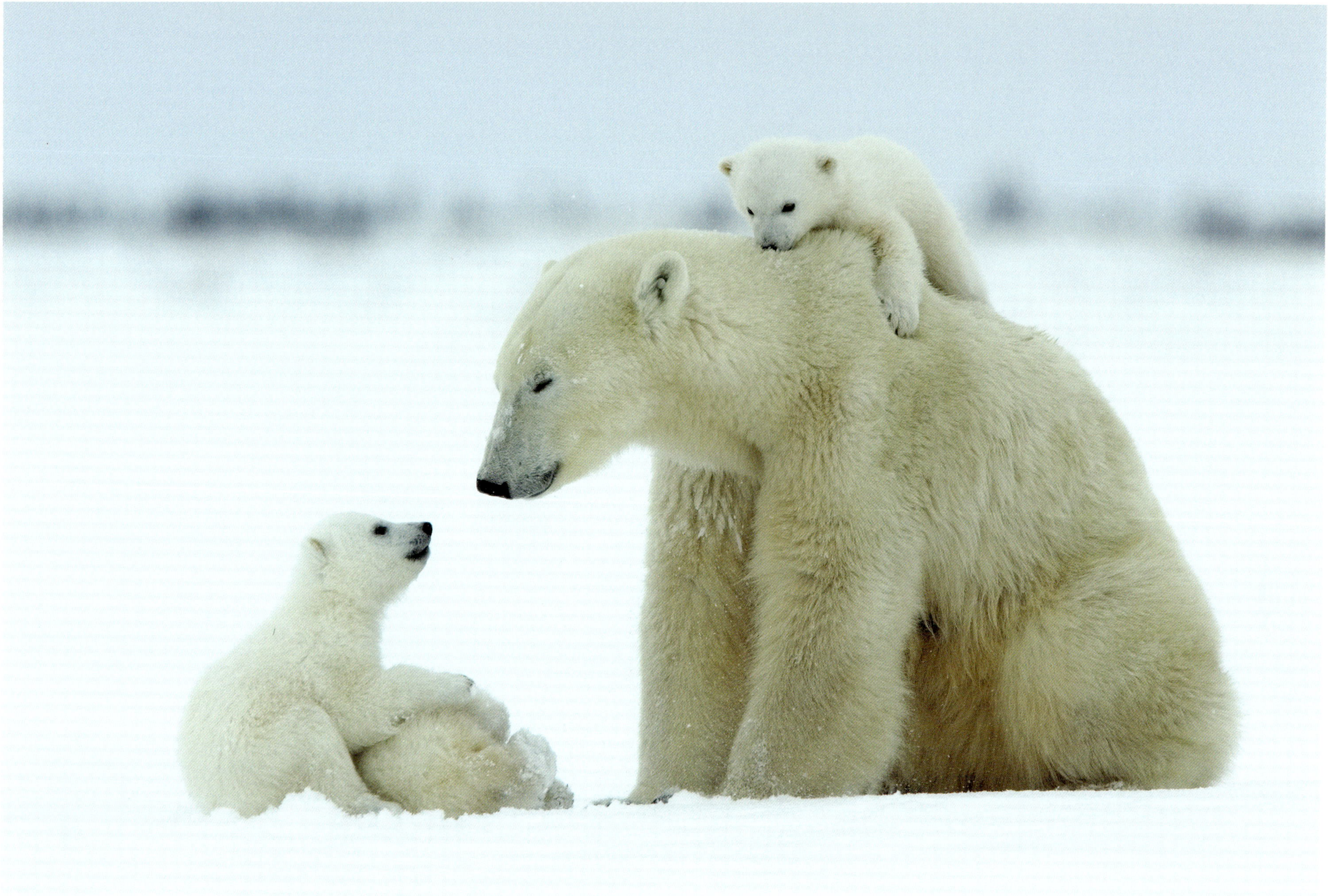

Polar bear cubs are adventurous creatures, and their attentive mother is happy to let her little ones climb all over her.

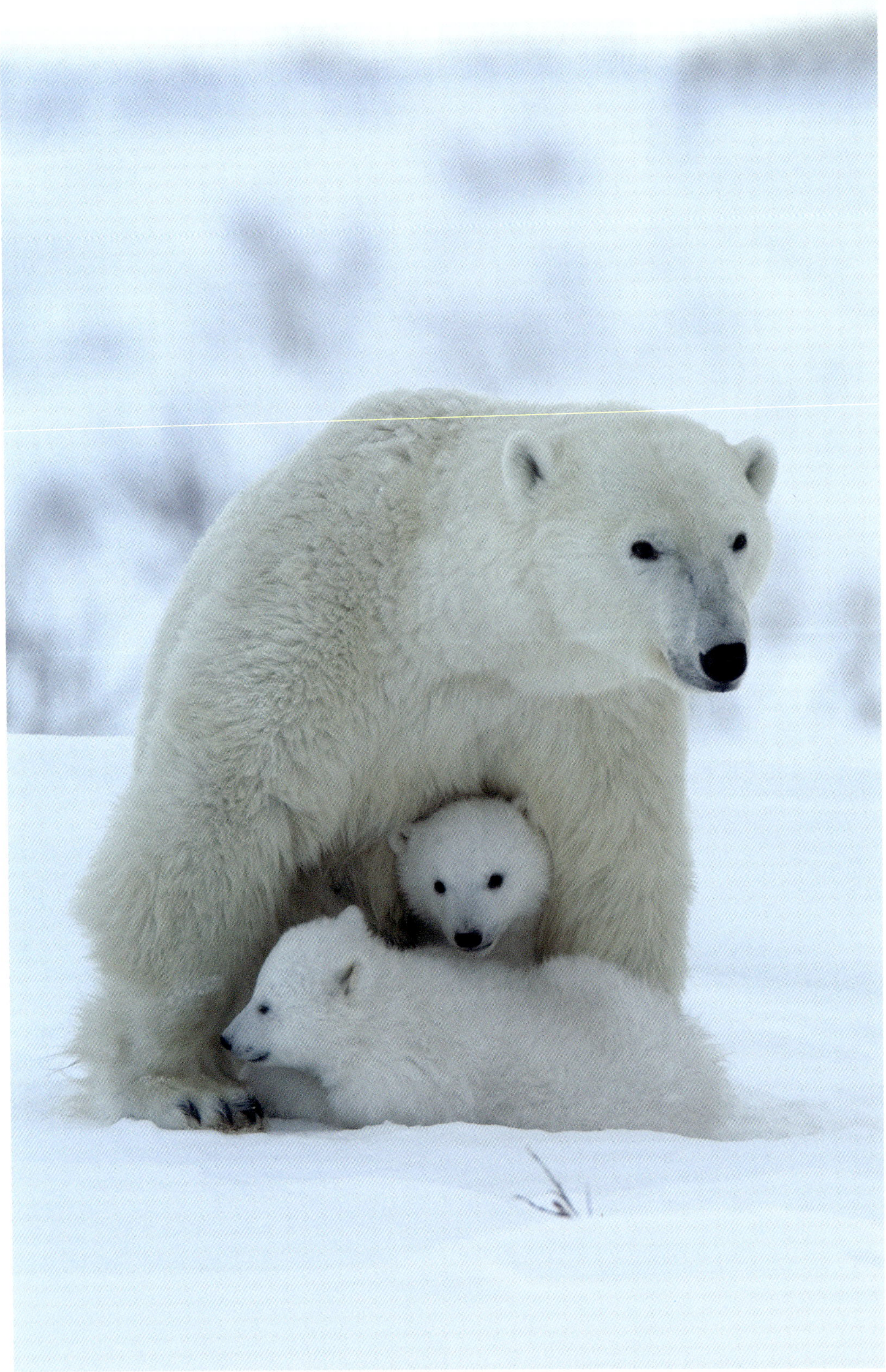

of her body, pressing the cubs to her teats. Polar bear milk is probably the richest food any mammal can give its young, with a fat content of 33.5 percent and a corresponding effect on growth. After only a month the young bears have quadrupled in weight, can hear, see and smell. In the second month they grow fur and teeth, and at three months they are strong enough to walk.

When the mother leaves the den with her chubby, furry babies, they are around four months old and weigh a good 10 kilos. Their mother, however, has become thin; after fasting for eight to nine months she has lost around three quarters of her body weight. But her strict diet has one advantage: all she has lost is fat. Her powerful muscles are intact. She needs them to defend her cubs against male bears on the ice, to drive marauders away from her catch when she makes a kill, and to replenish her own stores of fat as soon as possible.

The young bears usually require a further two weeks before they are fit enough for the trek to the ice. They still spend over 80 percent of their time in the den, nursing six times a day and gathering initial impressions of their world of white. They understand that they must come to their mother immediately when she calls, and that treading in her broad pawprints is the best way to travel on short excursions.

After such a long time underground, the female bear revels in the sun, the fresh air, the scents on the wind and the opportunity to move freely. She frisks in the snow, rolling on her back and kicking up her paws, and infects her cubs with her playfulness. Soon the young bears are clambering over her, pretending to bite the huge pads, tugging at their mother's neck fur, wrestling and flinging crusted snow into the air. Playing strengthens their muscles and they gradually learn how to place their paws more carefully as they acquire the characteristic polar bear gait: first front right, then back left, back right, then front left.

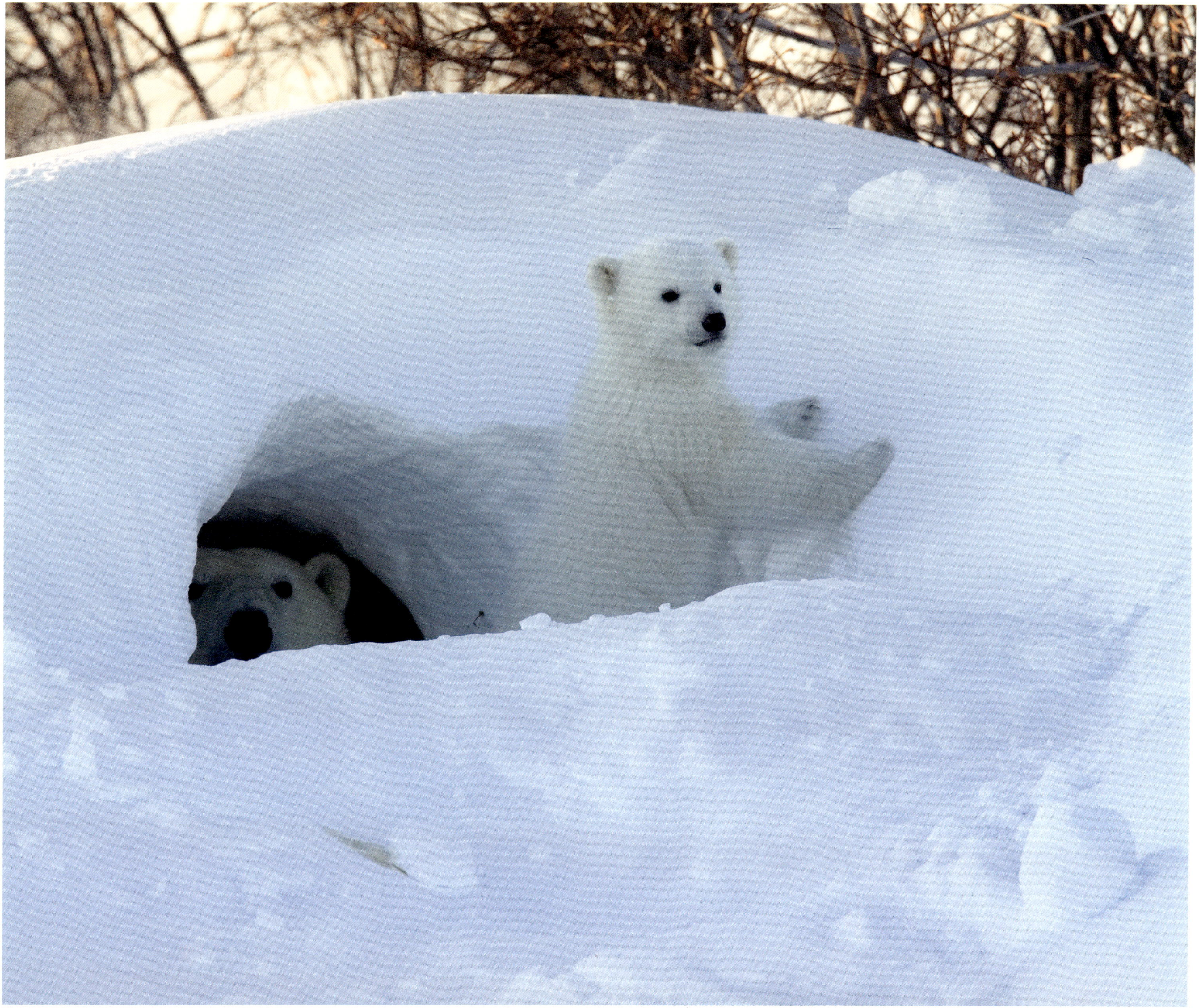

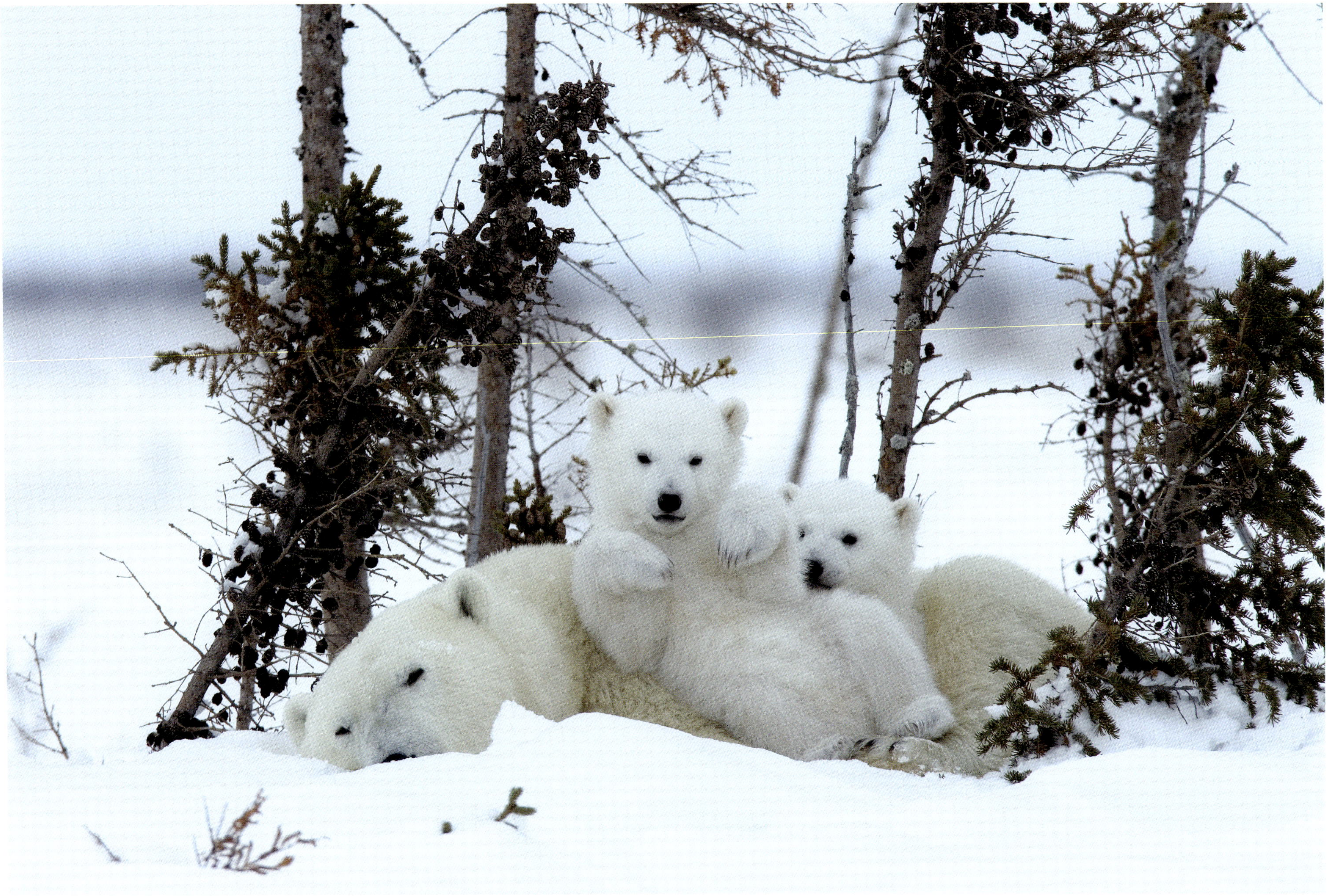

Snowdrifts tower on the bank of a frozen lake. The family rests, sheltered from the biting wind.
The twin cubs snuggle into the cozy fur of their mother's belly between her mighty paws.

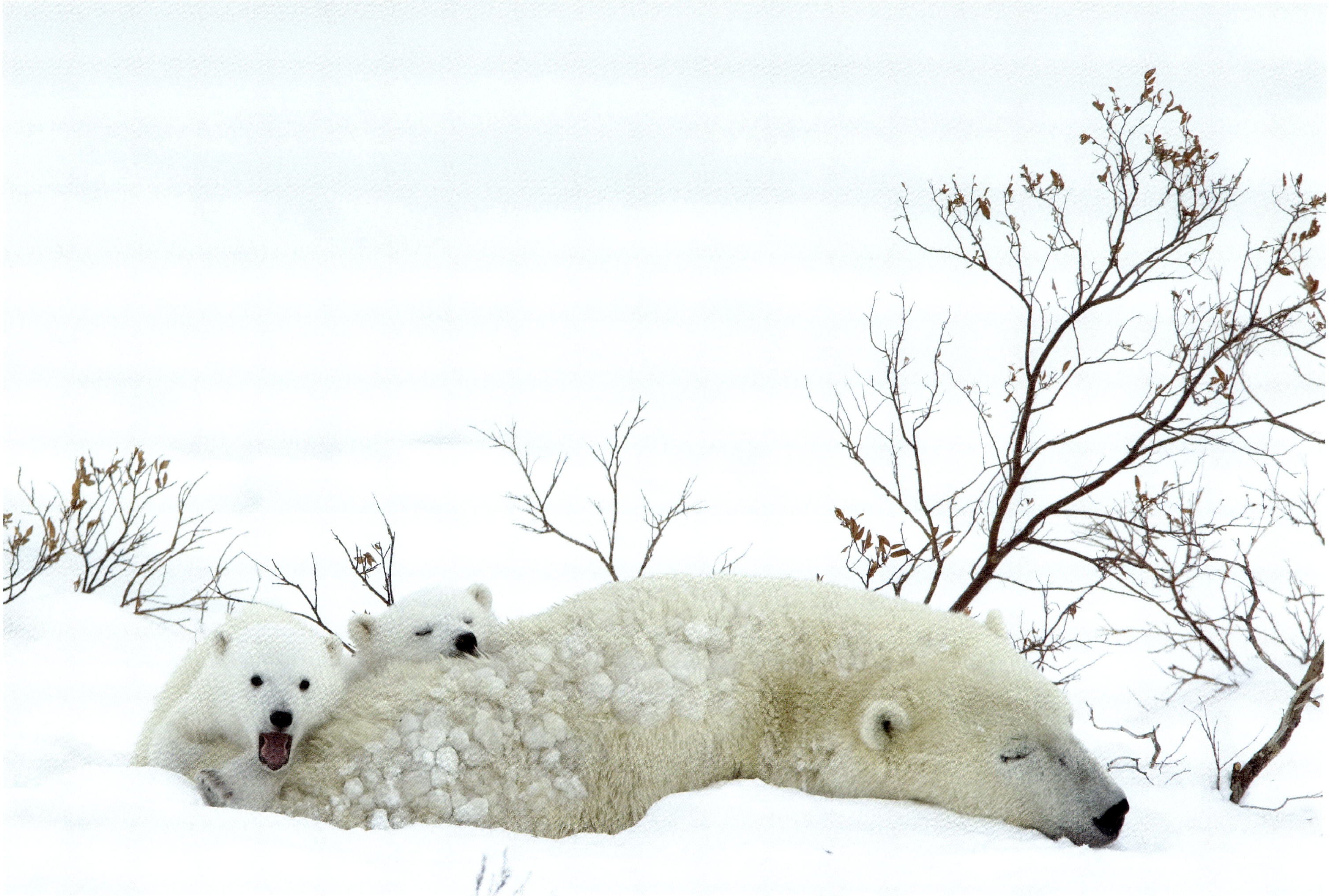

The mother bear takes regular breaks on the long trek from the birthing den to the coast of the ice-bound bay. The cubs are not yet strong enough for such long expeditions

The cubs have hardly learnt how to walk before the family embarks on its journey to the coast. However hungry the mother is, and however greedy for fresh meat, she has endless patience with her little ones. She regularly stops for a break, nurses the cubs, envelops them tenderly in her fur, and digs out one temporary shelter after another in the deep snowdrifts piled behind groups of conifers and bushes. The cubs must be protected at all costs from freezing in the biting winds that sweep unbroken from the North Pole.

What the mother expects of her cubs on this march certainly taxes their strength, but not excessively. They become tougher and more powerful with every day that passes. The mother subjects her young to an intensive training course; for example, they are permitted to head off in pursuit of something which has whetted their curiosity – albeit only if she accompanies them. They gradually discover new-found abilities, practice dealing blows with their paws, leaping and biting, and pursue phantoms. The route to the icy Arctic becomes a training ground for their skills as hunters, long before they have even seen or smelt – let alone tasted – their first seal.

Few animals are as uninhibited in play as young polar bears. Around 20 percent of their limited energy resources are wasted – or so it might seem – in repeated bouts of romping and gamboling. In reality, however, the intense sensory and physical stimulation accompanying their frolics encourages a host of junctions to form in the brain, which serve in turn to enhance the motor skills of the young animals.

The development of the neurons in the cubs' nervous systems does not by any means end at birth. Their brain cells require endless amounts of stimulation and encouragement from their environment in order to function precisely.

Young animals in particular play with such animation because countless synaptic connections are established during this period, making the most of the full range of their physical and mental potential. They grow into indefatigable young predators, able to respond like lightning to new situations. This is an advantage for their future. Animals that have practiced assiduously and exercised vigorously from a young age have superior skills to those that don't start till later.

The bear cubs' frolicking not only enhances their stamina, memory and flexibility, but also generates reverse connections. In other words, specific muscle groups which will be vital later in determining the bears' success as predators are strengthened at the expense of other, less important muscles.

Through their play, the triplets learn skills which they will not dare to put into practice in the real world for some time. Protected by their mother, they prepare for the challenges they will face in the harsh world of the Arctic, learning the use of their paws, pouncing, biting the throat – while also mastering the control of their own strength. After all, their aim is not to injure their siblings, but to exploit them as sparring partners. While romping, the three begin to iron out their baby clumsiness, correct their eye for distances, explore the uses of their sharp claws. Again and again they experiment with individual movements, reveling in the skill of their own bodies. Until they have finally mastered every movement. And one day, when life has become a serious affair, whatever they have learnt will come to them automatically, with the effortless elegance and apparent ease that is typical of their kind.

Equipped with the virtual repertoire of the predator, the little ones and their mother finally reach the pack ice that will be their future hunting ground. In the crystalline landscape of yawning chasms and towering icebergs, they finally experience for themselves what it means to tear at the blubbery neck of a ringed seal with their sharp teeth, and to take up their position at the top of the food chain. ■

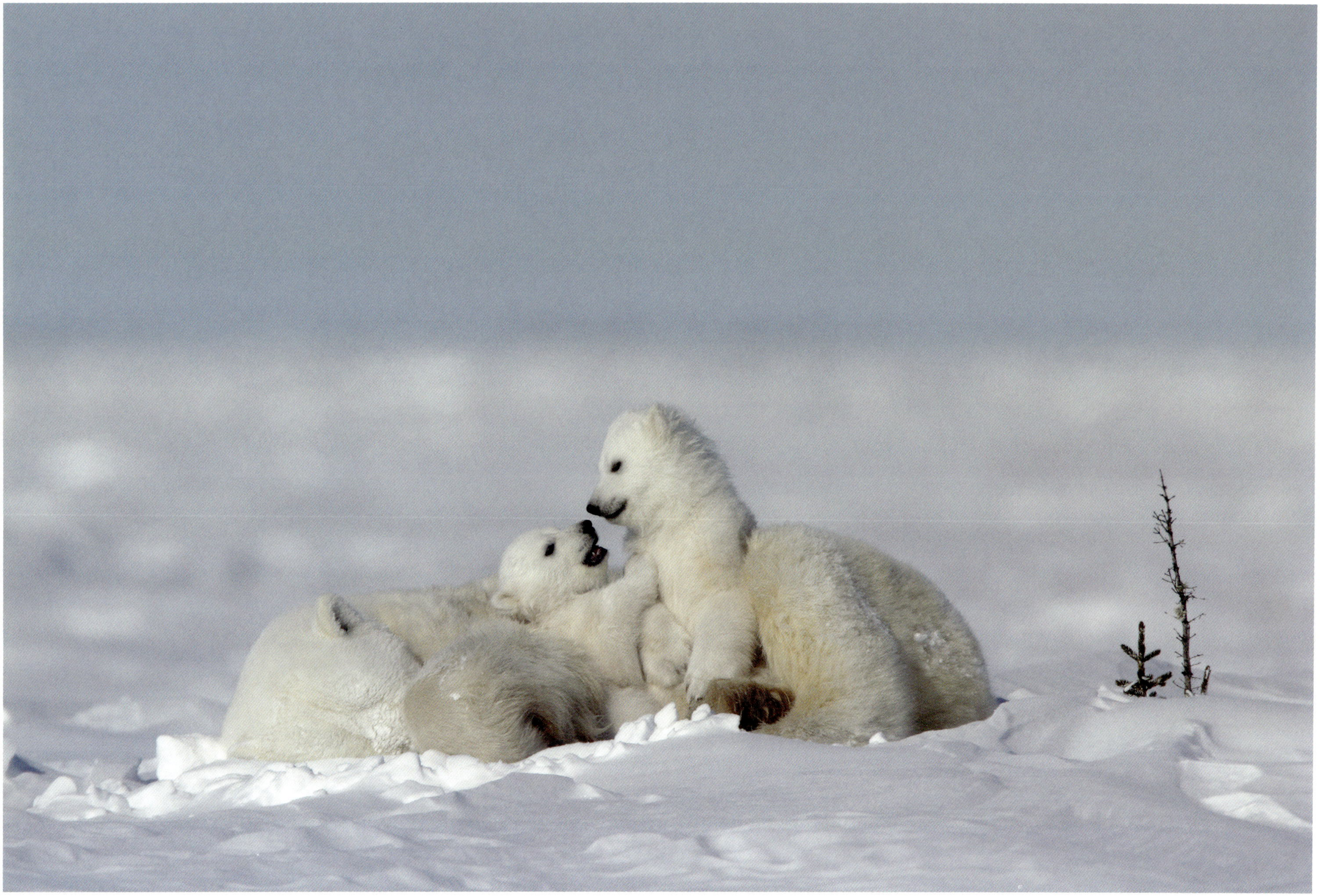

The 200-kilo female polar bear needs only to roll over a couple of times to create a cosy hollow in a snow drift. Lying on her side, her furry body encircles a sheltered playground for her frolicking cub.

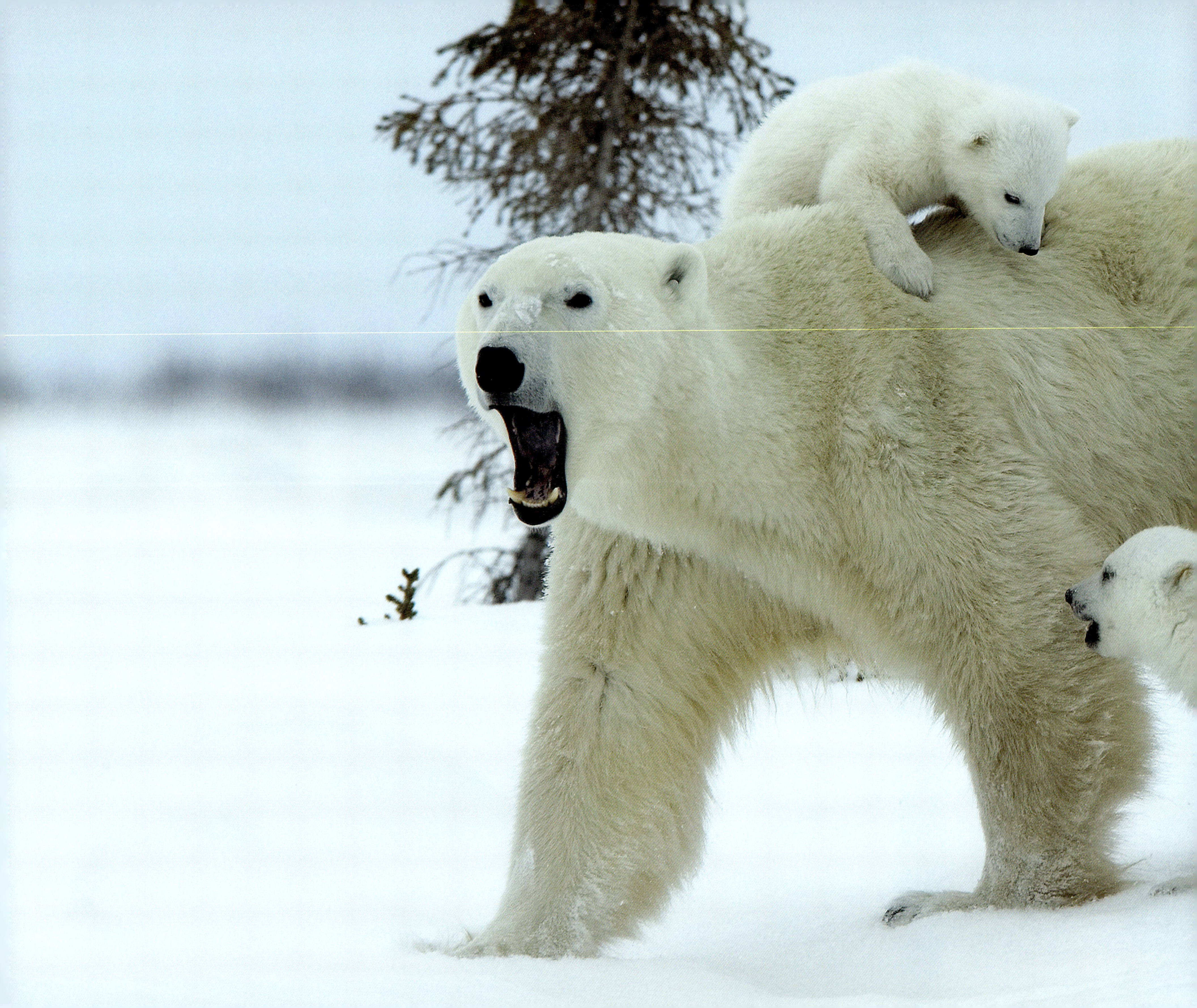

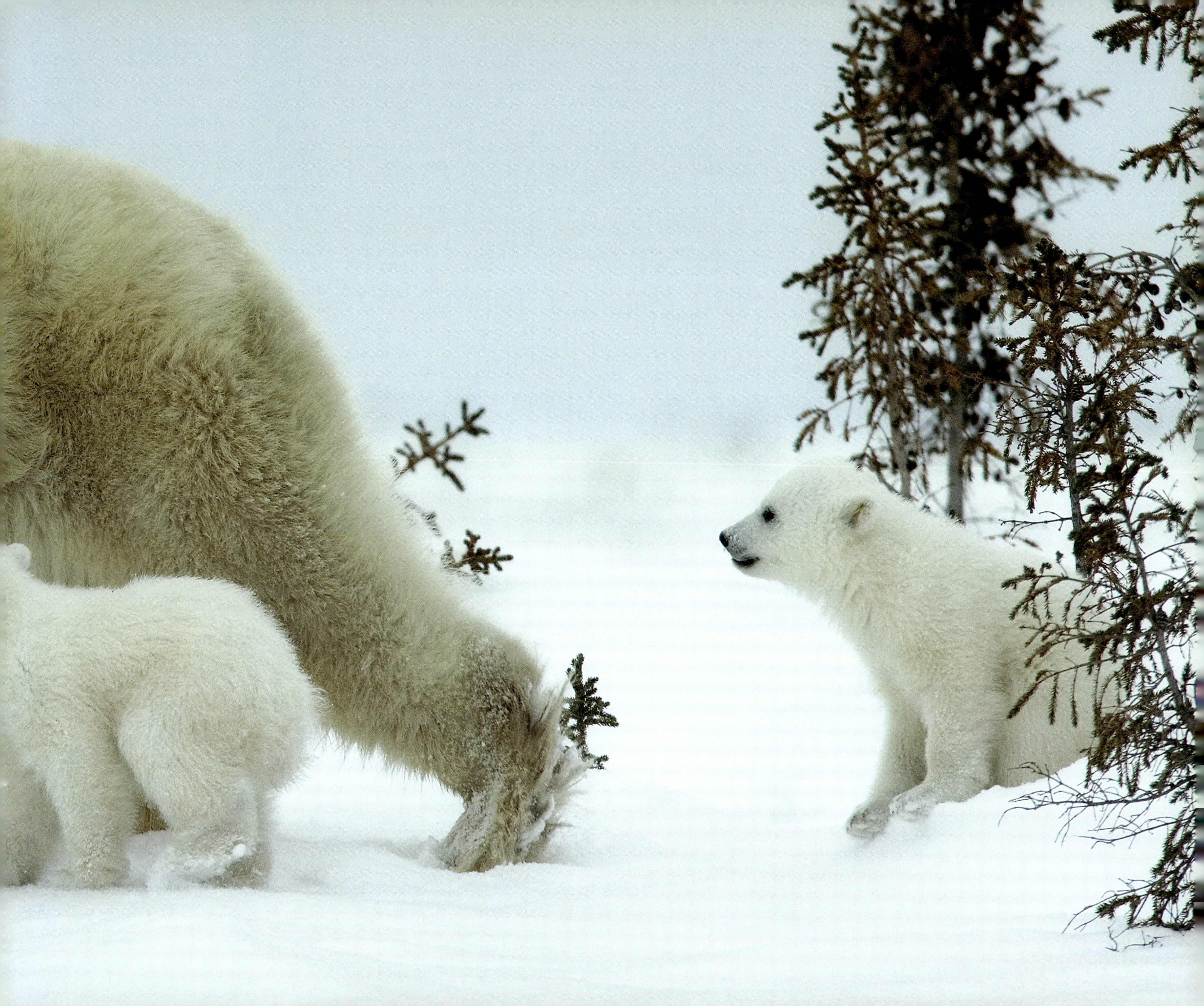

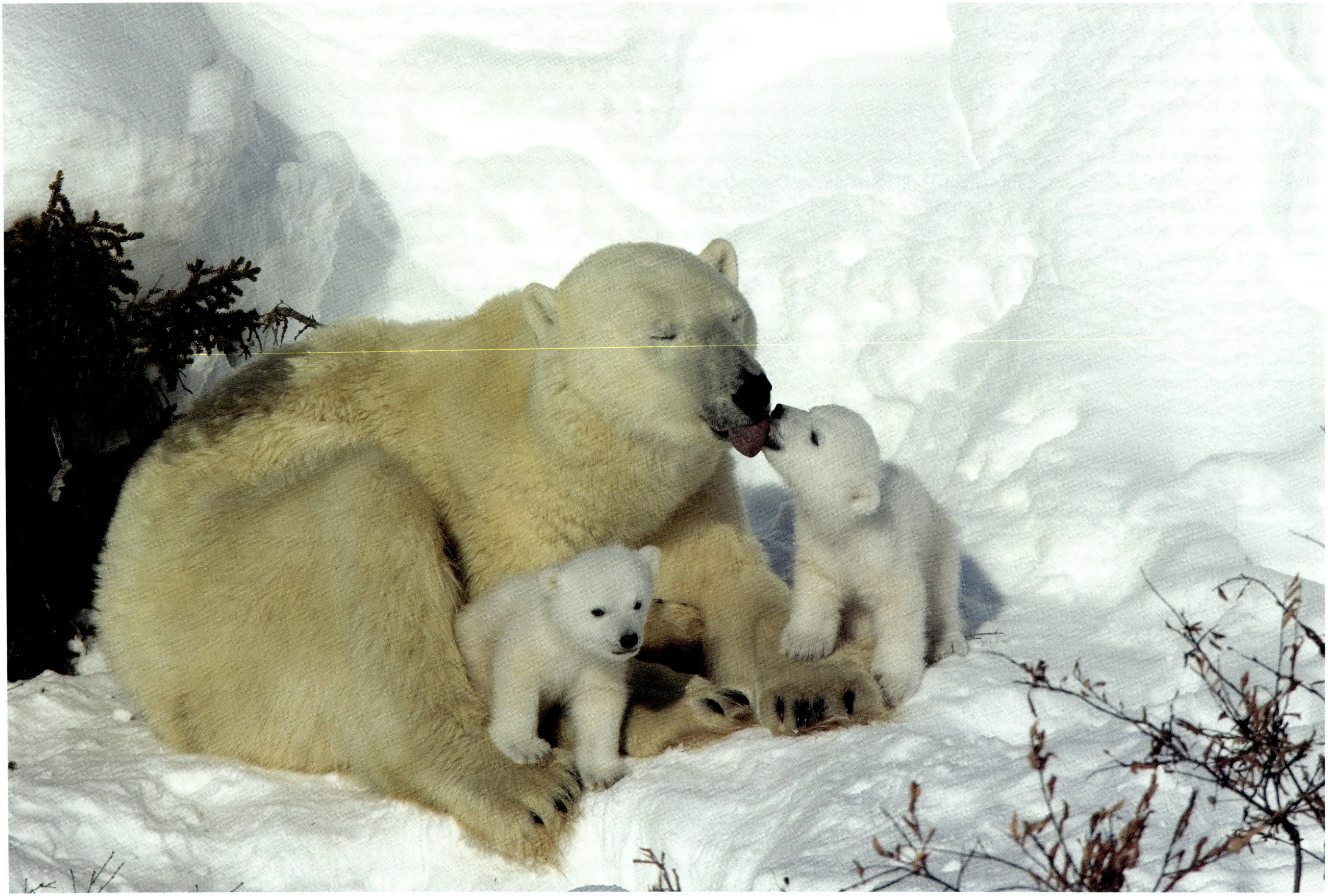

Polar bears are scrupulously hygienic. Because the cubs are not yet skilled at cleaning themselves, their mother regularly licks them clean. After the months of darkness in the den where the cubs were born, the mother's coat has taken on a yellowish tinge.

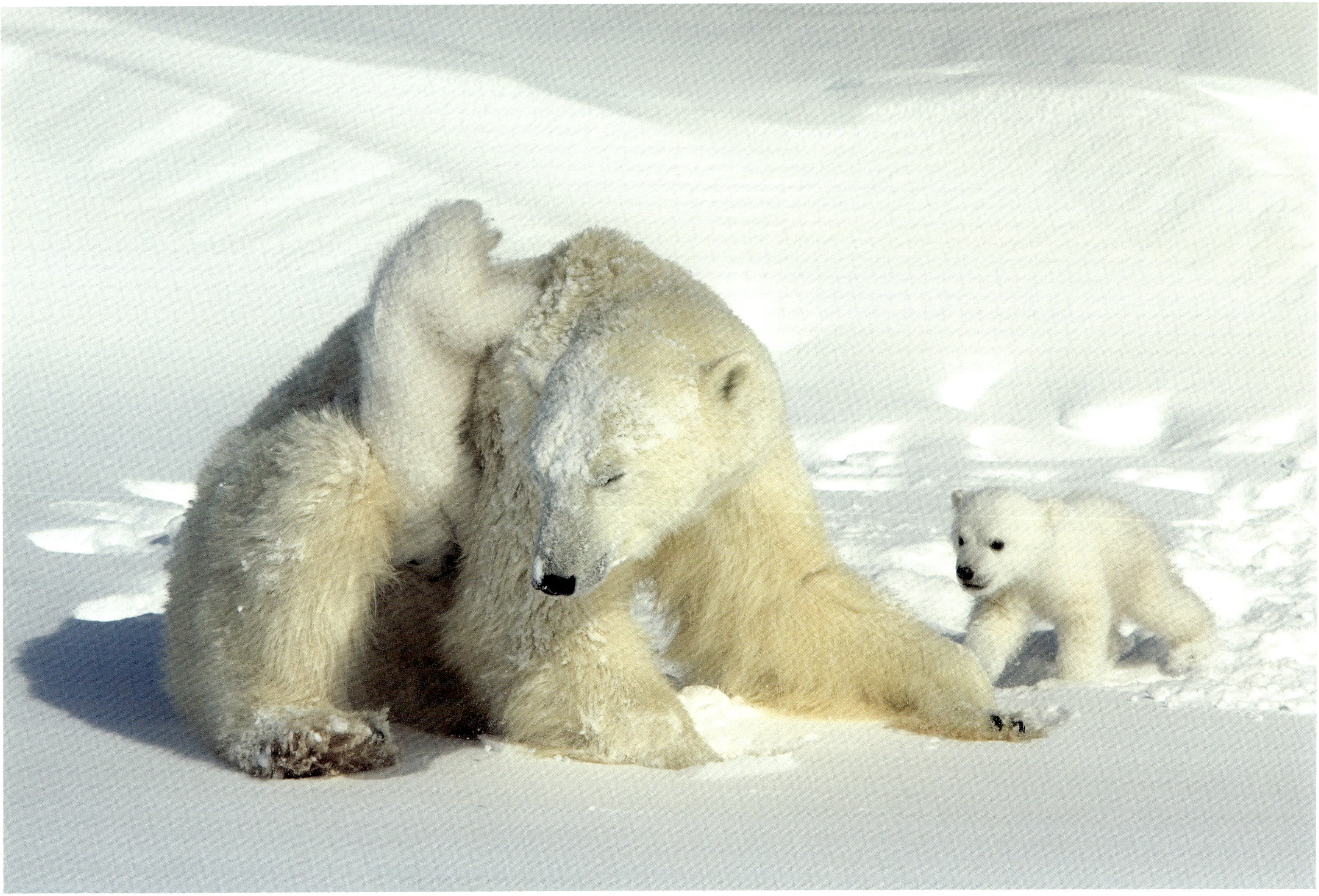

Although these cubs are still small, they are enormously exuberant, romping through a snowdrift and using their mother as a springboard. Polar bears are cautious mothers, preferring to keep their young close to them to protect them.

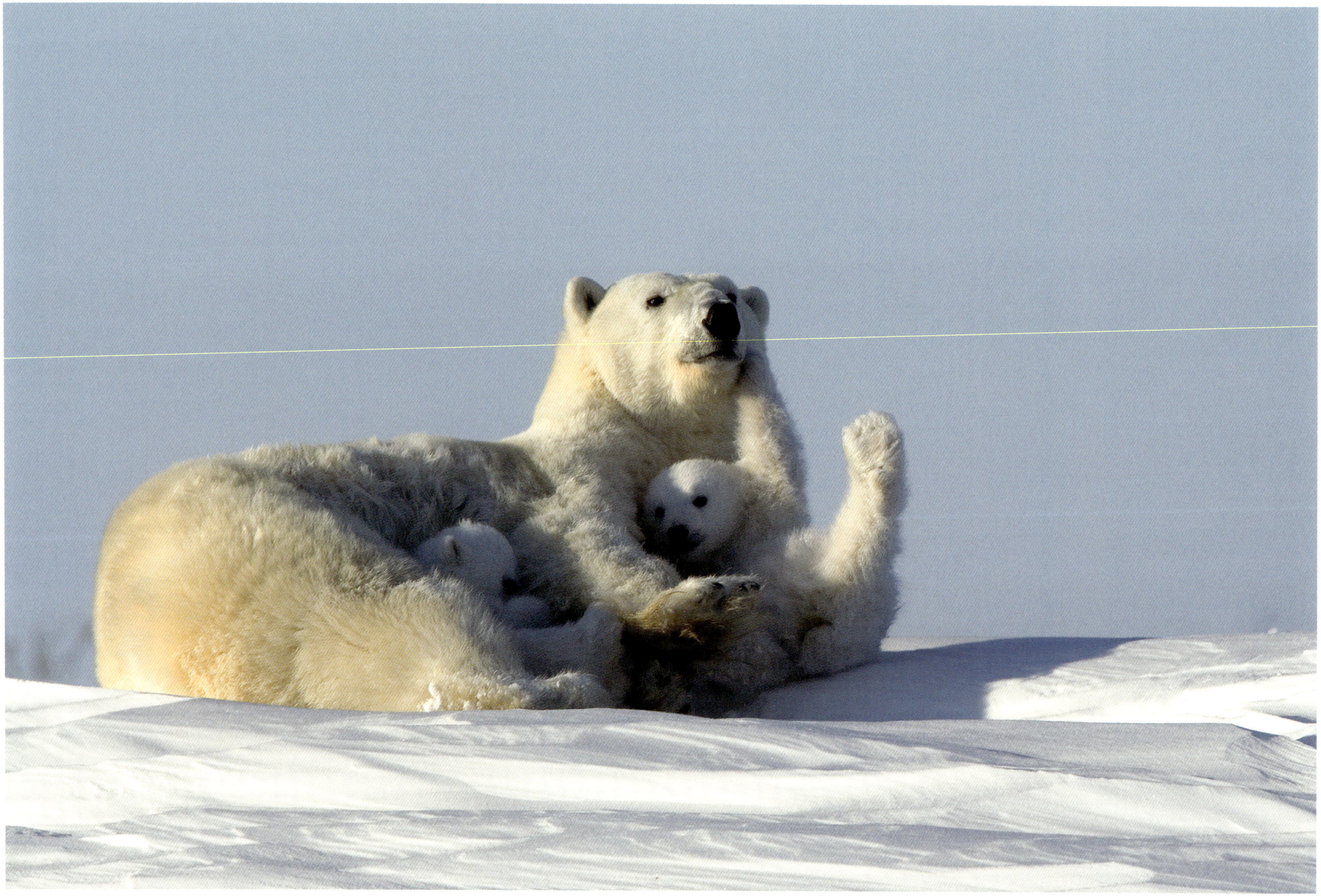

The mother bear has climbed a small hill to survey the landscape. She is in a hurry to reach the ice of Hudson Bay and start hunting, after months of fasting while she was giving birth to her young in her den and nursing them. Nevertheless, the mother is patient with her cubs, for they still need frequent rests on their long trek to reach the ocean ice.

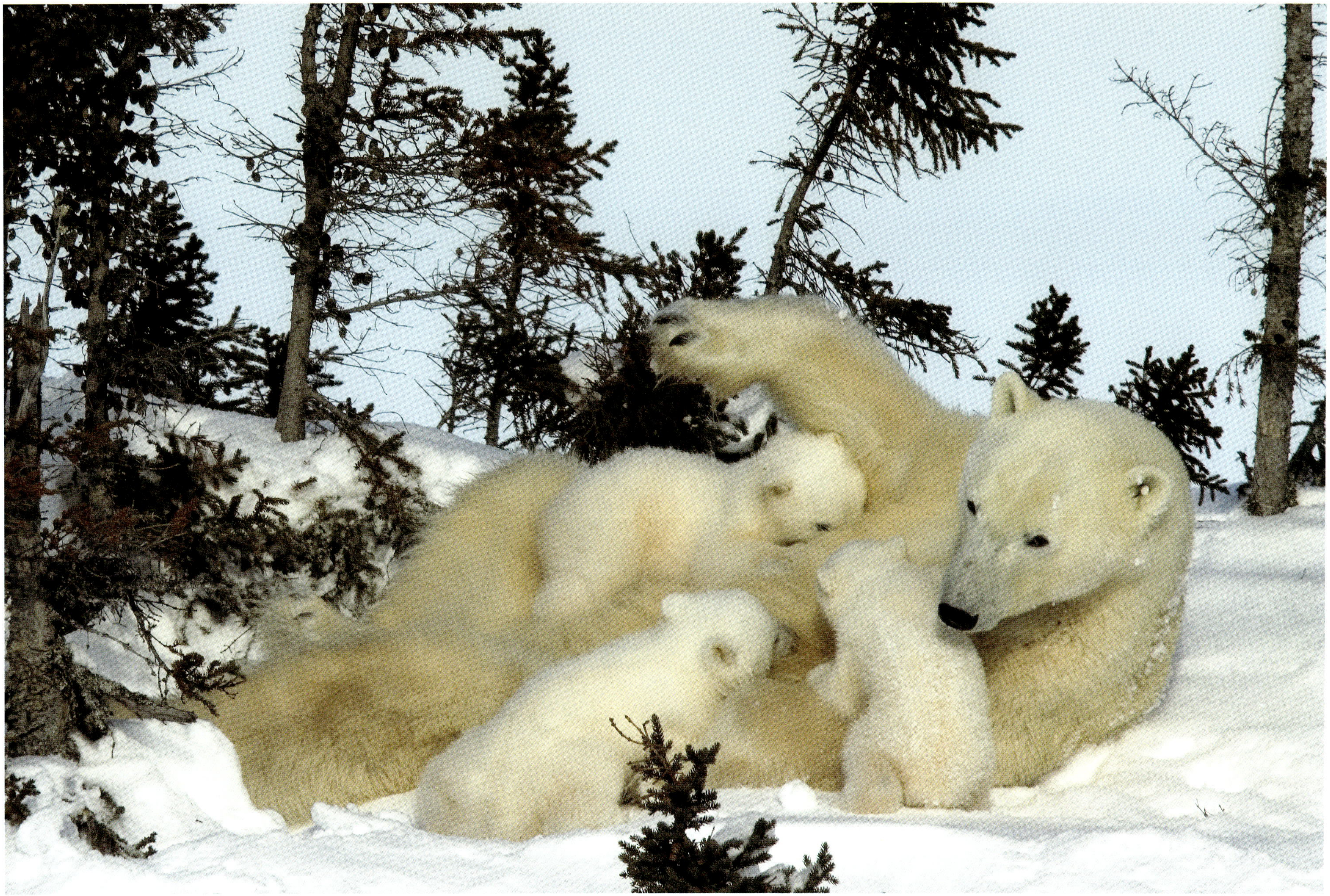

A mother bear lies in a snowdrift nursing her cubs. In the first few months of life the little bears grow rapidly and become stronger – all thanks to their mother's rich milk. As soon as the mother bear has killed her first seals, the cubs will also begin their lives as carnivores.

Polar Bears – at a glance

Their place in the animal kingdom

- They belong to the phylum of vertebrates
- to the class of mammals
- to the order of predators
- to the family of bears

Their scientific name

Ursus maritimus

Their closest relatives

Polar bears are a relatively recent species, evolving scarcely 10,000 years ago from a line of brown bears that became isolated by increased glaciation in the northern hemisphere 2.5 million years ago. The population adapted to their new habitat of ocean ice, and soon began to exhibit features of an independent species.

Their habitat (population numbers)

Polar bears (22,000) live around the North Pole. Their territory comprises the pack ice of the Arctic Ocean and the mainland ice of the coastal regions. The five countries where polar bears live are the USA, Canada, Russia, Denmark and Norway.

Polar bears in figures

- Polar bears are the **biggest land carnivores** in the world.
- They cover enormous **distances** of around 8,000 kilometers (5,000 miles) per year.
- Their **maximum speed** over short distances is 50 kilometers (31 miles) per hour.
- A male polar bear can grow four meters (13 feet) **tall** when upright, with females up to 285 centimeters (9 feet) tall.
- Males can **weigh** from 650 to 800 kilos, while females are seldom heavier than 500 kilos.
- Female polar bears have **four teats** and can therefore nurse up to four cubs simultaneously.
- A polar bear's layer of **subcutaneous fat** is up to 10 centimeters (3.9 inches) thick.
- Polar bears can **swim** up to 100 kilometers (62 miles) without resting.
- They have an incredibly fine **sense of smell**, which extends up to 30 kilometers (19 miles).
- Polar bears reach **sexual maturity** at the age of four to six.
- They have an average **lifespan** of 30 years.

Polar bears' characteristic features

The distinctive appearance of the polar bear, with its narrow skull and "Roman nose," long neck and straight back, sets it apart from its nearest relative, the brown bear. Polar bears' teeth are typical for a carnivore; the broad back molars used by their brown cousins to grind tough plant fibres are no comparison with the polar bears' incisors – powerful sabres used for slicing through meat. The canines with which they grasp their prey are also longer and more powerful than those of brown bears. The most obvious feature of the polar bear – its white fur – is the result of light refraction, not white pigment; the fur is actually transparent. The skin under the fur is black, as can be seen on the tip of the nose and the lips.

What polar bears eat

Polar bears feed at the top of the Arctic food chain. They are hunters, and can smell a seal pup many kilometers away, concealed under snowdrifts. Breaking through the wall of ice with a bound, they can kill their prey with one blow of their paw. A polar bear will wait for hours at a breathing-hole which a seal has carved into the ice and to which it must sooner or later return. Again, one blow is usually enough to kill the seal, which is then dragged out of the water. Polar bears are not fastidious eaters, and will devour whatever they find: crabs, shellfish, walrus calves, beluga whales or carrion – and even birds, eggs, berries or seaweed if necessary.

Polar bears' lifestyle

Polar bears are nomadic and active in the winter season. They do not mark and defend their territory. Southern populations such as those of the western Hudson Bay region return to the mainland in summer, well fed after successful hunting, and fast until the sea freezes again in the late fall. Polar bears are loners; male bears seek partners only from March to May when the females come into heat. Fertilized ova do not implant themselves in the female uterus until four months after mating.

How polar bears raise their young

Taking care of the cubs is the female´s responsibility. Females usually give birth to about three cubs around December. Weighing scarcely 500 grams at birth, the young are nourished by their mother's fat-rich milk and grow rapidly. When they take to the ice with their mothers in April they weigh 10 kilos. Everything they need to know as Arctic hunters is taught to them by their mother. Young bears are not fully independent until the age of around 30 months.

Dangers to polar bears

Six out of ten cubs starve to death in their first year of life. Many others are killed by male bears which attack and eat the young.

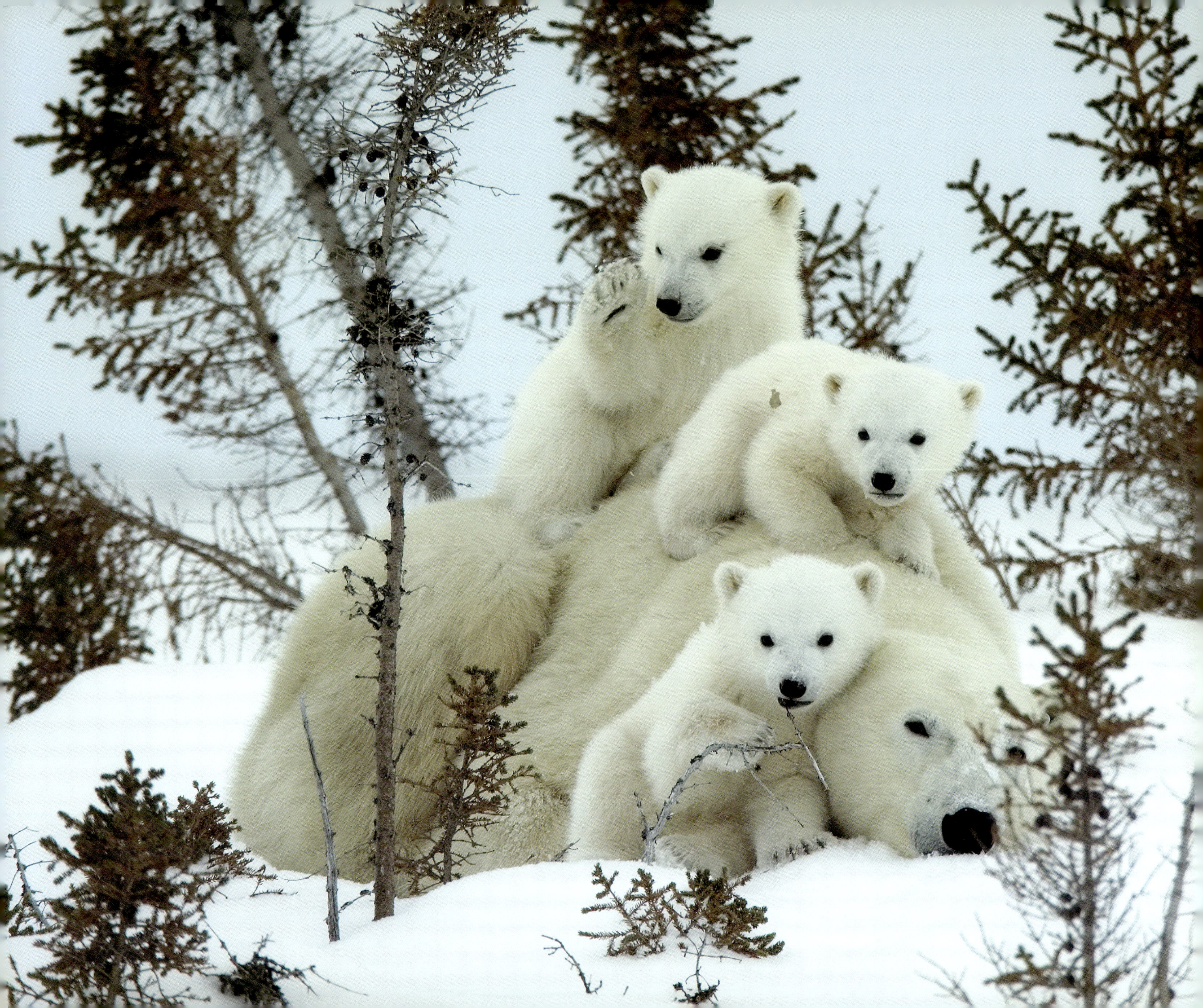

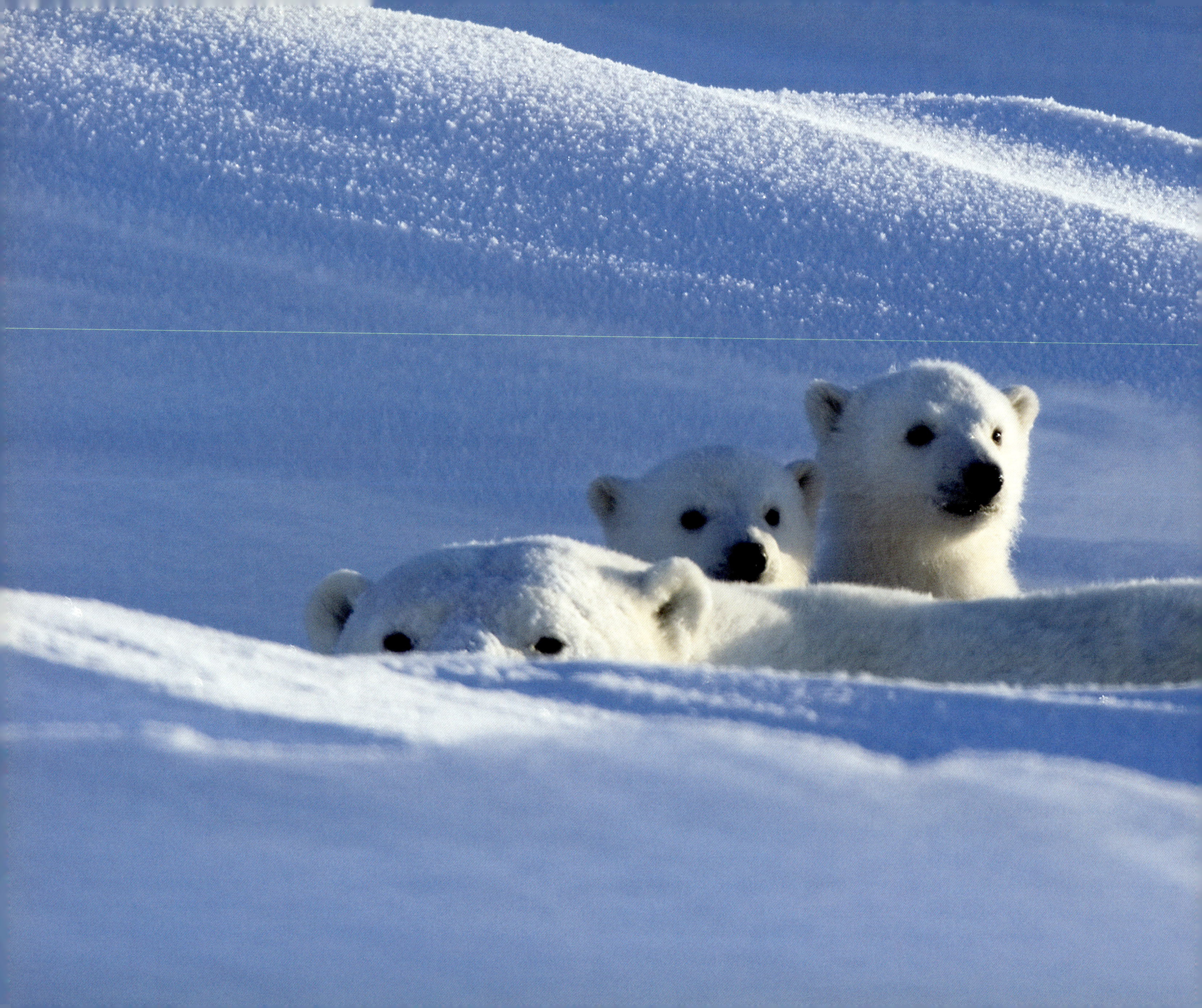

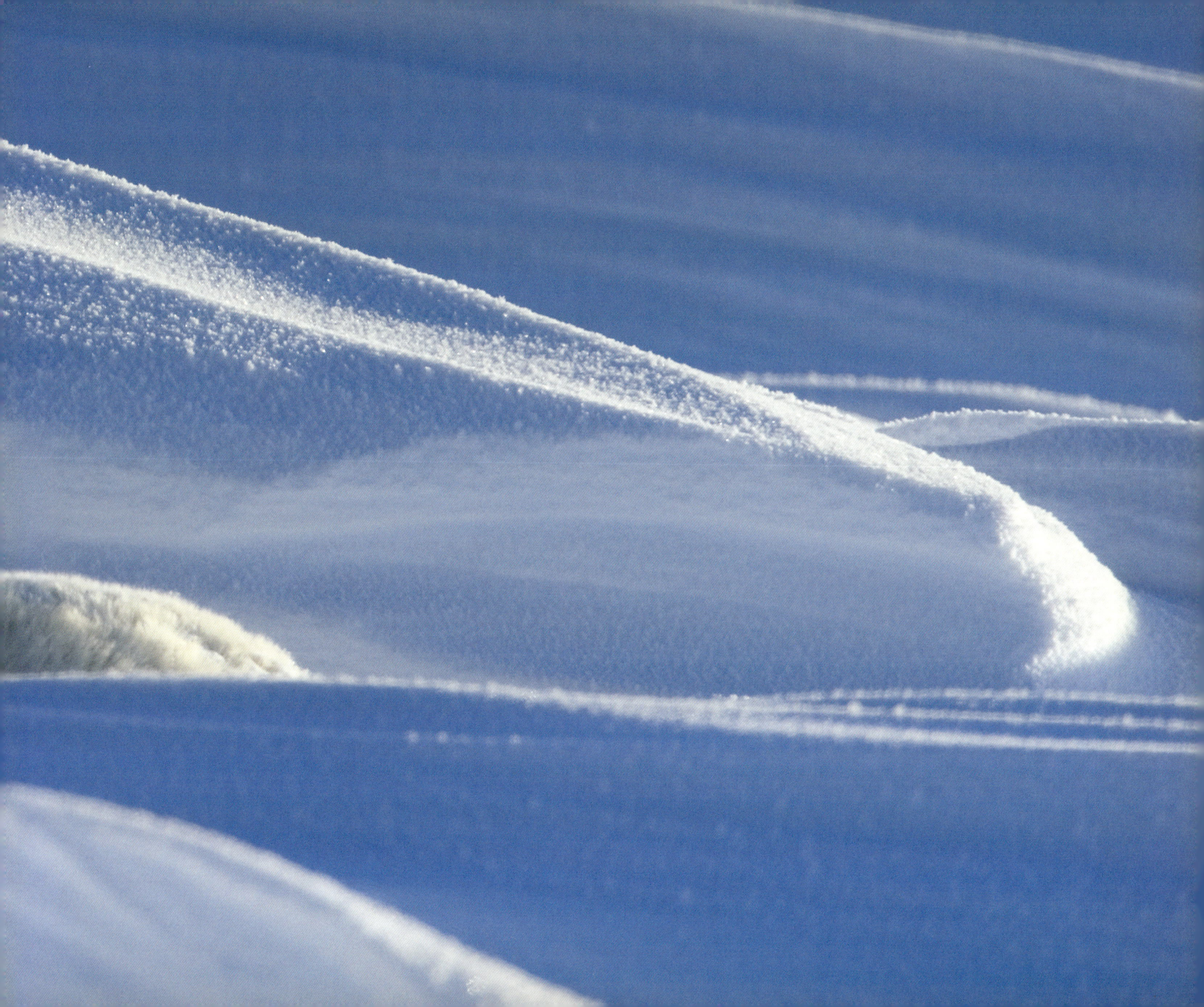

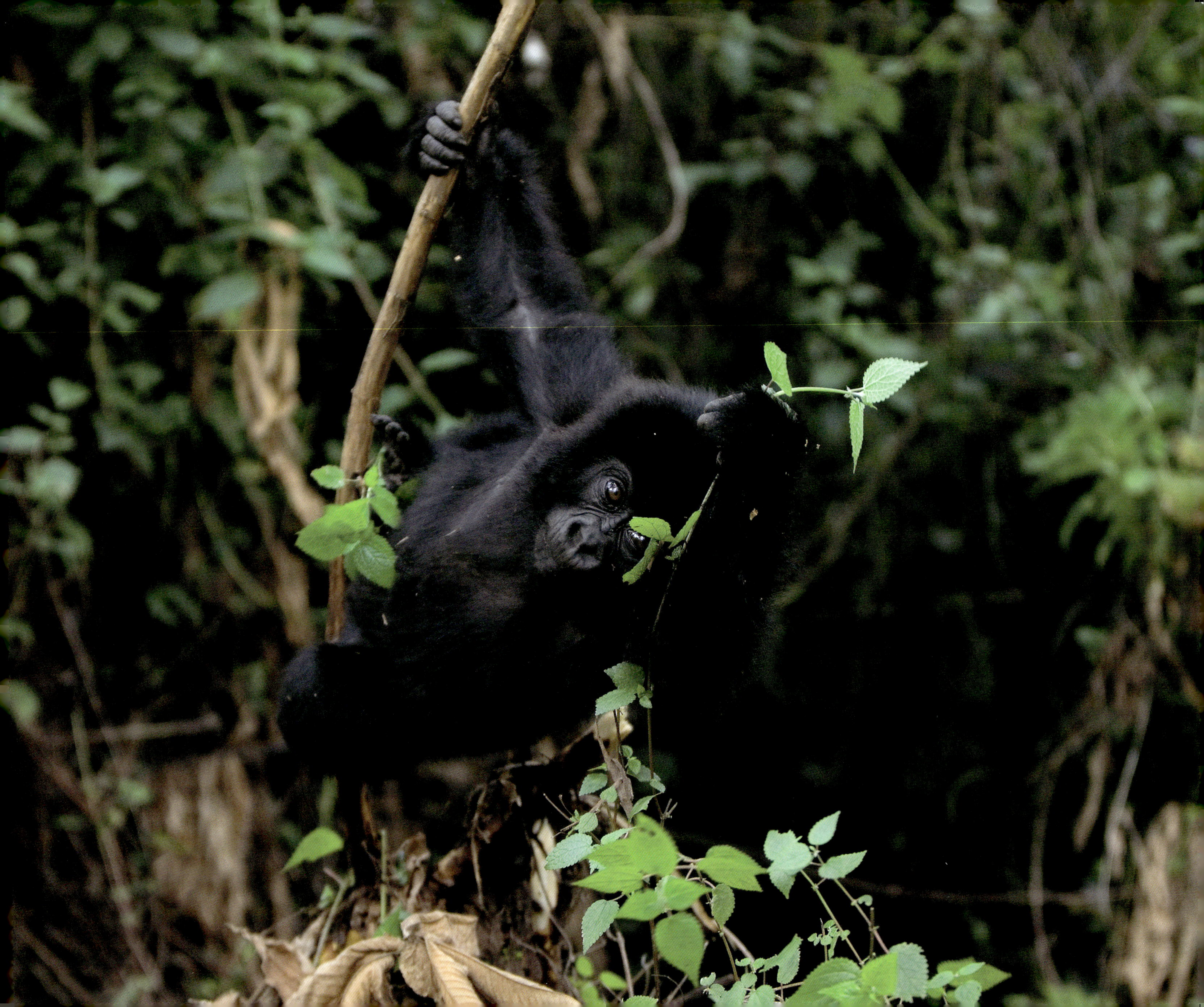

Mountain Gorillas

Natural Psychologists

Only a moment before, he had felt the warm belly against his back and tried to fall asleep again, lulled by the feeling of utter security. But it's no good. As soon as the sun rises the familiar crackling and snapping of twigs can be heard, as if a buffalo were barging through the jungle next to him. The mattress of vegetation under his body lists dangerously and the usual morning shower drenches him as a scatter of dew is shaken from the overhanging branches: his father is awake.

The young primate, more or less an adolescent at the age of six, sits up and blinks over the rim of the nest. In the hollow of the mountain, 3,000 meters (9,840 feet) up, the other members of his family snooze in their nests like black fruit in green pods. The young gorilla turns his gaze to his father, stretching up to his full height of 1.75 meters (5.7 feet), a mighty gorilla. A ragged mist has strewn pearls of dew over the fur of this colossus, 180 kilos in weight. His son's eyes rest in fascination on the saddle of grey-white hairs covering the broad back of his sire. How he admires this symbol of maturity and potency. It is the result of a change in fur color experienced by male gorillas when they reach adulthood – roughly twice as old as he is now. His father is a 22-year-old silverback.

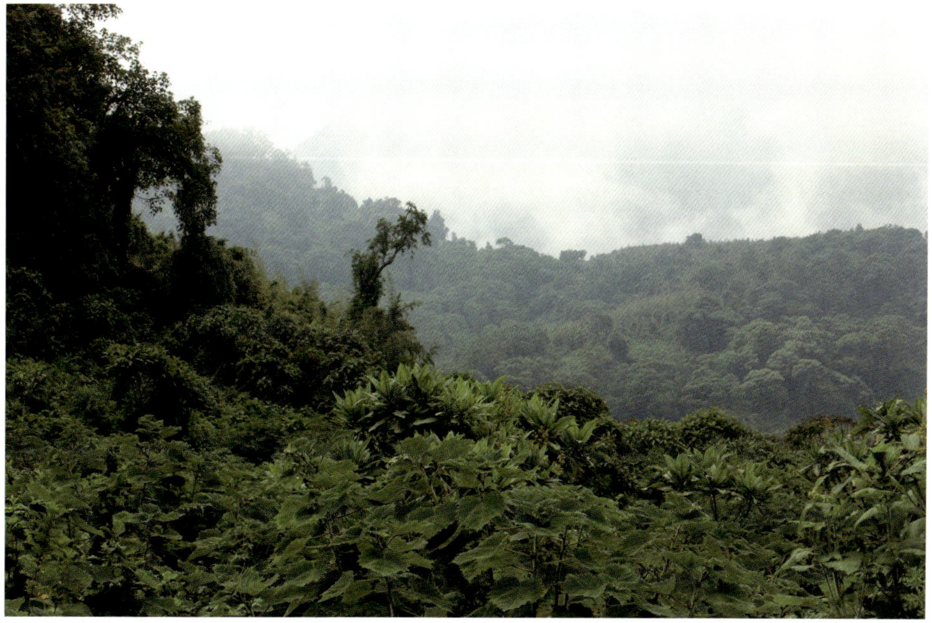

But not just any silverback. And certainly not one of the partnerless vagabonds that roam the forests. Indeed not! His father has reached a status dreamed of by male gorillas: he heads a group of 20 of his kind, made up of aunts, nieces, nephews and, above all, a harem of five females and their common children. He is responsible for protecting them all – for example, from attacks by silverback strangers.

In return, he expects his clan to respect him as the patriarch and follow his orders. Such as now. A deep, belching "harrumph" rises from his throat. Immediately the sleeping family begins to move, emerging from their beds of vegetation and following the silverback already waiting on the fringes of the forest. None of the animals has eaten since yesterday afternoon. And the powerful alpha male, whose diet consists of a good 30 kilos of greenstuff every day, is particularly hungry.

The six-year-old knows they are going to the saddle of Bisoke, a volcano in the region where bamboo grows. The family already eagerly awaits the new shoots, inspecting the progress of the seasonal delicacy every few days. Today the silverback appears convinced that the first tips are ready for plucking.

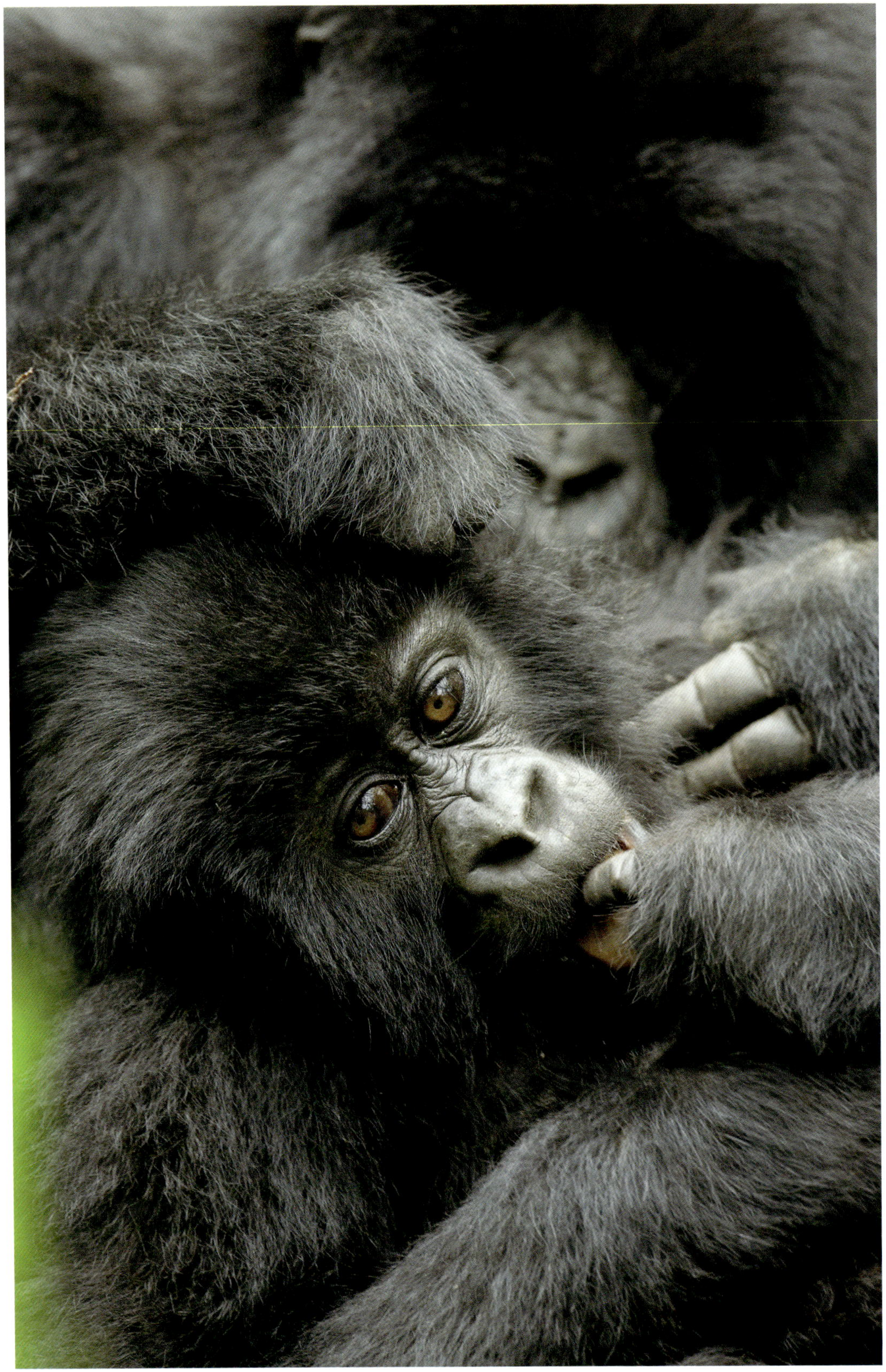

There will certainly be a fight over the juiciest stems – the six-year-old is sure of that, too. Like all young gorillas, he is growing up into a complex web of relationships, reading moods and even intentions in the familiar expressions of his relatives, and learning how to move smoothly through the minefield of conflicting priorities created by twenty individual personalities. He has developed into a natural psychologist, an expert in the delicate areas of demarcation between friendship, enmity, coalitions, and ties of blood. He has experienced the touchiness that can seethe under the skin of normality like a festering wound, ready to burst open at a thoughtless touch.

While the group is foraging for bamboo shoots the oldest female in particular will quite clearly demonstrate to his mother which of them is higher-ranking – a rivalry deeply embedded in the young gorilla's earliest memories. As a baby clinging to his mother's fur, he already sensed her tension and fear of this matriarch and her young.

At the time, his mother had only recently joined the group. Attracted by the young silverback, she abandoned her family and chose him as a mate, accepting the frosty reception she received from the other females in the harem. The reception was all the colder since the silverback took her part from the beginning, when the others jostled her aside. He protected her, his newest, youngest mate. And nothing has changed. He calms every conflict that flares up, ensures harmony within the family.

The young gorilla senses that he is an offspring of this love. Almost daily, as far back as he can remember, his father has demonstrated his affection. He remembers how the serious expression of the alpha male would relax into one of gentleness when looking at his son, how the great gorilla crouched down to the level of the small one, his smiling, open mouth signaling that it was playtime.

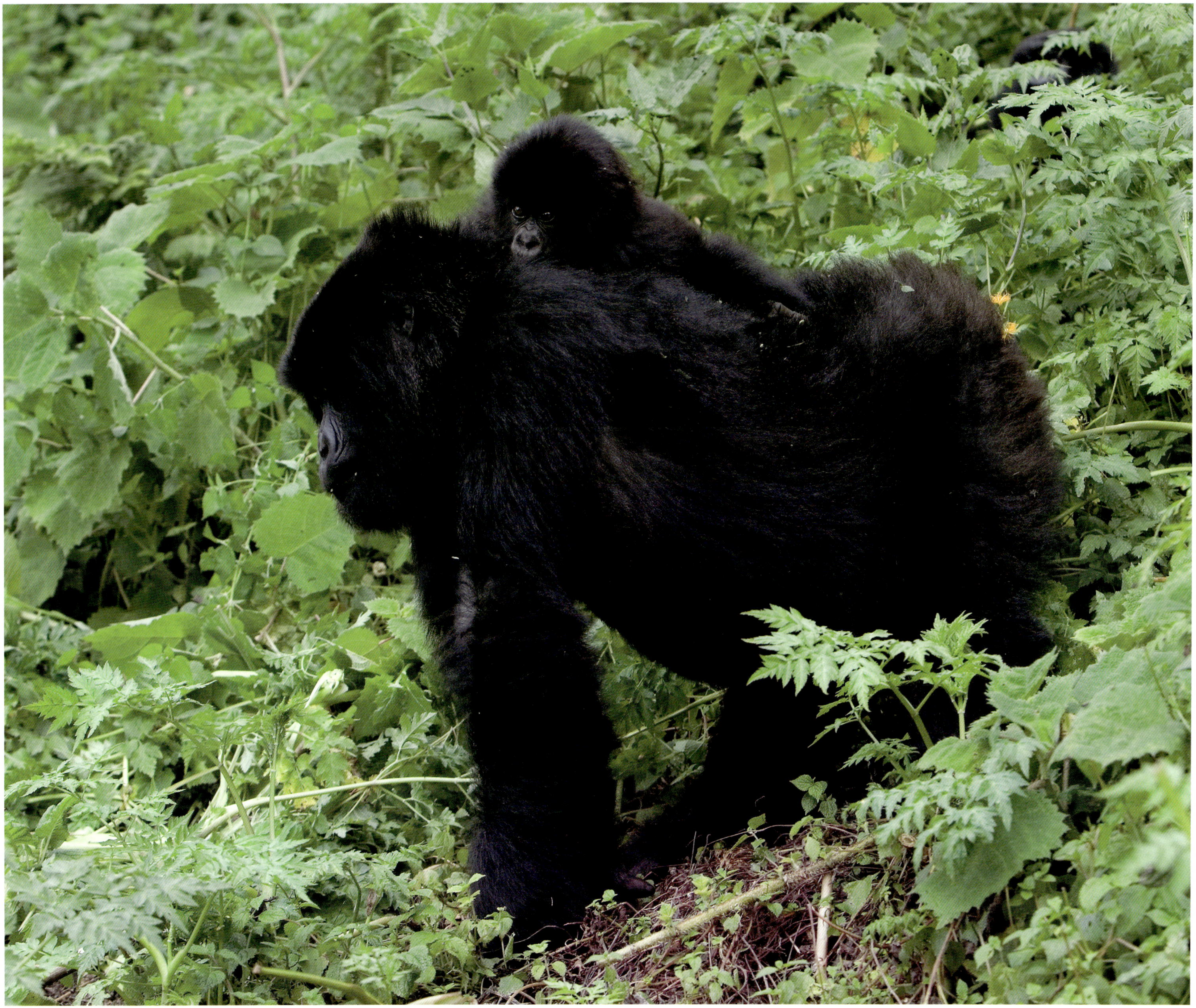

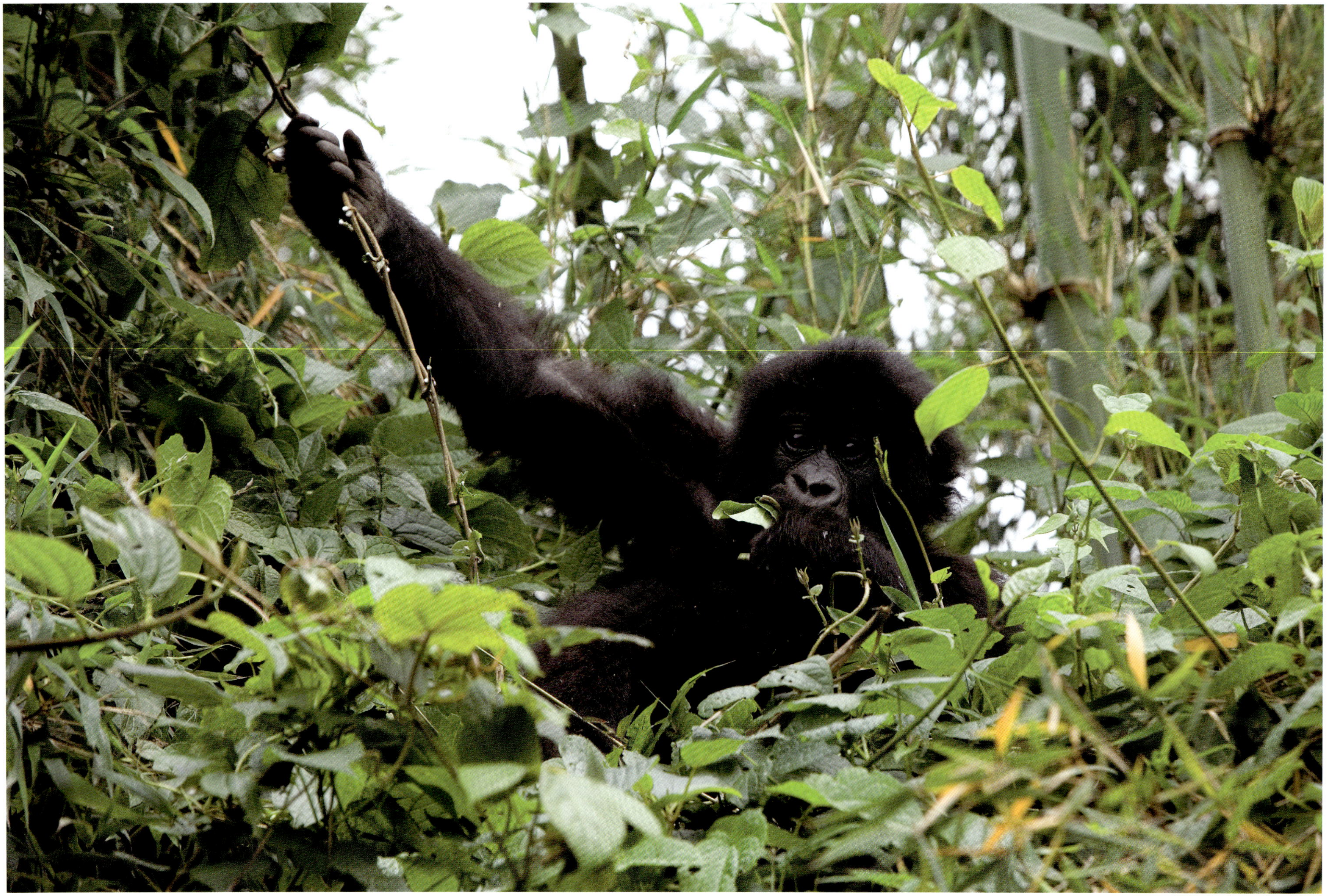

At eight months, young gorillas begin to sample what grows around them.
Constantly with their mother from birth, they learn from her which plants are suitable for a gorilla's diet.
The young animal skilfully plucks young leaves from a twining galium vine.

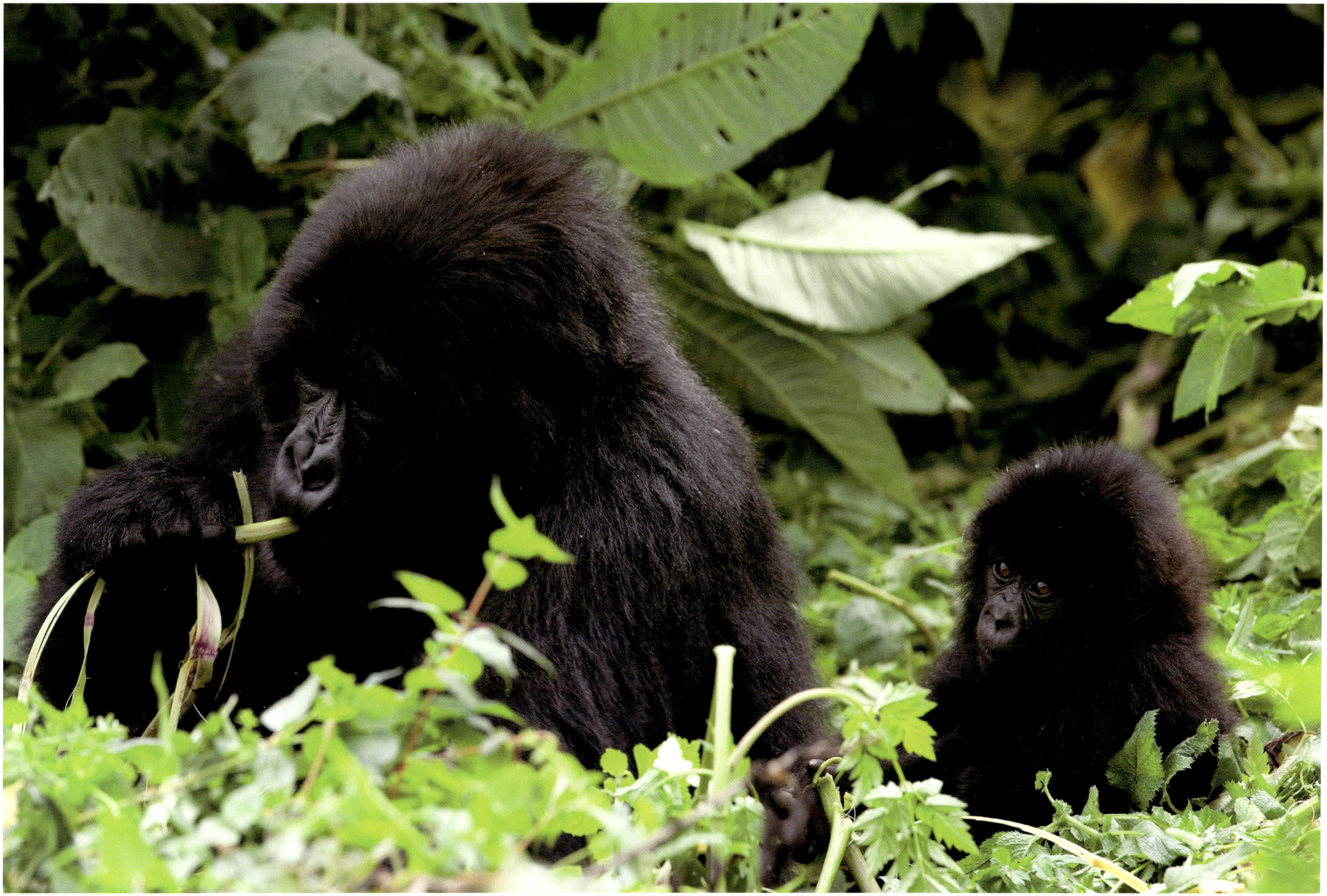

Fresh bamboo shoots are a delicacy for mountain gorillas.
The families make regular excursions to the bamboo groves on the slopes of the Virunga volcanoes and examine the ground for new shoots, occasionally excavating the juicy stalks from the earth.

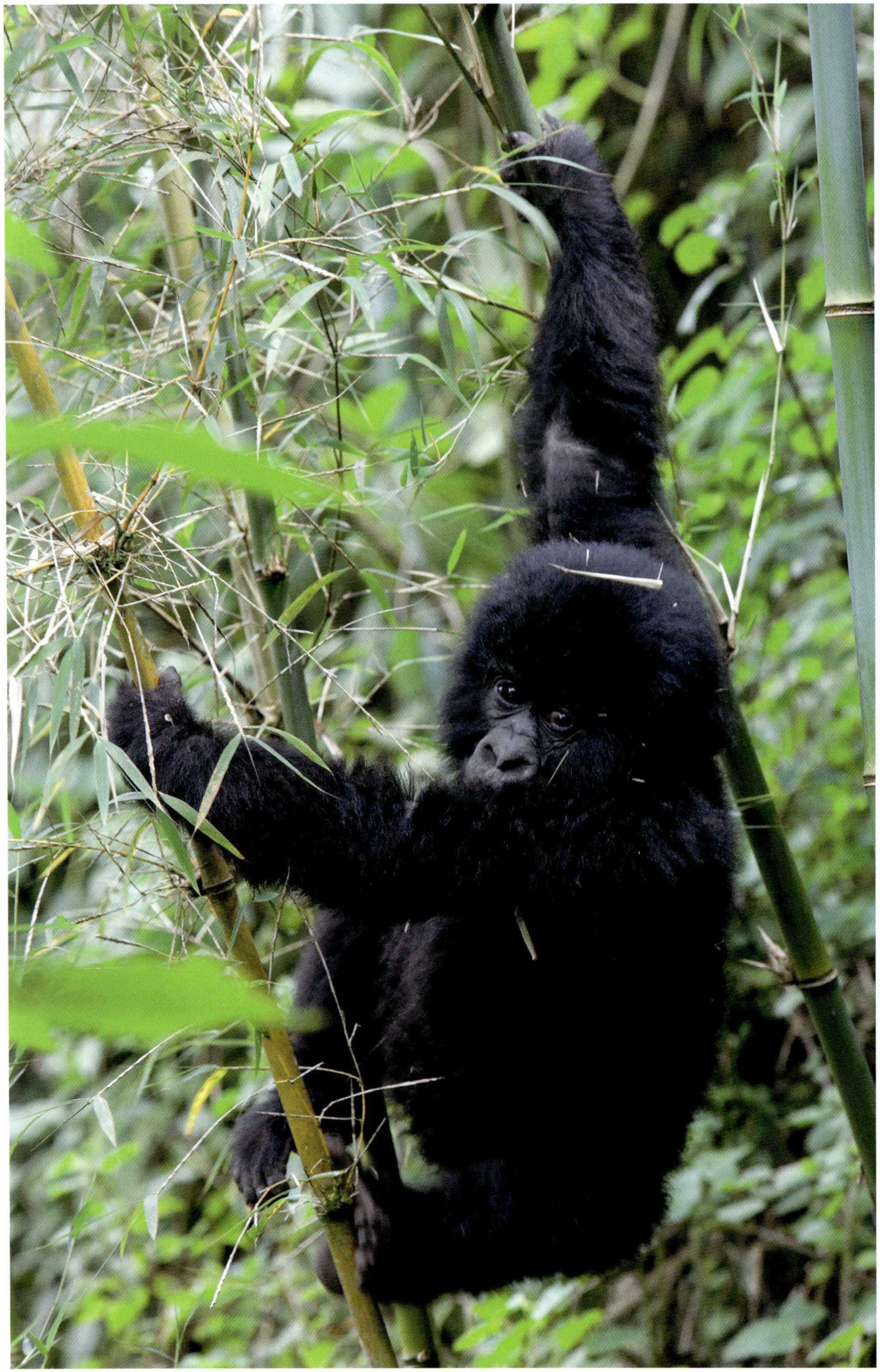

At the age of one the son was allowed to ride on the silverback's shoulders, and at two he even dared to plant a punch on his father's smooth, leathery nose with his tiny fist, receiving not so much as a grunt for this lack of respect.

The inquisitive six-year-old goes to his mother and bends over the baby in the crook of her arm. The female gorilla remains seated for a while for the sake of her child – a tiny daughter. Her brother cannot take his eyes off the baby, fascinated by the enormous nostrils, pinkish-gray skin and spindly limbs. He watches fascinated as the baby's head, with its shock of curly hair, bobs questingly to and fro until her cheek grazes a nipple. Immediately her mouth opens and clamps itself around the fount of milk, drinking deeply of the elixir of life. A moment later she is asleep.

Since his sister was born a week before, and because all baby gorillas spend their first six months in constant contact with their mother's body, the six-year-old youth has had to yield his place in his mother's sleeping nest. Other young gorillas in the group have slept alone since they were three; this young male, however, has a particularly close relationship with his mother, and he found even this late separation so difficult that his father actually took him in for a few nights. Soon it will be time for the six-year-old to build his own bed and sleep there alone.

For a while the young gorilla accompanies his mother, who supports the baby clinging to her stomach fur with one arm as she follows the group. Soon, however, the unhurried pace is too tedious for the six-year-old. Encouraging a few other youngsters by giving them friendly claps on the back, he bounds up the slope, drops into the lush vegetation at the peak and rolls down the hill, crowing in delight. Three adolescents plunge after him until they form a heap of black bodies at the bottom. Then they repeat the procedure.

On arrival at the bamboo grove, the fears of the six-year-old are confirmed. Only a few of the fleshy shoots are visible, enough for all, but not enough to satisfy their hunger completely. His mother reaches for the first shoot. But the matriarch has had her eye on the same one, and the females begin to grunt threateningly, each tugging at the thick stem. The silverback is already there. Silence immediately falls at his powerful presence and the low, gruff sounds emanating from his throat. The matriarch withdraws her hand, adopts an air of innocence and reaches for another bamboo shoot as if she had simply made a mistake.

The young gorilla is impressed at the composure with which his father smoothes over such conflicts. Every member of the group ultimately trusts in the silverback's sense of justice. He always defends the underdog – particularly in the case of newly arrived females that have no points of contact within the group. If they were always forced to back down in battles with the group's longer-standing members, they would leave. In the long run, this would weaken the silverback's position and impair his prospects of fathering as many young as possible.

Once the crisp appetizer has been demolished, the group moves to the nettle patch, spreading out throughout the area and devoting the next two hours to their main course.

Mountain gorillas have carved out an exclusive territory on the slopes of the Virunga volcanoes. True, there is little fruit to be found here; but they can choose from more than 60 edible plants whose leaves and juicy stems are rich in proteins and minerals. This abundance largely eliminates the need for battles over food – with the exception of special delicacies – and promotes the formation of stable bonds in the group, a luxury few species enjoy.

Mountain gorillas live in a salad bowl, so to speak. But the plants they crave do not yield their precious stores of nourishment without a struggle. Tree bark must be ripped open with powerful jaws to allow the gorillas to pick out the insect larvae which have burrowed deep into it. Other plants require skilled manipulation by hands, individual fingers or sharp incisors.

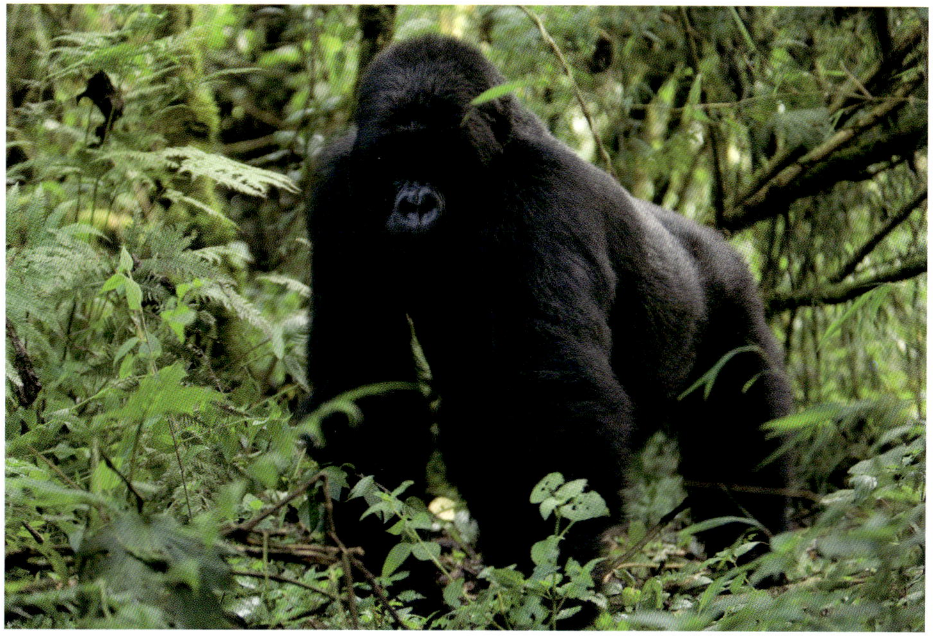

More than 40 movements of the hands must be carried out in the correct sequence to strip the leaves from the especially vicious nettle stalks, stack them and hold them firmly in place. During this procedure, the primates touch only the backs of the leaves, where stinging hairs are few. At last the stack is wrapped in a final leaf, smooth side to the outside, and put whole into the mouth.

Fragments of vegetation fall onto the babies grasping their mothers' fur. From an early age they discover which plants are edible, identify their scent and learn how much effort is necessary to prepare a single portion. At the age of around six months the young gorillas begin to sample the greenery themselves, later watching and imitating their elders to learn the repertoire of moves required for the preparation of their meals. By the time they are weaned at the age

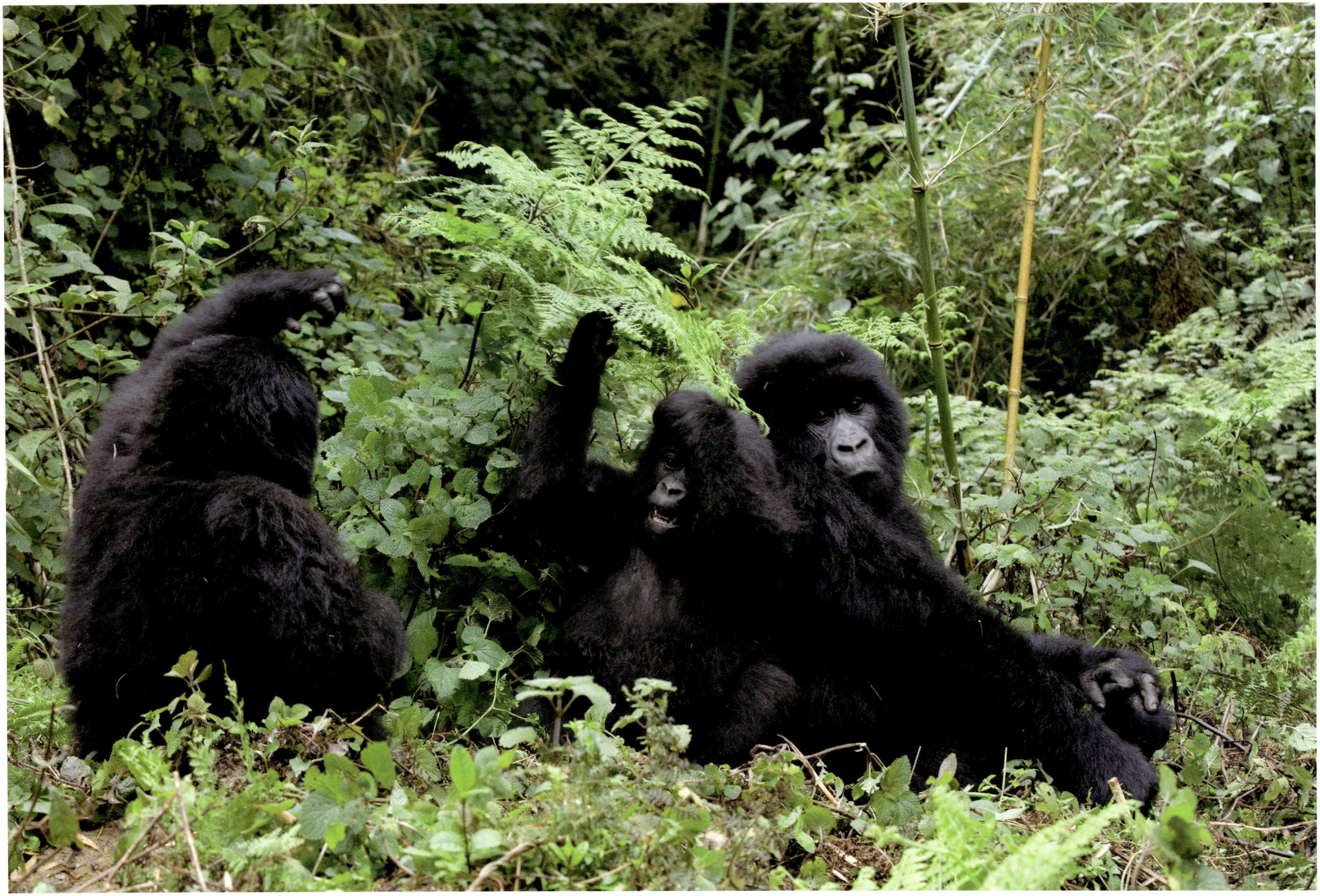

Young gorillas are extremely boisterous and enjoy competing with each other. The little ones are engaged in slapping their heads with both hands alternately, while the more sedate four-year-old watches them in surprise.

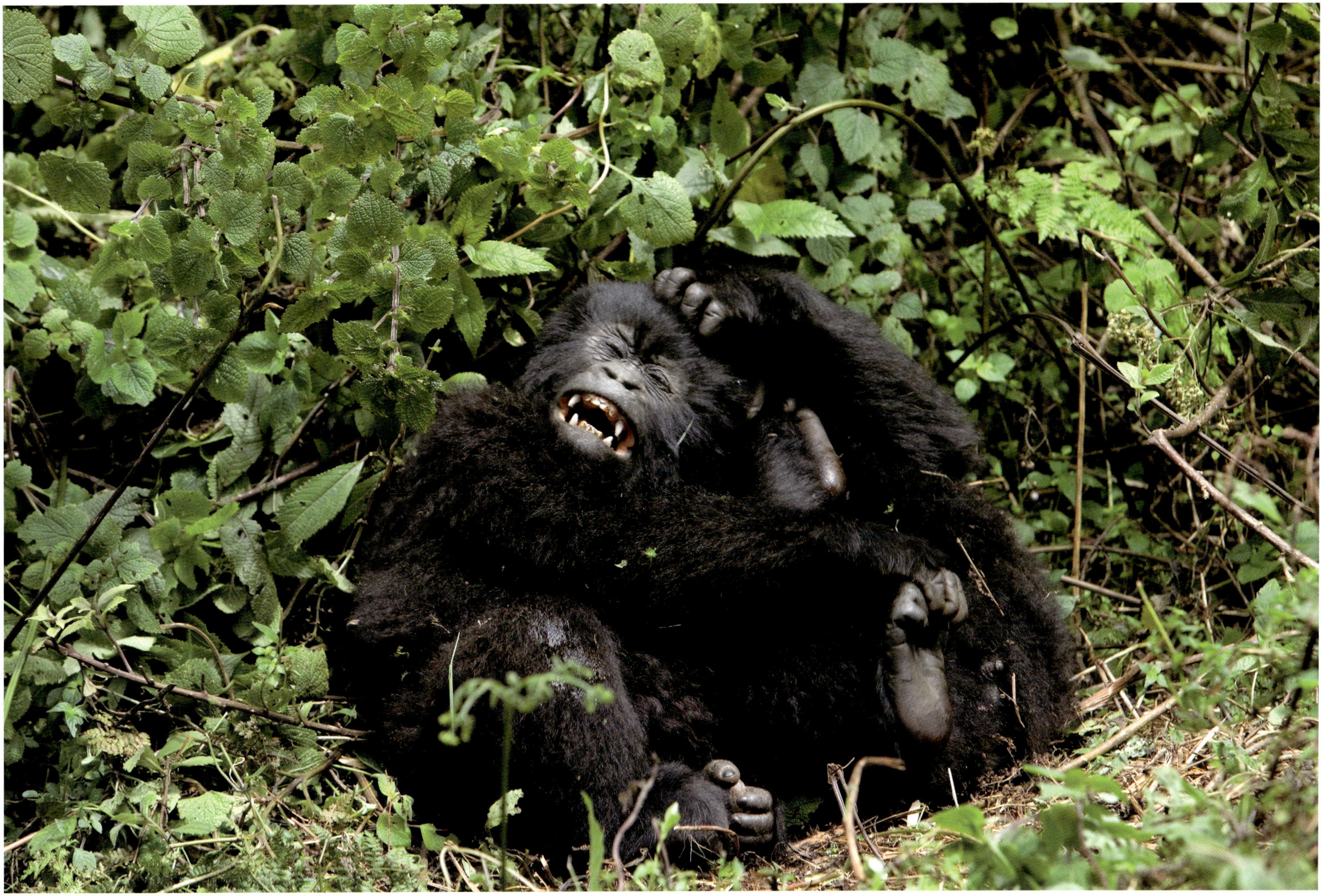

Although the two adolescent gorillas appear to be wrangling vigorously in a battle of strengths, one shows a typical "play-face", which clearly reveals that their tussles are only in fun.

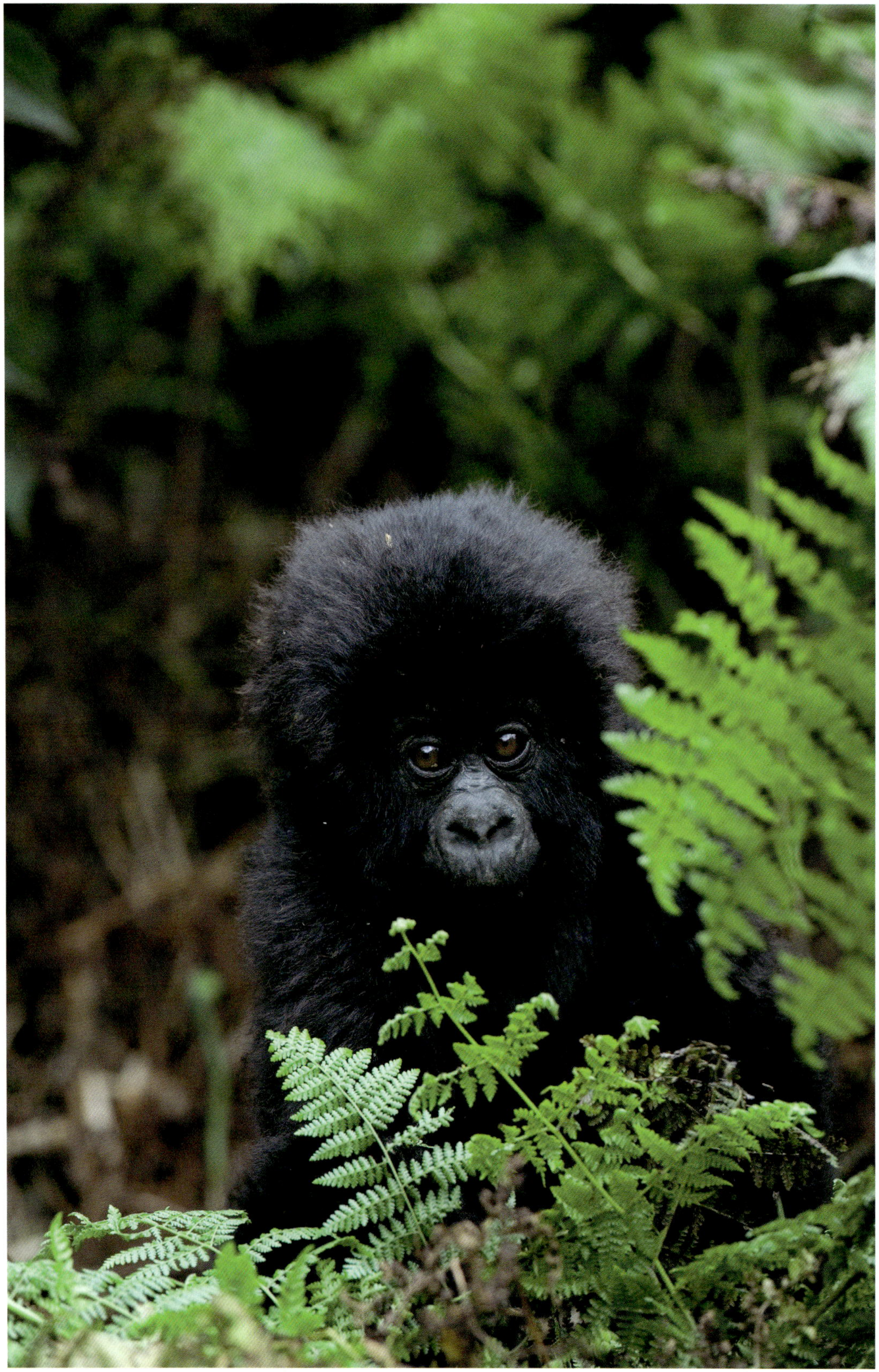

of four, they have mastered the actions customary in their group and are able to "disarm" their favorite delicacies themselves.

From the branch of a hagenia tree, the young gorilla watches astonished as the new female in the group attempts to devour her nettles. Again and again she pulls a face as her lips brush the edges of the leaves. Every bite is the same. She does not know how to bundle the leaves neatly, assigning different tasks to her left and right hands; instead, she rolls torn-off leaf tips into balls and stuffs them into her mouth. The baby at her breast, perhaps two months old, cowers constantly under the shower of nettle scraps.

The female evidently comes from a part of the rainforest where no nettles grow, and has never learned the correct harvesting technique from her mother. She has no chance of making up for lost time in her new family of nettle-eaters; mountain gorillas maintain a distance of around 30 meters (100 feet) between each other while grazing, giving each other a wide berth. In the thickly overgrown, rocky terrain, they lose sight of one another and rely on sound alone to detect the position of their family.

But when it is time for the midday siesta, their social event, they move together all the closer. Now the primates are at leisure, with time to spend on defusing tensions, strengthening relationships, playing with their young or watching them from a relaxed position. The silverback is enveloped in a web of affectionate, attentive gestures. The females build their day nests in his vicinity, painstakingly groom his coat, demonstrate to him how they appreciate him and rely on him as their protector. The young gorillas clamber over him, play around him and try to get him to join their games. But he abandons his role of guardian only for a short while to allow the new female's baby to swing from his powerful finger.

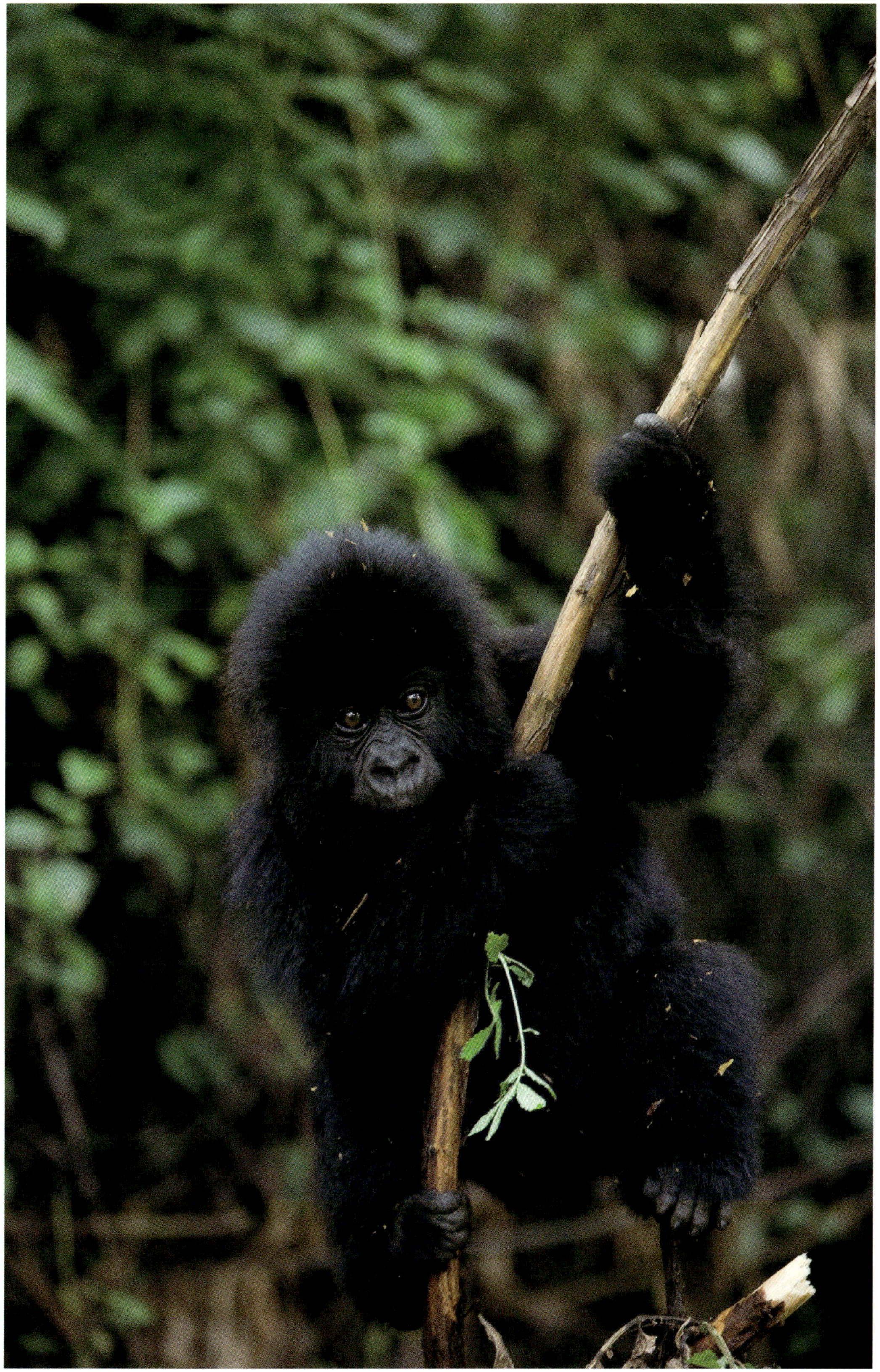

All adult animals tolerate the wild antics of their young, even when their great bodies are used as climbing frames. The primates' ministrations betray the vulnerability of their babies; only half of all baby gorillas reach the age of three. While many die of respiratory diseases, the majority fall victim to foreign silverbacks who approach the group to carry off females ready to mate and are uninterested in children that are still being suckled.

The young gorilla would like to examine the new female's baby more closely. However, as an attentive pupil in social studies, he knows that he must not approach the baby's sleeping nest directly. The young mother is still insecure. The six-year-old can imagine her feelings, and devises a strategy to ensure that she does not misinterpret his curiosity as aggression. He builds himself a sleeping-nest around eight meters (26 feet) away from her, and sits there for a few minutes. Then he stands up, moves one meter closer and builds a new nest. Nothing could be more innocent. Around 40 minutes and six nests later, he is sitting at the new female's side and gazing into the bright eyes of her shock-headed baby.

The day is sunny, the mist has long dispersed. The six-year-old leans back in his nest and soaks up the warm rays on his black fur, feeling happier than ever before. His family is grouped around him. His father guards them all. He himself has eaten well. He feels a sound growing in the pit of his stomach, rising higher and higher until it bursts out of his throat into the bright air. It is a humming or growling or howling, an ululating sequence of high and low notes. And suddenly, from the right and the left, he hears similar sounds, the murmuring choir of 20 contented animals. ■

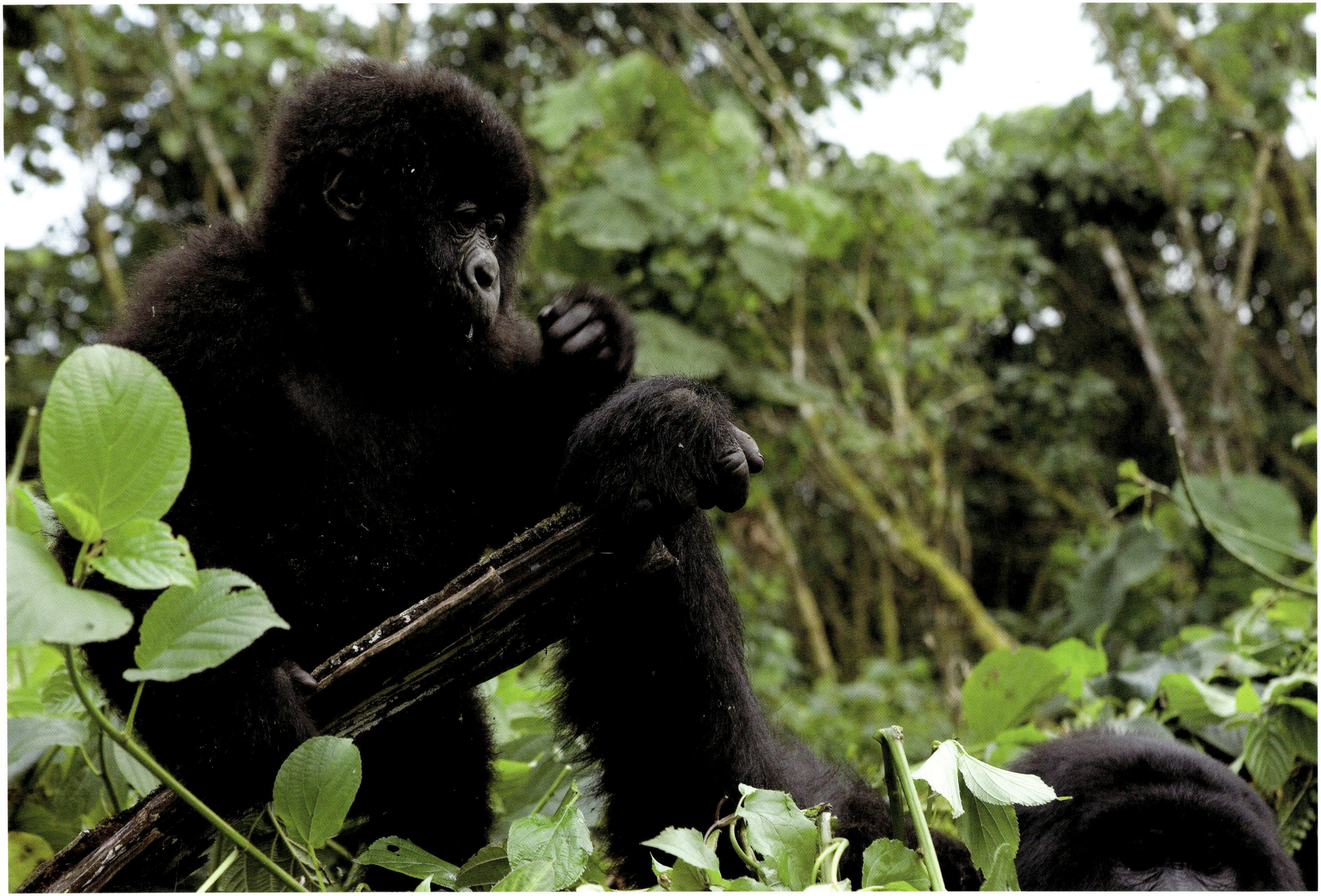

As mountain gorillas move through the rain forests, they leave a trail of devastated vegetation behind them.
The powerful primates even break tree trunks to get at the juicy pith.
But within weeks the vegetation has recovered and the scars in the forest are overgrown.

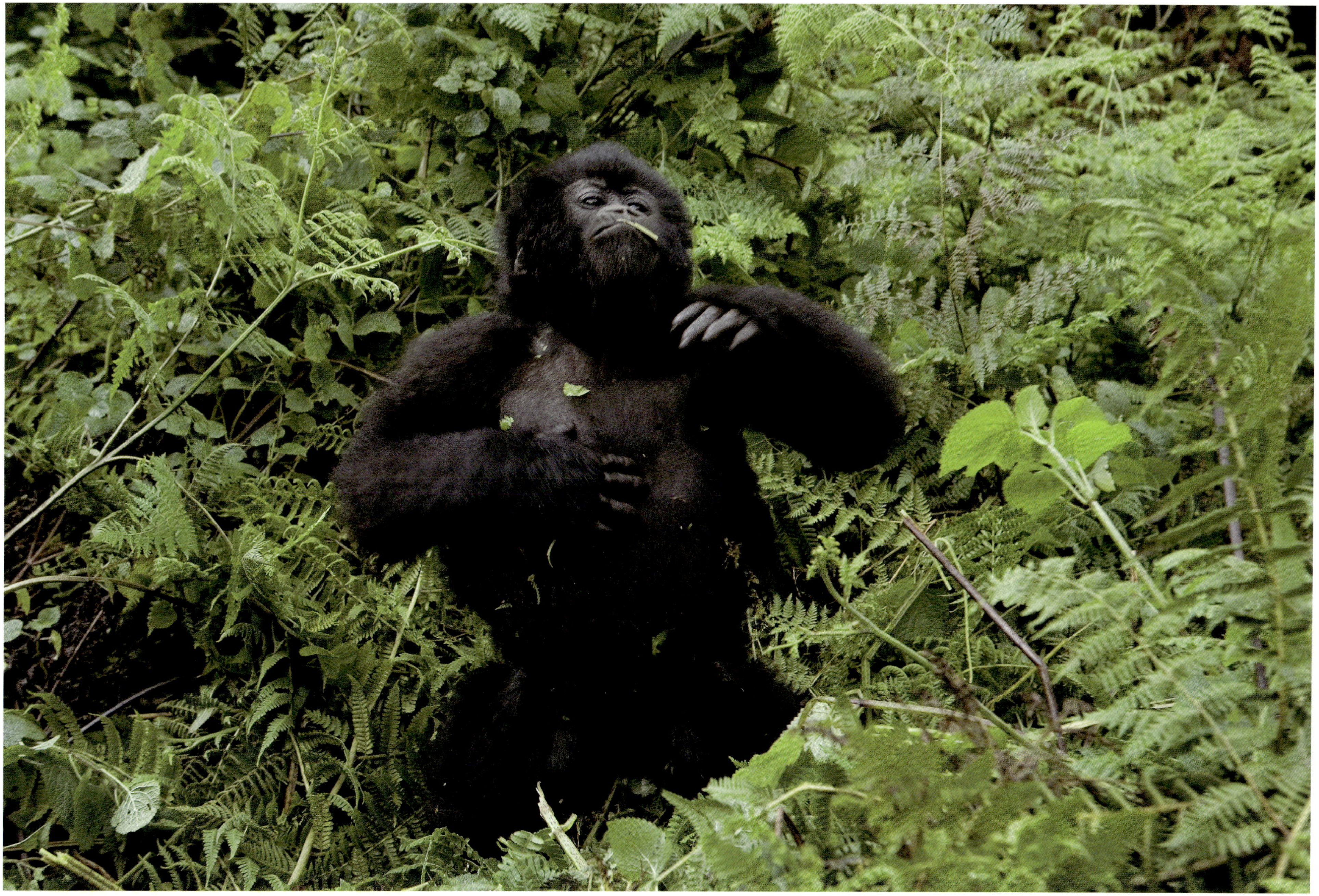

Even at the age of one, a gorilla is already familiar with the repertoire of male braggadocio. When neighboring clans encounter one another in the forest, their patriarchs stage a show of strength, rising to their full height and beating their chests.

Mountain Gorillas – at a glance

Their place in the animal kingdom

- They belong to the phylum of vertebrates
- to the class of mammals
- to the order of primates
- to the family of apes

Their scientific name

Gorilla gorilla beringei

Their closest relatives

Mountain gorillas are one of three subspecies of gorilla which live in various geographical regions of equatorial Africa. Like orang-utans, chimpanzees and bonobos, gorillas are large primates, evolving ten million years ago from the group of African Old World monkeys – the same group from which human beings evolved only three million years later.

Where mountain gorillas live (population numbers)

Mountain gorillas (700) live on the cloud-forested slopes of the Virunga volcanoes in Uganda, Rwanda and the Democratic Republic of the Congo. They are the only large primates to have adapted to life in these extreme vegetation conditions at an altitude of 3,500 meters (11,500 feet).

Mountain gorillas in figures

- Male gorillas are almost twice as big as females. A silverback standing upright from its usual knuckle-walking gait can reach a **height** of over 180 centimeters (around 6 feet), while females grow to only 150 centimeters (around 5 feet).
- Differences in **weight** are even more extreme, with males reaching 230 kilos and more, but females usually only 70 to 100 kilos.
- The **territory** of a gorilla family rarely extends beyond 8 square kilometers (around 3 square miles).
- Female gorillas reach **sexual maturity** at the age of nine, males not until the age of twelve.
- Mountain gorillas have a **lifespan** of 35 to 60 years.

Mountain gorillas' characteristic features

Mountain gorillas are among the most powerful primates. Their black skin is hairless in the facial regions, hands and soles of the feet. Otherwise they are covered in a thick, silky fur which is blue-black or gray-brown in color. Their build is sturdy and thickset, with a bulky body and short muscular limbs. Their powerful hands and feet can skilfully grip and manipulate thanks to their opposable thumbs and prehensile big toes which can be folded across the palm or sole. When walking, gorillas support their heavy torsos on the knuckles of their inward-folded fingers. All gorillas become "silverbacks" when they reach sexual maturity at the age of twelve: a broad saddle of white hair grows across the back and down to the flanks.

What mountain gorillas eat

Mountain gorillas are almost exclusively plant-eaters. Half of their twelve-hour day from six in the morning to six in the evening is occupied by eating. Leaves, stems, shoots, seeds, bamboo shoots, celery, nettles, and galium vines are their main diet, encompassing more than 60 types of vegetation and supplemented by rare delicacies such as fruit, insect larvae or termites. Adult males eat up to 40 kilos of plant material per day, females 20 kilos.

Mountain gorillas' lifestyle

Mountain gorillas live in families of ten to 30 members. The group is given cohesion by the bonds between a harem of females and the silverback. He is generally the father of all young born to the group. Usually he tolerates only blackbacks – young adolescent males – besides him in the family, but some large groups may have more than one alpha. Silverbacks are the undisputed leaders of their family and defend their group with their lives. Young males and females leave their families shortly before they reach sexual maturity. Females join other families, while males roam as bachelors, hunting for females with which to form families of their own.

How mountain gorillas raise their young

In the first few months of life, a new-born gorilla is constantly in contact with its mother. Baby gorillas learn to walk at the age of five months and regularly eat vegetation at eight months, although they are nursed up to the age of three years. Even older, independent gorillas have strong ties to their mothers, who teach them which plants are edible and how to breach the plant's defences. The second key relationship in young gorillas' lives is with the head of the group, their father, who is also their protector and chief authority. Young gorillas learn the rules of community life from the other members of the family, and are brought up to be sensitive and socially adept.

Dangers to mountain gorillas

Silverbacks unattached to a family group roam through the jungle and attempt to snatch females, using violence if necessary and generally killing the females' young to enable the new male to sire his own young as soon as possible. Poachers kill gorillas for the bush meat trade.

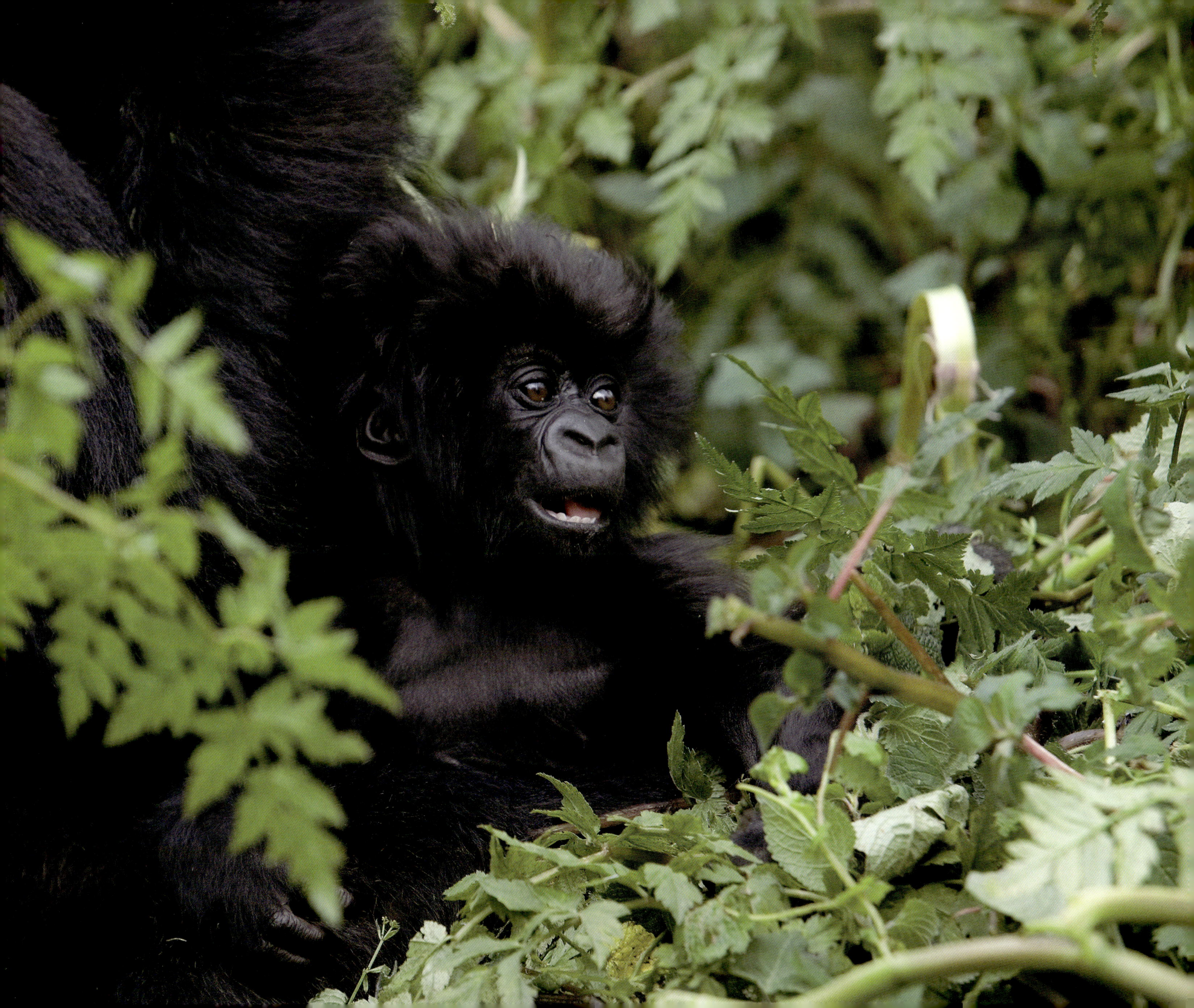

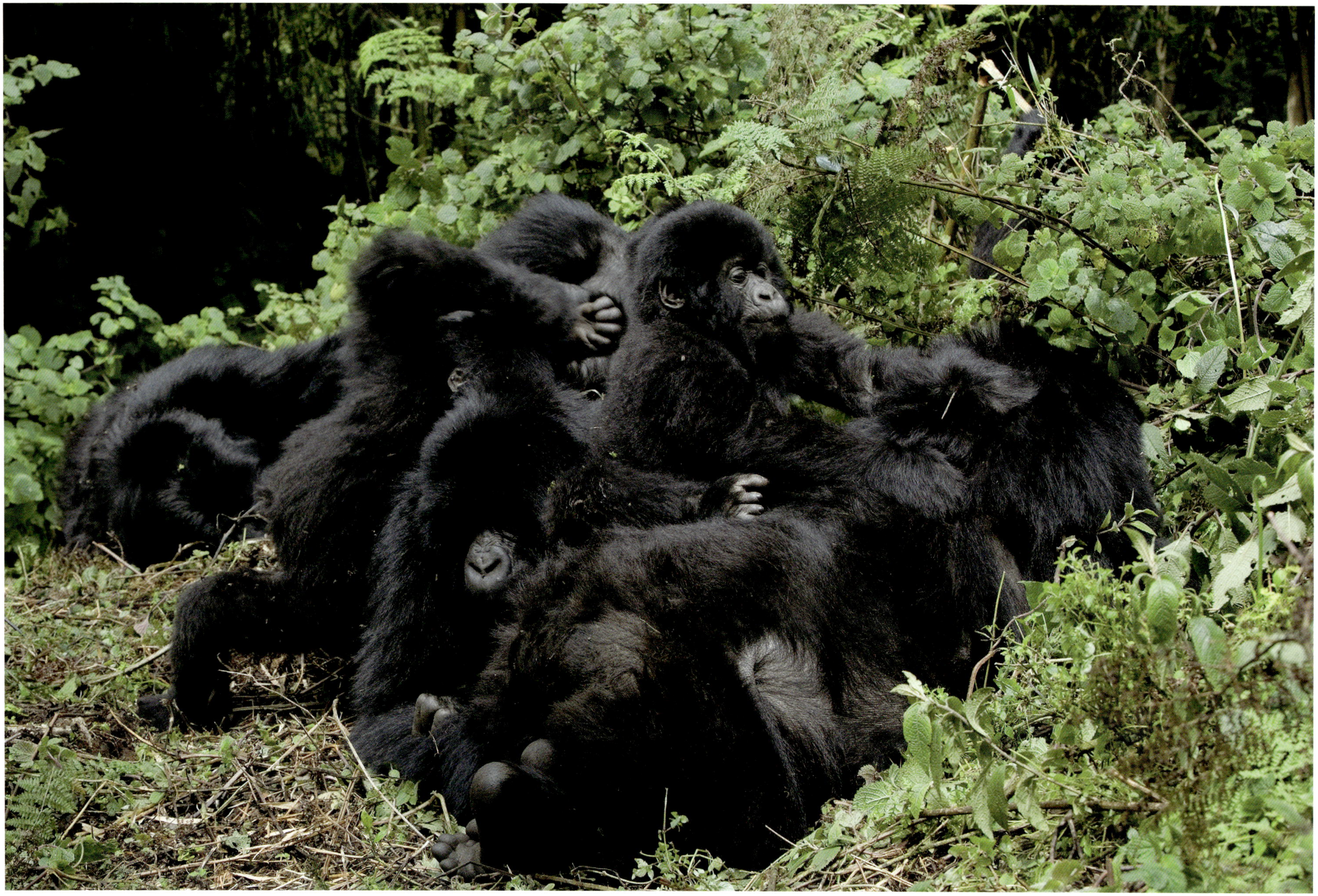

After eating, which accounts for around half of a gorilla's day, the family settles down for a companionable nap. The younger members take advantage of the relaxed mood to wrangle amicably and achieve maximum physical proximity.

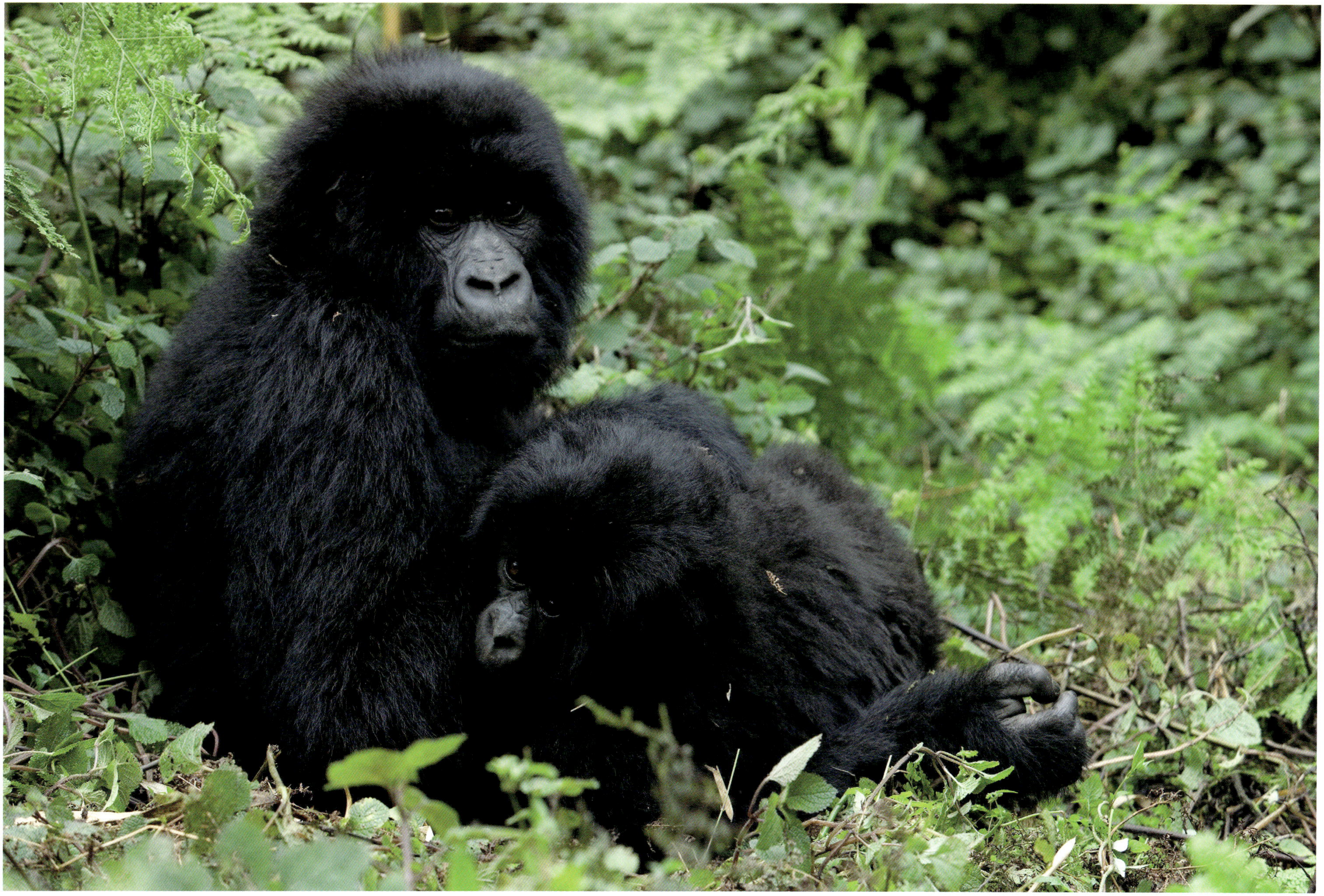

During the midday siesta, members of a family group take the opportunity to cement relationships. Assiduous grooming fosters trust – and pleasure. The eight-month-old baby relishes its special treatment by a caring two-year-old.

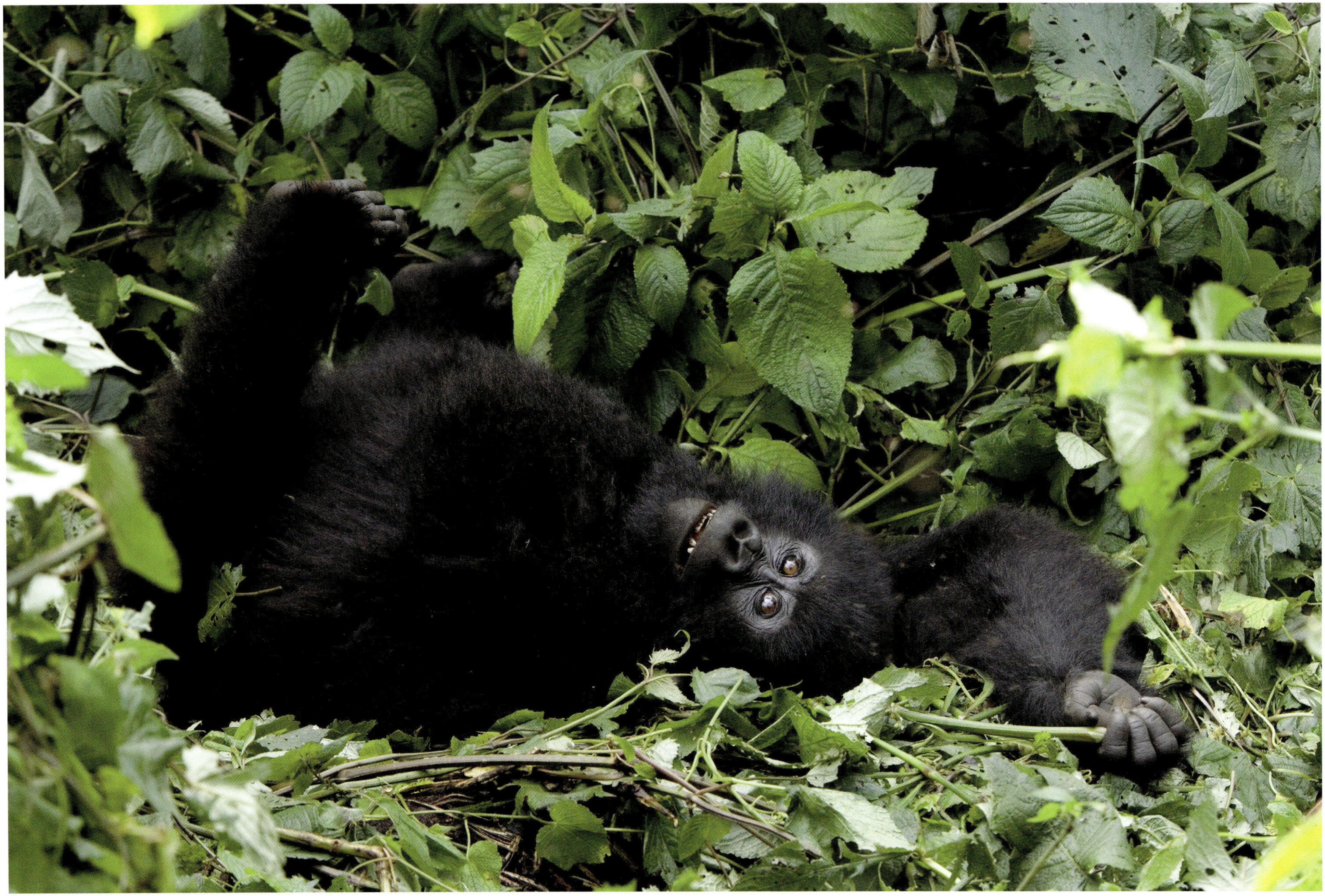

In the midst of romping, a baby gorilla plumps down into the lush vegetation and fixes its companions with an insistent stare. They immediately translate the gaze into a request for cuddling, tickling, grooming – in other words, physical contact with a close relation from its family, preferably its mother.

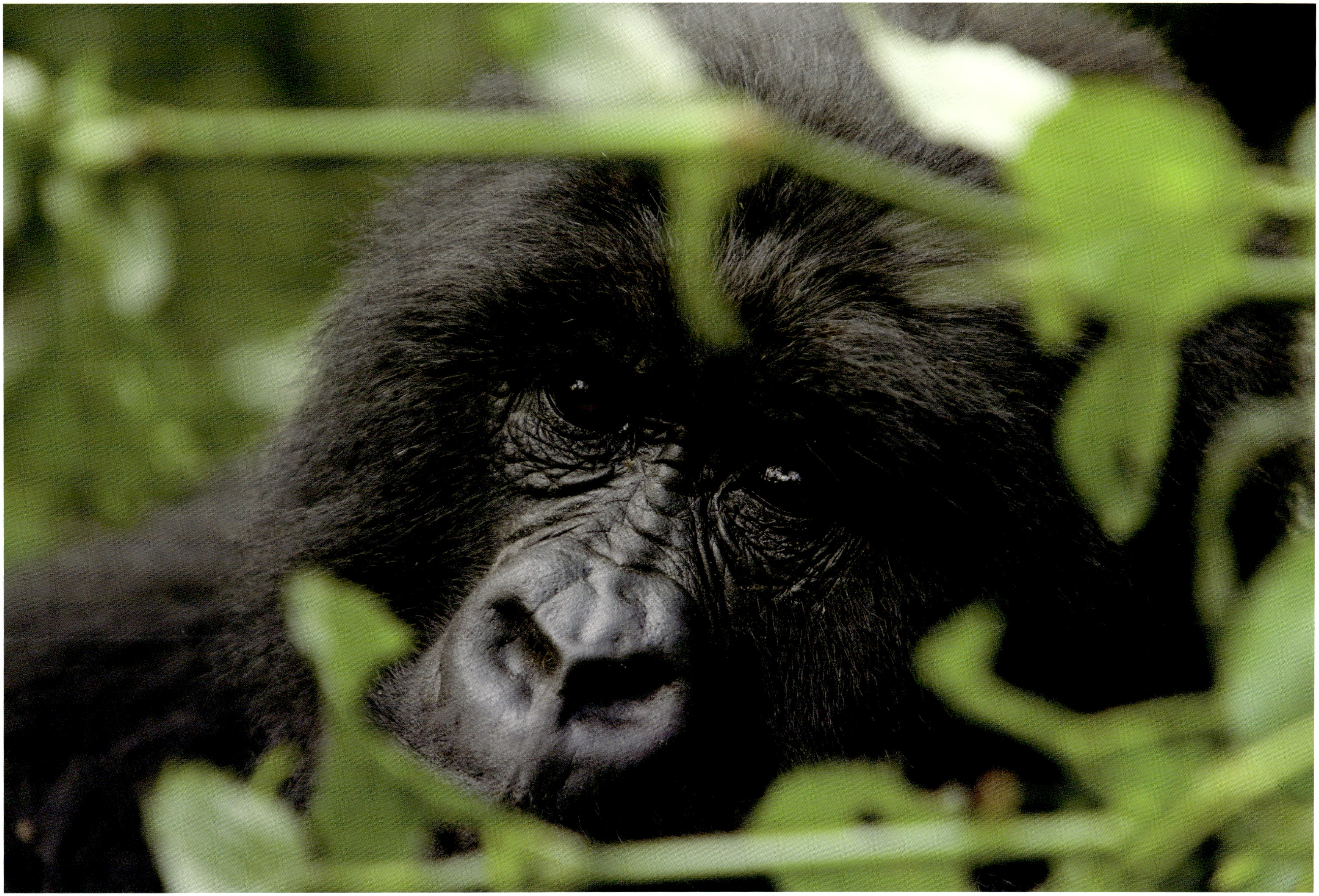

Every gorilla has a unique pattern of wrinkles across the bridge of its nose. Field researchers use these "nose prints" for identification, entering them in the identity cards in which they record the individual animals' unique features.

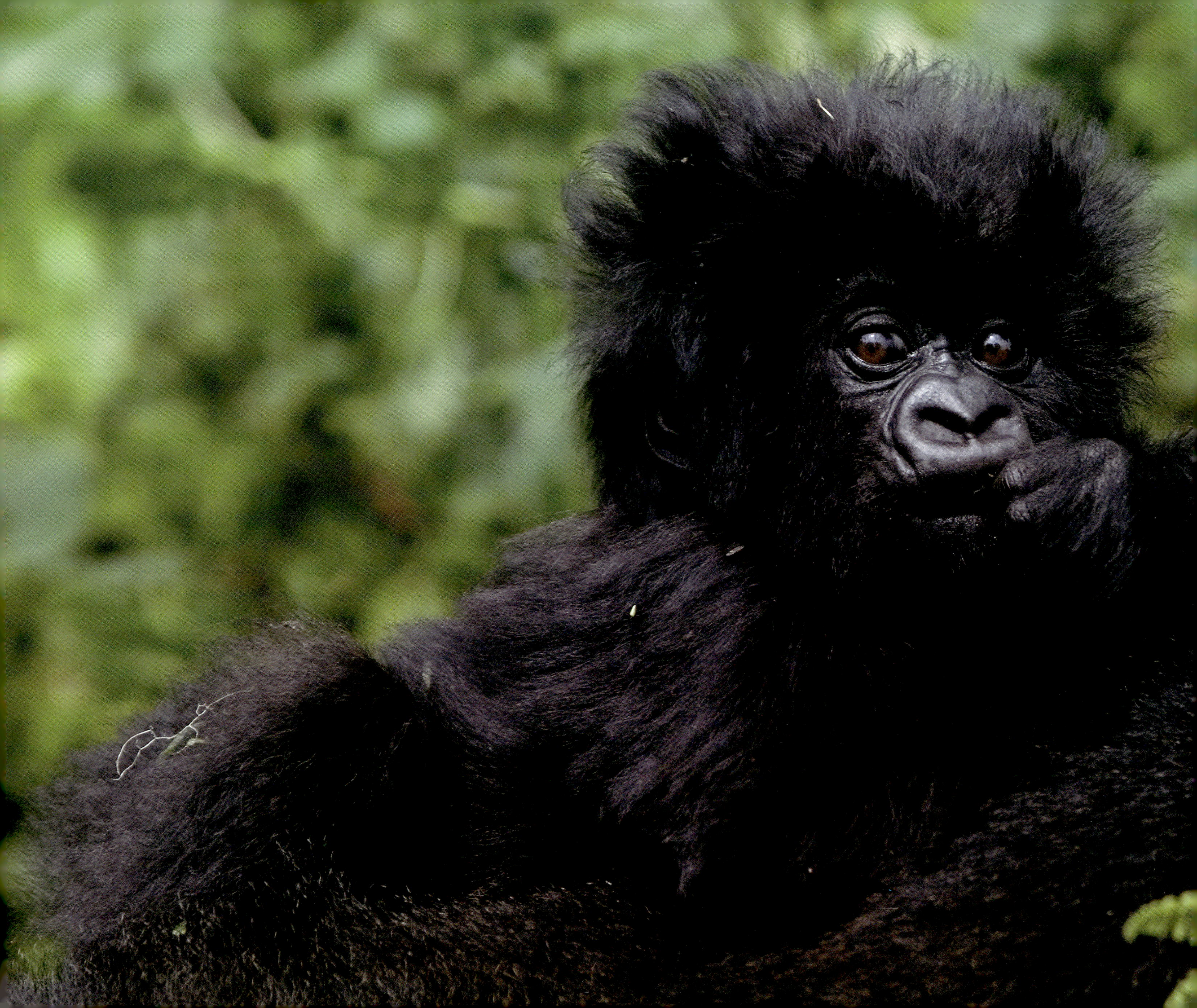

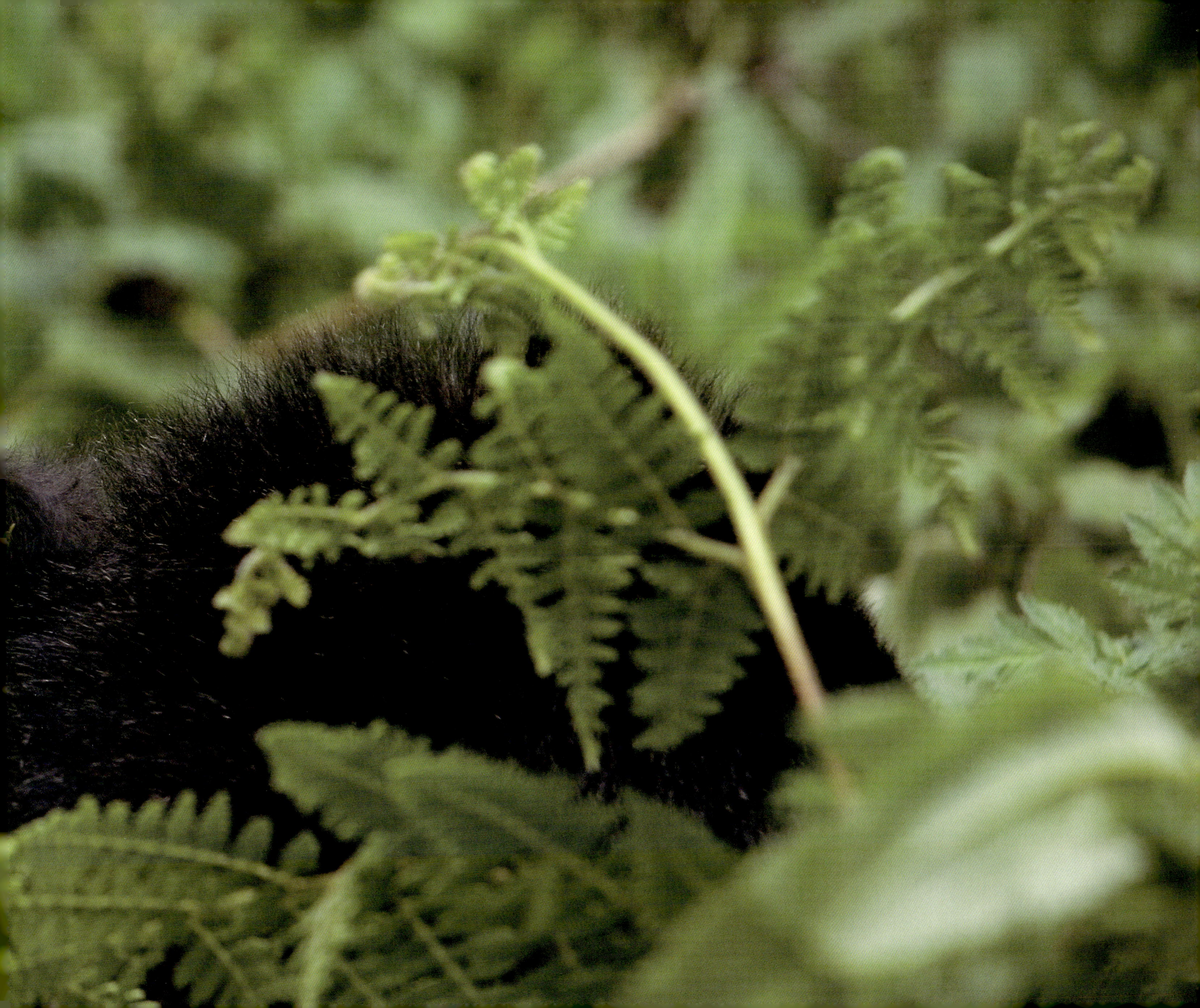

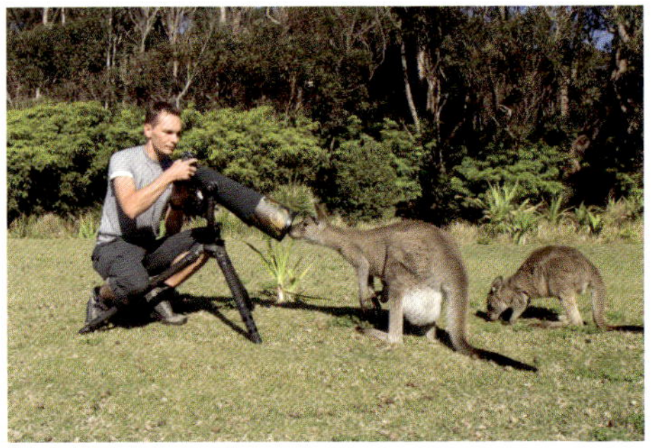
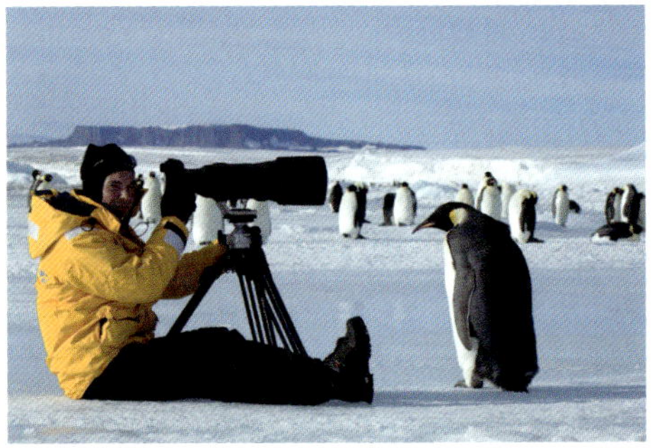
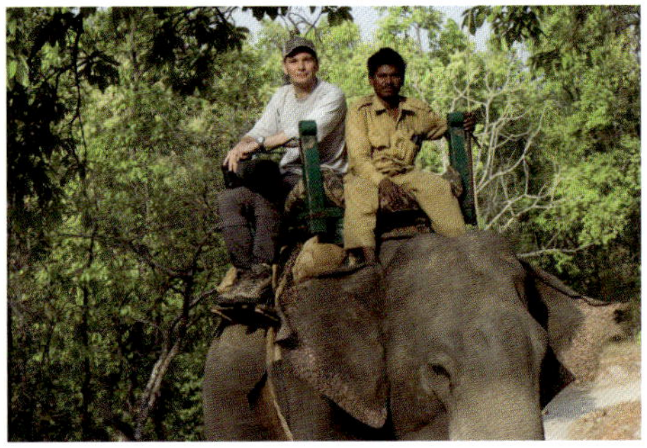
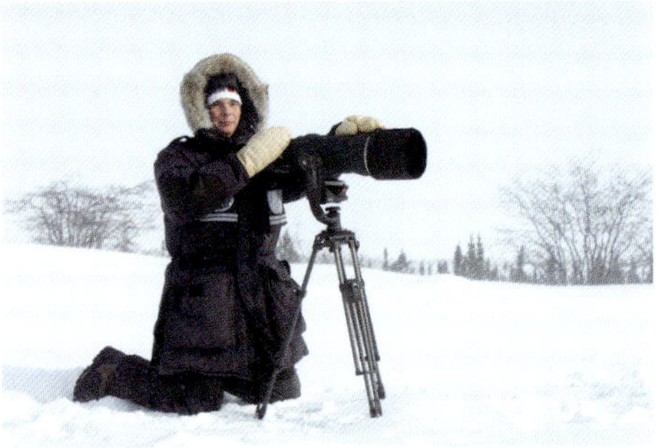
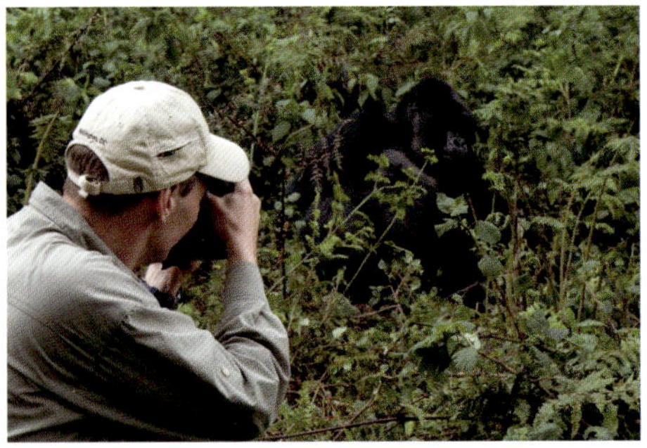

The Photographer in the Field

EMPEROR PENGUINS, Snow Hill Island, Antarctica

Admittedly, it's a long way to travel. But once we've reached Ushuaia at the southern tip of Argentina and are aboard the icebreaker "Kapitan Khlebnikov", we can leave everything else up to the Antarctic professionals of Quark Expeditions. The travel experts were the first to discover the emperor penguin colony at Snow Hill Island in the Weddell Sea in 2004. Their icebreaker approaches to within around ten miles of the breeding ground. After a 30-minute helicopter flight to the landing-pad and base camp, a 45-minute walk brings us to the first outposts of the penguin colony. The birds are fearless, inquisitive and, after a short time, so trusting that it is difficult to avoid taking a string of close-ups of eyes and beaks. At least as breathtaking as the penguins themselves, attired in formal black and white, is the cacophony of calls from thousands of throats.

In October in the Antarctic, cold is less of a problem than heat. Sun protection is essential, since the glaciers and ground ice reflect the sun's rays.

Save your batteries when the sun is out. You'll get the best light for taking pictures either when the sky is overcast or in the early hours of the morning or evening.

POLAR BEARS, Wapusk National Park, Canada

The destination is remote. A snow-covered fencepost in the heart of the tundra signals the railway station at Chesnaye, a two-hour journey from Churchill. Thank heavens the trekking team's snowmobile is already waiting. 30 minutes later we reach Wat'chee Lodge, a former military barracks now converted into a base camp for visitors to the National Park and the starting-point for tours into the conservation area and the birthing dens. Trackers are in constant contact with the Wat'chee team, using satellite phones to supply up-to-date GPS data of mother bears leaving their den with their cubs. Aspiring photographers need to use powerful telephoto lenses of around 600 mm (23,6 inches) to ensure that the mandatory minimum distance of 100 meters (328 feet) from the bears is always maintained. The animals are not shy, and unhurriedly adopt lying or standing poses. The main problem is the cold; after five hours, an ambient temperature of minus 40 degrees Celsius and severe north winds penetrate even the thickest down jacket. Fortunately, thanks to digital camera technology, any worries about tearing films are now a thing of the past. However, every 30 minutes the rechargeable battery should be exchanged for a warm battery from a jacket pocket.

And never touch the metal parts of the camera equipment without gloves (which are essential anyway!) or press the camera to your face without a mask.

MOUNTAIN GORILLAS, Parc National des Volcans, Rwanda

The starting-point for mountain gorilla tours is Ruhengeri, a busy town 1,700 meters (5,577 feet) above sea level and two hours' drive from the capital of Kigali. The park is inhabited by seven gorilla groups which are "habituated", or accustomed to humans. Trackers locate individual gorilla groups and report back by phone to the park entrance at daybreak. There, the visitors – never more than 56 at a time – are assigned to the seven groups of gorillas. A maximum of eight human observers is permitted per group, and visits are limited to one hour per day. The march to our wild relatives on the slopes of the volcano can involve a climb to 3,500 meters (11,482 feet) and take anywhere between twenty minutes and six hours. Paths are muddy, steep and often fringed with stinging-nettles.

Gloves are essential. Daytime temperatures in the cloud forest reach 30 degrees Celsius. But despite the effort it requires, an encounter with the largest of all the primates is a moving experience, an insight into our own biological origins. Even though human observers are required to keep a distance of seven meters, the apes break this rule with impunity. Occasionally curiosity gets the better of the young gorillas, or they deal a playful slap here and there. The greatest problem concerning photography is the sun. In full sunlight the forest foliage is radiantly white, the gorillas black. Early mornings and afternoons or cloudy conditions offer the best opportunities.

CHEETAHS, Khomas Hochland, Namibia

The hilly uplands of Namibia's center with its capital of Windhoek are, like so much of the country, divided into farms. Areas of open wilderness are almost non-existent. The 2,500 or so West African cheetahs are thus forced to live in coexistence with the farmers' livestock within fenced corrals – although these may be up to 20,000 hectares in area. Some farmers tolerate cheetahs, and others even run guest farms where cheetah-spotting is offered. These cats are used to people and are even fed occasional chunks of meat by the farmers. The farm I visited has a tracker with 30 years' experience in spotting single cheetahs for visitors. Thanks to him, I found out about a cheetah with four cubs. I pitched camp near her hide for a week until the cubs were so trusting that they dared to emerge from the long grass and came up inquisitively, soon even playing with my shoelaces. The alert mother lay nearby but did not view me as a threat.

The best time to take photographs was the time before sunrise and two hours after that

GREY KANGAROOS, Wilsons Promentory National Park, Murramarang National Park, Kangaroo Island, Australia

The national parks of eastern Australia but also the arid regions of the hinterland are home to millions of Grey Kangaroos. They are least shy in the reserves, where shooting is prohibited. On Kangaroo Island they were so trusting that I felt I had been accepted into their group. One evening I was crossing the campsite when I felt a paw on my shoulder. From then onward, "my" kangaroo would come daily to my camper van at twilight and spend a couple of hours with me. The relationship was strengthened by scraps of vegetables and salad. My new friend discouraged competition by applying a few of the kangaroos' famous boxing punches. By day, a mother kangaroo would hop past with her young to inspect my lens shade at close hand.

INDIAN TIGER, Bandhavgarh Tiger Reserve, India

Getting there is simple. A night train runs from Delhi to Umaria in the state of Madhya Pradesh, from which the park is a thirty-minute drive. 1,131 square kilometers (439 square miles) in area, it was once a hunting reserve of the Maharajas of Rewa and has been a conservation area since 1968. The park is believed to have the largest tiger population in India. From November to June is the best time to watch tigers – including mothers with their cubs who often simply laze around or rub against each other as cats do. Watching tigers feeding or bathing in one of the many waterholes are among the more thrilling natural spectacles that the park offers in abundance. All tours are accompanied by trained, expert interpreters and rangers. In the mornings and evenings, visitors can travel by off-road vehicle or elephant to specific conservation areas; during the noontime heat, both wildlife and visitors need a break. Tripods are useless in a swaying vehicle – or when you are on an elephant. Bean-bags are the best way of containing camera shake. And strong nerves are also a good idea; the mighty tigers are confident beasts and don't hesitate to look humans straight in the eye – often from a distance of only a few meters.

My Camera Equipment

1) Various lenses and cameras by Canon, such as:
Cameras Canon EOS 1DS MKII, EOS 1D MKII, EOS 1DS, EOS 5D, EOS 10D, EOS 1 V; EF 15 mm/2.8 fisheye, EF 16-35 mm/2.8 L, EF 24-70 mm/2.8 L;
TSE-24 mm/3.5 EF 70-200 mm/2.8 IS L, EF 100-400 mm 4.5-5.6 IS L, EF 300 mm/2.8 IS L, EF 500 mm/4.0 IS L, EF 600 mm/4.0 IS L; teleconverter 1.4 x and 2.0 x and flashes 550EX and 580EX.

2) Technical equipment:
A Heiler carbon tripod with Wimberly head; a beanbag 30 x 30 cm; collapsible Rainer Burzynski sunshades; memory cards from 1 GB to 8 GB; a mobile Rugged 160 GB hard disk drive by LACIE; a MAC Powerbook G4 laptop plus Peli waterproof case and ThinkTank backpacks.

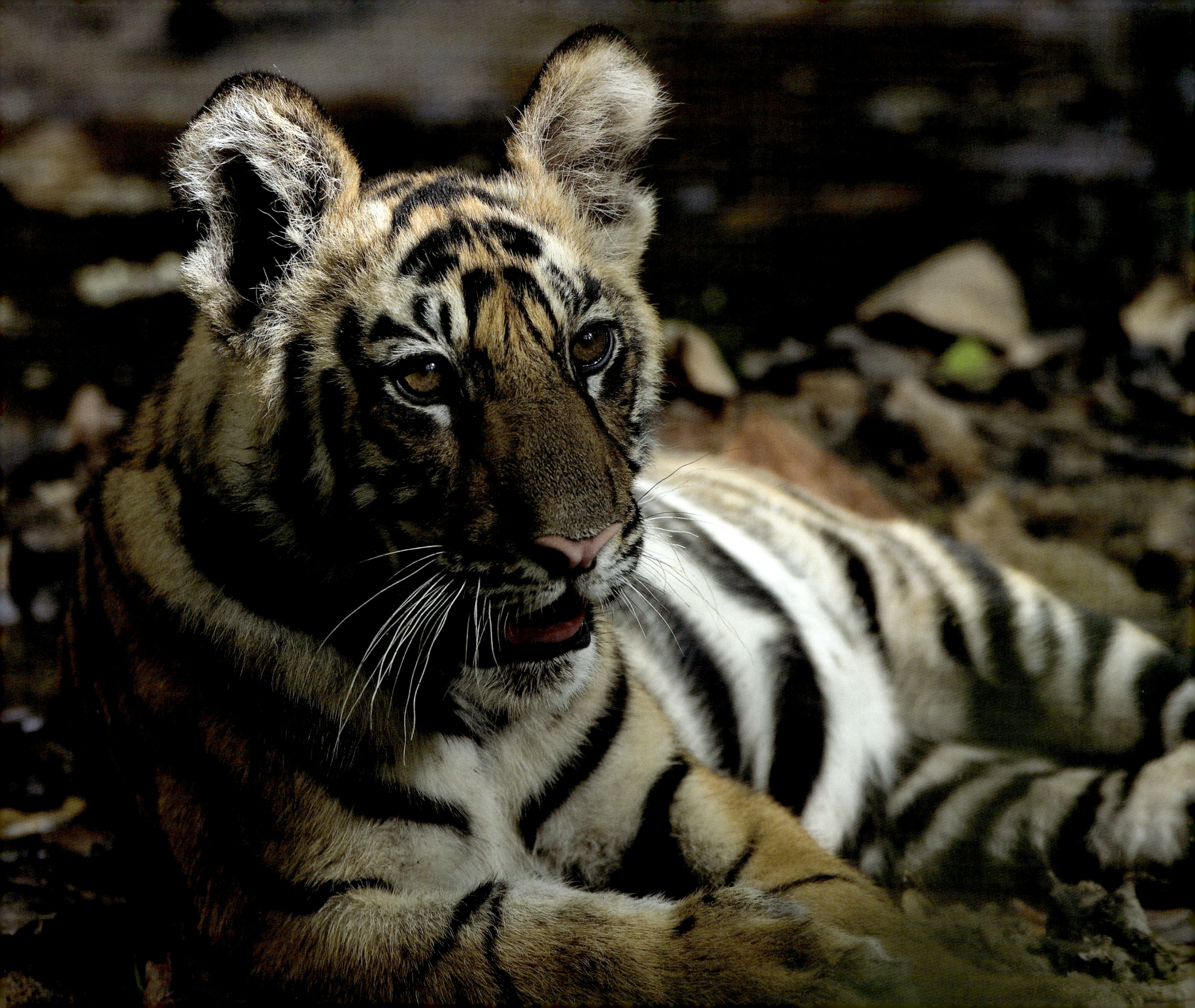

Wildlife Conservation

Planning, traveling, funding, hiring guides and drivers and recruiting field expertise to put this book together would have been in vain if the stars of the show had refused to take the stage. It is their tolerance of human spectators while going about their daily business, their generosity in overlooking inquisitive eyes and camera lenses, that made it possible to recount intimate stories of the animals' private life in words and images. It is their tolerance of human proximity in the neighborhood of the last refuges for polar bears, Indian tigers, mountain gorillas, cheetahs, eastern and western grey kangaroos and emperor penguins that enables projects like this one to succeed.

Not all of the six species described here are faring well. Although millions of eastern grey kangaroos graze in eastern Australia, millions are shot every year. A total of 200,000 emperor penguins and roughly 20,000 polar bears still inhabit our planet. But these figures should not deceive anybody. The effects of global warming (see further information at the International Polar Year website *www.ipy.org*) have reached the most isolated wildernesses. Breeding-grounds on ice melt too soon, hunting grounds are swallowed by the sea, and the offspring of many wild animals are doomed for years to come.

The populations of mountain gorillas, Indian tigers and cheetahs are even more at risk. Here the survival of every youngster counts towards increasing the dwindling numbers.

There is thus reason for concern for each of the species and their young presented here. But there are also opportunities to do something for them. Professional aid workers and members of national and international conservation organizations are working in situ to protect these representatives of our biodiversity.

To give financial support to the conservation organizations or find out more about their work, contact them at the addresses given below.

INDIAN TIGERS

The organization "Terre et Faune" works in the field and pursues two objectives. It equips the Tiger Reserve's ranger patrols with motorbikes and vehicles to discourage poachers. And it also reimburses the poor farmers living around the park if their goats are lost to tiger attacks. The population is thus encouraged to let the tigers live, because the tigers are improving the livelihood of their human neighbors. ➥ ***www.terre-et-faune.org***

MOUNTAIN GORILLAS

The mountain gorilla population is most seriously threatened in Virunga National Park, by frequent poaching. An effective special ranger unit has been trained to protect the animals from the attacks of armed soldiers and other military forces. This training is partly funded by Zoologische Gesellschaft Frankfurt (ZGF). ➥ ***www.zgf.de***

CHEETAHS

The largest population of these fast cats can be found in Namibia. And if today an increasing number of farmers are willing to tolerate cheetahs on their land to attract tourists, it is due to Laurie Marker. 17 years ago, she founded the organization "Cheetah Conservation Fund" and succeeded in winning round many farmers by educating them and supplying practical suggestions. She has encouraged the farmers to buy Anatolian guard dogs to protect their livestock. These dogs effectively scare any cheetahs away without harming them.
➥ ***www.cheetah.org***

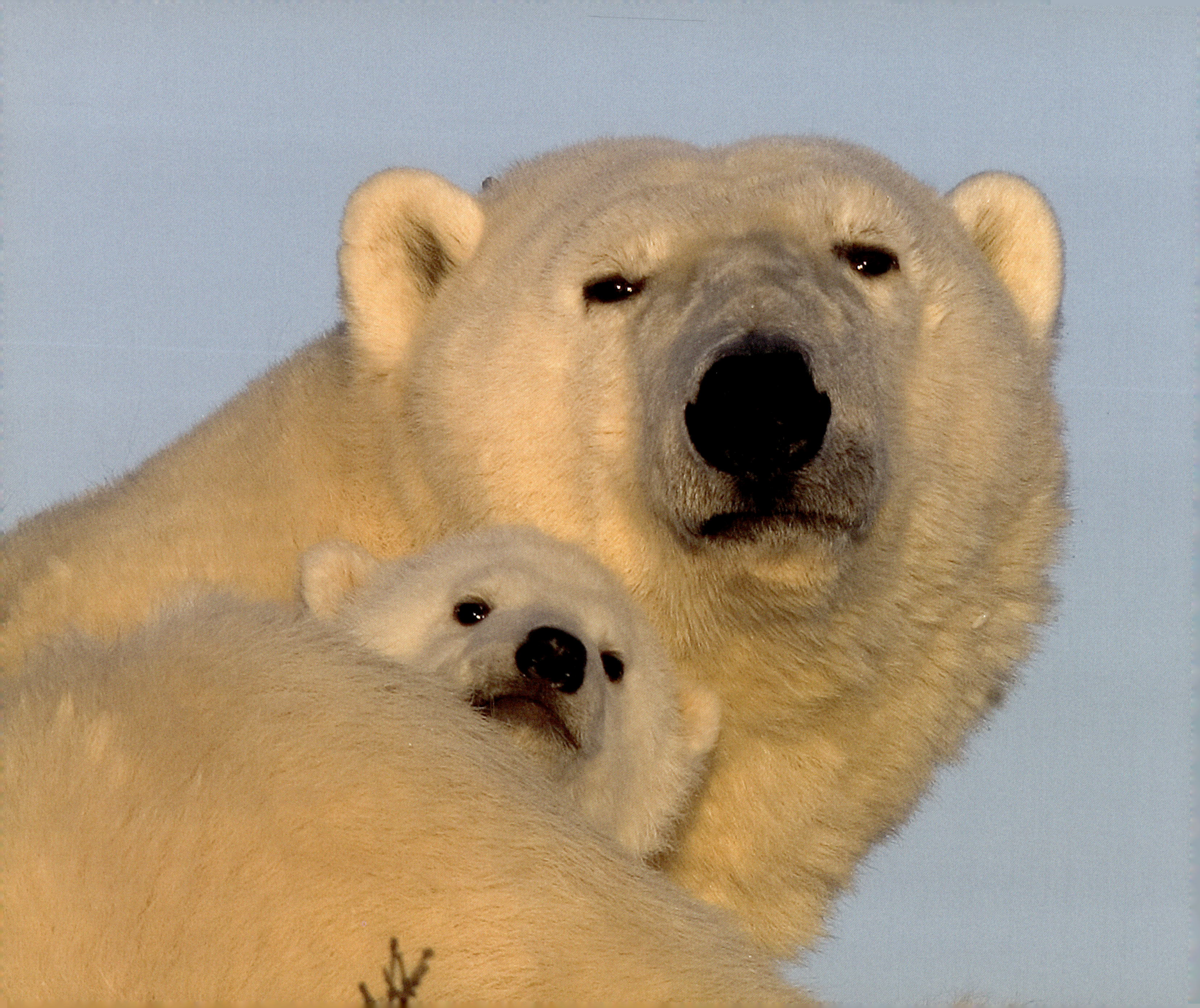

Acknowledgements

Many people have helped to make this book possible. My deepest thanks go to Steffi, who held the fort at home while I jetted from location to location. And at every stopover in Germany she served me the best pizza north of the Alps. In addition to working for her own agency, Alex designed the book, creating a wonderful backdrop for my pictures with her infallible sense of graphic style and layout, and constantly inspiring me with new ideas. Uta found the words hidden in my photos, creating – to continue the natural metaphor – a fruitful combination that will hopefully be followed by many more joint projects.

Gerhard Grubbe makes me feel at home with C.J. Bucher Publishing. He readily allows himself to be infected by my ideas for books, and provides me with attractive opportunities to make them happen. My thanks go to him and the staff of Bucher for their assistance and support.

I am similarly obliged to Ruth Eichhorn, Director of Photography at GEO magazine, who wrote the foreword for the German edition, and Sophie Stafford, Editor-in-Chief of BBC WILDLIFE magazine, who supplied the foreword for the English edition.

My thanks also go to the entire Canon team for their support and reliable servicing of my equipment.

My gratitude goes to all those who assisted me during my travels, giving me advice and encouragement and providing me with their inside knowledge and their time. They helped me to encounter animals in the wild and to make my pictures possible. I should like to thank the following individuals and institutions specifically for their generous assistance:

- In Canada: Morris and Michael Spence, the finest guides, polar bear experts and friends, and both their families; Lawreen Reid for her reliable organization; the trekking team of Wat'chee Lodge; the park rangers of Wapusk National Park.
- In the Antarctic: Jonas, Danielle, Jaclyn, Mick, Tim, Akos, Jason, Damien, Saskia, and the crew of the "Kapitan Khlebnikov" from Quark Expeditions.
- In Australia: the Director of Flinders Chase National Park and his rangers.
- In India: Rajvardhan Sharma, Manager of Nature Heritage Resort and a tiger expert of 20 years' standing; Bablu and Pappu, my drivers; Daya Ram, the mahut; Field Director Assem Shrivastava of Bandhavgarh Tiger Reserve and all Forest Department guides; Shalini Shukla for the superbly organized travel.
- In Rwanda: the administrative staff at the National Park "Parc National des Volcans"; Samuel Gasana, the driver; Diogène Kwizera and François Bigirimana, the guides; Dieter Müller from Duma Reisen for the organization.
- In Namibia: farmer Johann Vaatz; Elias, the tracker; Dieter and Dongina Risser from Ondjamba Safaris for their organization.

Imprint

The photographer

Thorsten Milse is an internationally renowned nature and wildlife photographer. His photographs have appeared in magazines such as *GEO, Nature's Best, Illustreret Videnskab* and *BBC Wildlife*. He has won several awards – including a prize at the *BBC Wildlife Photographer of the Year* Competition and the Grand Prize of the photography competition held by the American magazine *Nature's Best* – for his photos of polar bears cubs. He published the immensely popular book *Little Polar Bears* with Bucher last fall.

The author

Uta Henschel is a science writer, specializing in natural history and behaviour. She has been covering these fields since 1978. She is author of several books and has been writing regularly for *GEO* magazine among other renowned European publications. She has won several awards for her work. In 2007 she was nominated for the *Henri Nannen-Prize*.

Photo credits

pp. 138: © Stephanie Weber (2), Prem, Martin Eisenhawer, Diogène Kwizera
Jacket flap: © Stephanie Weber, Ron Moorhouse

All others © Thorsten Milse.
www.wildlifephotography.de

With the friendly support of
Canon Deutschland GmbH, Professional Imaging

CPS

This work has been carefully researched by the authors and kept up to date as well as checked by the publisher for coherence. However, the publishing house can assume no liability for the accuracy of the data contained herein.
We are always grateful for suggestions and advice.
Please send your comments to:
C. J. Bucher Publishing, Product Management
Innsbrucker Ring 15, 81673 Munich, Germany
e-mail: info@bucher-publishing.com

Project Director: Gerhard Grubbe
Product Management: Dr. Birgit Kneip
Translation: Alison Moffat-McLynn, Munich
Proofreading: Rosie Jackson, Munich; Danko Szabo, Munich
Design and DTP: Alexandra Finke, Lemgo
Production: Bettina Schippel
Printed in Germany by Passavia Druckservice, Passau

ISBN 978-3-7658-1636-9